Other titles by the same Author

The Mask of Ra
The House of Death
The Godless Man

Forthcoming

Isabella and the Strange Death of Edward II

The Mysterious Death of
Tutankhamun

The Mysterious Death of
Tutankhamun

Paul Doherty

CARROLL & GRAF PUBLISHERS
New York

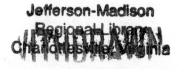

Carroll & Graf Publishers
An imprint of Avalon Publishing Group, Inc.
161 William Street
New York
NY 10038—2607
www.carrollandgraf.com

First Carroll & Graf edition 2002

First published in the UK by Constable,
an imprint of Constable & Robinson Ltd 2002

ISBN 0–7867–1075–6

Printed and bound in the EU

Library of Congress Cataloging-in-Publication
Data is available on file.

To the memory of Vincent Wells of Ilford,
pupil at Trinity Catholic High School
September 1990 to July 1997.
A lovely young man, beloved son of
Julia and Charles, Vincent was caught up
in the tragedy at the World Trade Center
on Tuesday 11 September 2001.

Contents

Illustrations

Between pp. 180 and pp. 181

Colossal statue of Tutankhamun (Werner Forman Archive/The Egyptian Museum, Cairo)

Tutankhamun and Ankhesenamun hunting scene (Werner Forman Archive/The Egyptian Museum, Cairo)

Nubian battle scene (Werner Forman Archive/The Egyptian Museum, Cairo)

Relief of Nubian slave (Werner Forman Archive/St Louis Art Museum)

Valley of the Kings (AKG London/Erich Lessing)

Relief of women mourners (Werner Forman Archive/Schimmel Collection, New York)

The Sun God travelling through the underworld (Werner Forman Archive)

A funeral procession (Werner Forman Archive)

Tomb of Tutankhamun (AKG London/Erich Lessing)

The mask of Tutankhamun (Werner Forman Archive/The Egyptian Museum, Cairo)

The goddess Nephthys guarding the tomb of Tutankhamun (Werner Forman Archive, The Egyptian Museum, Cairo)

Detail from the chariot of Tutankhamun (Werner Forman Archive/The Egyptian Museum, Cairo)

Painting of Ay in Tutankhamun's tomb (Werner Forman Archive/E. Strouhal)

Detail of wall painting in Horemheb's tomb (Werner Forman Archive/E. Strouhal)

Horemheb and Horus (AKG London/Erich Lessing)

Maya (AKG London/Erich Lessing)

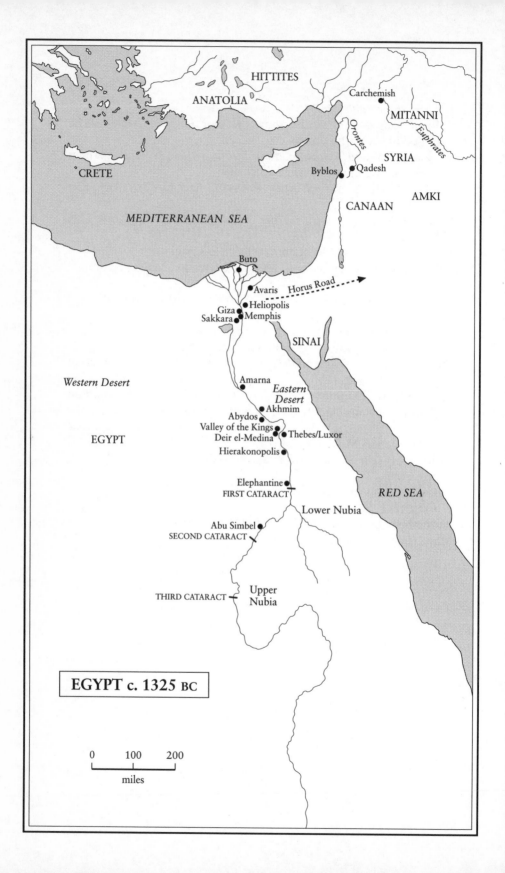

HITTITES

ANATOLIA

Carchemish

MITANNI

Orontes

Euphrates

CRETE

SYRIA

Byblos ● ● Qadesh

AMKI

MEDITERRANEAN SEA

CANAAN

Buto ●

Avaris ●   Horus Road

Heliopolis
Giza ●●
Sakkara ●● Memphis

SINAI

Western Desert

Amarna ●

*Eastern
Desert*

● Akhmim

Abydos ●
Valley of the Kings ●
Deir el-Medina ● ● Thebes/Luxor

EGYPT

Hierakonopolis ●

Elephantine ●
FIRST CATARACT

RED SEA

Lower Nubia

Abu Simbel ●
SECOND CATARACT

THIRD CATARACT

Upper
Nubia

EGYPT c. 1325 BC

0   100   200

miles

List of Historical Figures

Rulers and Politicians

Pharaohs of the Eighteenth Dynasty

Ahmose	1550–25 BC
Amenhotep I	1525–04 BC
Tuthmosis I	1504–1492 BC
Tuthmosis II	1492–79 BC
Tuthmosis III	1479–25 BC
Hatshepsut	1473–58 BC
Amenhotep II	1427–01 BC
Tuthmosis IV	1401–1391 BC
Amenhotep III	1391–53 BC
Amenhotep IV – Akhenaten	1353–35 BC
Semenkhkare	1335–33 BC
Tutankhamun	1333–23 BC
Ay	1323–19 BC
Horemheb	1319–07 BC

Pharoahs of the Nineteenth Dynasty

Ramesses I	1307–06 BC
Seti I	1306–1290 BC
Ramesses II	1290–24 BC

Queens of Egypt

Tiye: wife of Amenhotep III, daughter of Thuya and Yuya

Nefertiti: queen of Amenhotep IV/Akhenaten, daughter of Ay

Meritaten: daughter of Akhenaten, wife to Akhenaten's mysterious co-regent Semenkhkare

Ankhesenamun: daughter of Akhenaten, wife of Tutankhamun

Mutnejdmet: General Horemheb's second wife and sister to Nefertiti

The Akhmin Gang

Ay: minister under Akhenaten; first minister of Tutankhamun; later Pharaoh

Nefertiti: Ay's daughter

Anen: Ay's brother; a high-ranking priest in the court of Amun

Nakhtmin: kinsman of Ay, possibly brother, high-ranking general

Other Politicians

Maya: high-ranking official under Akhenaten, Tutankhamun and Horemheb

Huy: Viceroy of Nubia under Tutankhamun

Horemheb: military commander under Akhenaten and Tutahkhamun; later Pharaoh

Other Officials

Pentju: high-ranking official under Akhenaten and Tutankhamun

Mahu: chief of police under Akhenaten, probably continued in office under Tutankhamun

Foreign Rulers

Tushratta: king of the Mitanni

Suppiluliumas: king of the Hittites

Rib-Addi: prince of Byblos

Prologue

Towards the Far Horizon

Arms will be made out of copper,
Bread shall be demanded with blood,
One shall laugh with a sick man's laugh,
One shall not weep at death.
  R. B. Parkinson, *Voices From Ancient Egypt*

PHARAOH WAS DEAD! Tutankhamun, Strong Bull, Fitting-of Created Forms, Dynamic of Laws, He Who Calms the Two Lands, Who Propitiates All the Gods, He Who Displays the Regalia, King of Upper and Lower Egypt, The Lordly Manifestation of Re, The Living Image of Amun, had died in his palace of Malkata in the late spring of 1323 BC. Tutankhamun's journey into the Eternal West, towards the Far Horizon, the Kingdom of the Great Green-Skinned God Osiris had begun. He had died unexpectedly, this Pharaoh of little more than eighteen summers, a pretty youth with his elongated head, sloe eyes and sensitive, smooth face. The crowds who'd gathered outside the great double-barred gates of the House of Rejoicing, the heart of the king's palace at Malkata, had heard all the rumours and knew the gossip. Tutankhamun was of the Tuthmosid dynasty, the strange son of an even stranger father, Akhenaten. His original name had been Tutankhaten, The Living Image of the Aten, but all that foolishness was now forgotten. Akhenaten's heretical religious cult, based on his city Akhetaten, Horizon of the Aten, in the north, was now, like that city, a dusty memory, for Pharaoh had returned to Thebes and the temples of Karnak were thriving once again.

[3]

The people had hoped for a long life for their Pharaoh, a period of calm which would bring peace and prosperity to the nomes or provinces of Egypt, uniting once again, more firmly than ever, the Upper and Lower Kingdoms. Pharaoh's troops, his squadrons of war chariots, would thunder out along the Horus Road across Sinai, or beyond the Third Cataract, to smite terror into the hearts of Egypt's enemies and restore the flow of tribute. So much promise had disappeared so quickly, yet Tutankhamun, despite his girlish looks and slender appearance, had been vigorous enough. The crowds had seen his hunting parties go out into the Red Lands led by his Chiefs of Whips, Captain of the Chase, and the Keeper of his Berber Greyhounds. They had seen the long line of hunters return, their slung poles heavy with ibex, antelope, lion and any other beast rash enough to cross Pharaoh's path. Tutankhamun had loved the hunt: his splendid chariots, their bronze-electrum gleaming in the desert sun, pulled by swift horses, magnificent in their gorgeous housings and harness.

Nevertheless, despite such vigour, Pharaoh had died quickly, some seventy days earlier, in the Malkata palace, the House of the Brilliant Aten, built by the great Amenhotep III on the west bank of the Nile. A favourite imperial residence, the Malkata stood below the western hills so the rays of the setting sun could flood the House of Rejoicing. The light would illuminate its gorgeous Halls of Audience with their splendid coloured pillars covered in a variety of eye-catching hues; these, in turn, shimmered in the Pools of Purity and dazzled like rainbows in the marble, glass-like floors of that beautiful palace, decorated with the cobalt blue, so beloved of Amenhotep, which was everywhere to be seen, in paintings, pottery, dishes, jars and exquisitely carved glassware. The

[4]

young Pharaoh had breathed his last in the master bedroom which lay at the heart of Malkata. Despite the yellow and ochre carvings of Nekhbet, the Guardian Vulture Goddess, as well as the protective symbols of Ankh (life) and Sa (Protection), Pharaoh had grown worse. The doctors had been summoned, an army of physicians who tried their best, or so rumour had it: the ordinary physicians, the Saumus, as well as the exorcists, the uabus, the Doctors of the Right Eye and the Doctors of the Left. These would have brushed away the King's personal chamberlains, the Men of Pure Hands and all the other flunkeys of the court: the Keeper of the King's Diadem, the Keeper of the King's Perfume, the Holder of the Imperial Sandals. Officials such as these were no longer necessary for the breath-catching battle between life and death.

The physicians would have invoked the Delicious Breath of the north, the life-giving breeze of the god Amun to enter Tutankhamun's right ear and, by way of the nose, rejuvenate the weak, fluttering heart of their Pharaoh. They had struggled in vain. The breath had not come. Instead the Breaths of Death had entered by the left ear and the battle between life and death, at least in this earthly existence, was lost; despite their best ministrations, countless invocations and incantations, Pharaoh had died. Perhaps, as he slipped into unconsciousness, Tutankhamun recalled the vital spell, the prayer from the Book of the Dead he would need in the next stage of his existence:

Oh my heart which I had through my mother!
Oh my heart of my different ages,
Do not stand up as a witness against me!

[5]

Do not be opposed to me in the tribunal!
Do not be hostile to me in the presence of the Keeper of
the Balance!
For you are my Ka which is in my body.
The protector who made my members hale.
Go forth to the happy place, where to speed,
Do not make my name stink with the Entourage who
make men.

This spell, or prayer, represented the spiritual life of all Egyptians, be they slave or Pharaoh. Death was not an end but the beginning of a journey. For the well prepared this was a journey of triumph into Divine Light, for those who had failed, or were not prepared, a voyage into an eternal night. Eventually the exorcists and physicians from the House of Life had withdrawn so the priests could take over. If Pharaoh was to make his journey into eternity, his body had to be embalmed according to the strict Osirian ritual before being laid to rest in the Temple of Eternity where his Ka, his spiritual essence, would return in a bird-like form. Tutankhamun would then live in eternal glory surrounded by the symbols, artefacts and goods he would need in the after life.

The body and Ka of the young Pharaoh had separated for a while; to recover the Ka was to recover eternal youth and join Osiris in the Fields of the Blessed. The Ka had grown within him, the eternal soul, which did not grow old. In time it would return with the breath of life when the priests performed the ceremony of the Opening of the Mouth. If Osiris decided, Tutankhamun would be reborn to a blissful eternity, soaring through the sky with the sun god by day and returning

nightly to a well ordered tomb. This ideal could only be realized after the body had been suitably prepared and the correct
liturgical rites administered.

Tutankhamun had first to be 'justified' for this spiritual
journey. According to the Book of the Dead, he must proceed
to the Kingdom of Osiris. He must strike at the door of the
Kingdom of Justice, seek entrance, and make his way through
the Tuat, or Underworld, before he entered the Halls of
Judgement in the company of Horus. Here, he would face the
tribunal of Osiris which would judge the purity of his heart.
Surrounding this heavenly court would be the other forty-two
gods of Egypt ready to decide his destiny. In their presence
Tutankhamun would make his great confession:

> Oh Far Strider – I have done no falsehood.
> Oh Fire Embracer – I have not robbed.
> Oh Swallower of Shades – I have not stolen.
> Oh Dangerous One – I have not killed men.

This long negative confession would be heard in silence.
Afterwards, Thoth, the Ibis-headed Scribe of the Divine Court,
with the aid of the jackal god Anubis, Lord of the Mortuary,
would place Tutankhamun's heart, which was not removed
from the body, in the scales of Ma'at, goddess of Honour and
Truth, the Feather of Truth in the other. If the two scales hung
evenly, Thoth, the Scribe god, would deliver his verdict: the
deceased had been weighed in the balance, there was no sin in
him, his heart had recorded the truth. Osiris, the Far Strider
would then pronounce judgement: 'Let the deceased go out
victorious.' Tutankhamun would not be turned back by the
Keepers of the Gates to the West. He would not be seized by

[7]

Amemet the Crocodile-Headed Destroyer. He would not know the burning lakes of fire where flaming water was the only drink for the wicked. He would not be delivered to the cruel demons, tormentors of the damned, who dwelt in halls with floors of water, roofs of fire and walls of living snakes. The doctrine of eternal justification, as Spell No. 83 of the Book of the Dead proclaims, means going out:

> Into the day after death and transformed at will, being in the suite of Wenenefer, being content with the food of Osiris . . . of being vindicated with Osiris. Nothing evil shall have power over thee. A matter a million times true.

To ensure this was carried out, the King's body had to be ritually embalmed under the supervision of priests wearing the terracotta masks of the Jackal-Headed Anubis. In the Wabet or Clean Place Pharaoh's naked body was laid out on a stone of alabaster. The embalmers began their rite, handed down by tradition in the sacred texts. This ceremony had first been carried out by Osiris's devoted son Horus after Osiris had been slain by Seth. The mummification process was an integral part of Tutankhamun's struggle for blessed immortality: for the soul to be eternal, the body had to be incorruptible and the process of embalming ensured this. It had its own dramatic liturgy and rite: throughout the long seventy-day period of preparation, each step was accompanied by prayers, hymns, invocations, blessings and the recitation of spells. Amulets, charms and papyri inscribed with prayers and quotations from the Book of the Dead were liberally used. The priests were not dealing with a corpse but a sacred naos, or tabernacle, which had to be scrupulously prepared to receive back its eternal Ka. Incense would be burnt, lamps lit, flower wreaths laid, whilst priests of the mortuary chapels were commissioned to chant the litanies of intercession. The court would mourn but it would also watch and participate in this sacred ceremony.

The brain and other internal organs of the dead man were extremely moist and had to be removed immediately after death to avoid rapid corruption in the heat of an Egyptian spring. Around the alabaster slab would stand pots to receive the body fluids as they gushed out. The brain was first removed by inserting a long wire up into the nostrils, snapping the ethmoid bone, and so into the brain. This special wire was expertly twisted, reducing the brain tissue to an almost liquid state which would later drain out of the nostrils when the body was turned.

The embalmers then began the ritual cuts: the first, following a neat line drawn by a mortuary scribe, was four inches long on the left side of the belly. The priest made the incision chanting a prayer and using a special knife of Ethiopian stone. He then removed the intestines, stomach, lungs and liver. These were placed in bowls to be dried and sealed in four canopic jars. Each jar was protected by a son of Horus, in whose likeness the stopper to each jar was carved. The jackal Duamutef protected the stomach: the baboon Hapi the lungs, the falcon Quebehsennuf the intestines, Imsety, of human form, the liver. The body cavities were vigorously washed with palm wine and the orifices filled with spices and perfumed pads. Only Tutankhamun's heart was left intact, so he would be able to remember and recite those magical spells to animate life.

The corpse itself still had to be dried out. In order to remove

[9]

all moisture the embalmers covered the body in natron, a drying salt, for at least thirty-five days, after which most of the moisture would be drained. Once the natron had been removed, the body would be carried to the House of Beautification where the cavities in the chest, belly and part of the face were stuffed and filled out with fine linen and sawdust of scented wood. Tutankhamun's legs were placed together, his arms crossed in the manner of Pharaoh giving judgement. The craftsmen took careful casts for the coffins whilst the process of mummification continued. Each toe and finger was sheathed in gold, a small cap of white linen, bearing symbols of the Aten, placed on the shaven head. Over the face the embalmers laid a mask of pitch and a light piece of lawn. Other soft materials were carefully padded along the body which they now swaddled in linen wrappings whilst prayers were recited. Quotations from the Book of the Dead, spells and precious amulets were included as the wrapping continued, crossing and re-crossing, magic jewels being inserted in the folds. The wrapped body was then fully shrouded in its cloths. Over the face, head and shoulders was placed an exquisite mask of gold, beaten and burnished. The stripes of the nemes headdress were fashioned out of blue glass. The striking Cobra of Lower Egypt and the Vulture of Upper Egypt on the brow were of solid gold. Lapis-lazuli, quartz, obsidian, with coloured glass cloisonné work, were used to give the ceremonial mask an almost divine majesty. Artificial hands of burnished gold holding the Osirian symbols of the crook and flail were placed outside the bandages above the chest, under these a hieroglyph inscription, an invocation to Osiris, on a strip of gold: 'Thy soul liveth and thy veins are healthy.' A further lengthy inscription on

[10]

the shoulders and back of the mask identified each part of Tutankhamun's body with one of the gods.

Once the mummified corpse was ready, it was shrouded and placed in its casing of precious wood with gold plating. Pharaoh's head rested on a pillow under which lay a copy of the Book of the Dead. A soft, liquid, wax-smelling ointment was then poured in to keep the body stable and fixed in its resting place.

Seventy days after his death, according to the ritual, Tutankhamun's mummy was ready to leave for the Valley of the Kings. The doors of the great House, Pharaoh's Palace, were opened to reveal the mummy placed on a sledge under an ornately carved wooden shrine draped with flowers. Across the top of this shrine stood rows of elegantly carved wooden cobras symbolizing the uraeus, the Spitting Cobra, which decorated the Pharaoh's crown: these reared up, life-like, to protect their Prince on his final journey. Tutankhamun had died in the spring, so the flowers of that season had been cut and collected for garlands to drape the sledge, and to be carried by the mourners. The principal flowers were the mandrake, the blue water-lily, the nightshade, the olive and the willow which were woven together to form the Wreath of Justification, as well as neck and pectoral garlands.

The funeral cortege left the palace compound. Around the sledge of the corpse clustered the priests, heads shaven, the principal ones wearing panther or leopard skins over their naked shoulders hanging down to linen quilted kilts fastened about their waists. Some of the priests carried bowls of burning incense, others the waters of purification, white and red, which would be later used for the ceremonies at the entrance to the tomb. Priests from the mortuary chapels

[11]

carried their hand-clappers, or sistra, which they shook in mournful lamentation over their dead prince. Musicians of the harp, lute and the double and single flute also accompanied the cortege, as did carts and sledges stacked high with the treasures, goods and foods Tutankhamun would need in the after life: swords and daggers with hardened gold blades, elaborately carved ivory boomerangs, Pharaoh's leather scaled armour, self bows with arrows in elaborately inscribed wooden cases covered with linen, leather and gold-leaf decorations. The best of these was the Bow of Honour, sheathed in gold. The king's state chariots, lined with gold and highlighted with coloured inlays and heraldic devices showing Tutankhamun smiting the enemies of Egypt, were also included.

Heirlooms, had been assembled. the most precious being a small casket holding a lock of Queen Tiye's hair, Tutankhamun's grandmother. There were palettes and paints for writing, military trumpets of beaten silver, their bell rims and mouthpieces of gold, copper or bronze, ivory clappers, ebony boxes and game boards to play senet or the game of twenty squares, ivory jars of cosmetics, precious boxes, ointment containers of gold inlaid with coloured glass and semi-precious stones, mirrors and mirror cases, sandals, gloves and garments. There were beautiful collars shaped in the form of the Vulture Goddess, corselets, jewellery, earrings and ear-studs, couches and beds, guardian statues to protect the King's last resting-place. Ritual servant figures, the shabtis, some 413 in number, ranked prominently: these would form the dead King's retinue in the after life to do all necessary work for him. There were carvings of different gods. One in particular would protect the entrance to the tomb: a life-sized image of the black dog Anubis resting on a large ornate casket. This beautiful statue, carved from wood, was covered in black resin, its ears and collar picked out in gold leaf, its inlaid eyes of calcite and obsidian set into gold surrounds, whilst its nails were of solid silver. This statue would guard the treasury and the precious canopic jars.

The funeral procession would move along the principal highway towards the Valley of the Kings, that great rocky outcrop intersected by its maze-like lanes and dominated by its soaring peak or horn, the dwelling place of the goddess Meretseger, She who Loves Silence. Priests and acolytes from the House of Life and the temples would go ahead sprinkling the dust with water and milk. The entire procession of brilliant colours moved amidst billowing clouds of incense. The paeans and hymns of intercessions mingled with the noisy lamentations and keening wails of the mourners, as they processed towards the shingle-strewn entrance to the valley whose rocks could change colour so startlingly at dusk and dawn. To their right the Nile curled like a green snake; across the river, the gold-capped obelisks and temple cornices of Thebes glinted in the sunlight.

The entire procession would be guarded by hand-picked household troops: the Nakhtu-aa and Maryannou, the Braves of the King, foot soldiers in their white linen, padded armour and distinctive striped headdresses, armed with the bronze khepesh swords, spears and decorated, oval-shaped shields. On the flanks of this royal procession moved squadrons of two-wheeled war chariots, their six-spoked wheels turning slowly, the bronze and electrum of the carriages glittering and shimmering. These chariots would be pulled by the finest horses in Pharaoh's stables, decorated with exquisite housing

[13]

and gleaming harness. The drivers, selected for their bravery, would display the Gold of Valour over their coats of bronze scales and distinctive light blue leather collars. The chariots, under the command of their standard-bearers, moved slowly in time with the procession. The soldiers were arrayed to keep back the crowds and onlookers who had surged across the Nile to watch the Great Ones lay their Pharaoh to rest, the visiting merchants and traders, the sailors from the punts, skiffs and ships which plied along the Nile; the rabble who lived in narrow, fly-infested streets, eager to escape from their poorly built houses of dried clay and mud. The market officials and police, with their trained baboons, would drive away the yapping pie dogs and keep an eye on the Scorpion Men, those confidence tricksters ever ready to sell cheap good-luck amulets at such an inauspicious time.

Of course the great lords would not be concerned with this. Eventually they would leave the noisy throng behind them and enter the Valley of the Kings, moving slowly along its snaking, dusty trackways, past the tombs of previous Pharaohs. Near the bier would walk Pharaoh's immediate entourage. There would be Huy, Viceroy of Kush during Tutankhamun's reign, who had been sent south to crush rebellion in Nubia and oversee Egypt's free exploitation of that gold-rich area as well as ensure that tribute continued to flow as freely as ever. Beside him would be Taemwadjsi his wife and chief of Tutankhamun's harem. The Chief Scribe Khay and the Principal Steward and Fan-Bearer Ipy would also be leading mourners as would Nakhtmin, a senior military officer who'd provided five of the wooden shabtis for Tutankhamun's burial, and Maya, the Treasurer and Overseeer of Works for the Place of Eternity and, especially,

[14]

Ay, step-grandfather to Tutankhamun and certainly the dead Pharaoh's principal adviser, one of the great power-brokers of Egypt. Finally, there was Ankhesenamun, Pharaoh's wife, daughter of Nefertiti and the heretic Akhenaten, Tutankhamun's father. She was now a widow queen. She would walk slowly, joining in the hymns and participating in the ritual lamentation of the women.

Ankhesenamun would surely be thinking of happier days, when she and her husband, together with his pet lion cub, went fishing in a papyrus skiff, specially constructed by their grandfather Amenhotep, along the reed-choked rivulets. On such occasions Tutankhamun also hunted duck and geese, armed with his throwing stick or using his Bow of Honour, whilst she held the quiver of arrows. Perhaps she recalled other outings sitting in the shade of the pomegranate orchards of the palace where the grass and shrubs put out long, lovely and lush shoots in the rich black soil specially imported from Canaan; or happy festival days when they would sit and talk, surrounded by courtiers and their attention-seeking tame cheetahs or pet monkeys who were trained to climb the trees and bring back fruit for their master and mistress. They had participated in formal banquets and feasts in the great halls of Malkata, eating iced melon or drinking the rich wines, jars of which were now being carried to Pharaoh's last resting place, along with the funereal breads and meats. Now there would be no more banquets, no more festivals.

Ankhesenamun was grief-stricken. She was not only a widow but childless and, when her husband was laid to rest, his tomb would also include two small coffins carrying Tutankhamun's children; a foetus of about five months, born prematurely, and a child who'd died immediately after birth.

[15]

Ankhesenamun would feel the full horror of loneliness: for she was the last surviving member of the Tuthmosid line and this sad fact carried the seeds of further tribulation. She would feel the heat and dirt of the valley, grow faint after her long period of mourning and so welcome the cool, fragrant shade of the ostrich-plume fans, soaked in perfume, wafting above her.

As the procession went deeper into the Valley of the Kings, its strange red-brown stone gathering up like a sombre shroud around them, some of the retinue would be left behind as Pharaoh's entourage approached his House of Eternity, built close to those of his predecessors. Perhaps it was here that the ritual red oxen would be dispensed with and the sledge now pulled on the final part of its journey by twelve leading officials clothed in white, mourning bands of the same colour wrapped round their foreheads, the place of honour being given to Tutankhamun's viziers of Upper and Lower Egypt, Pentju and Usermont. Despite the heat and the dust, the chanting would continue, verses from the book of the Dead, the hymn to Osiris's divine company: 'Hail to you, you owners of souls . . .'

At last they reached the entrance to Tutankhamun's House of Eternity. In the sacred precinct before the tomb the most important ceremony would be carried out, the Opening of the Mouth, in order that the dead Pharaoh be able to breathe, unite with his Ka and intone the magic incantations from the Book of the Dead. The ground would be consecrated and purified with water from four sacred vessels. Incense-burners would send out gusts of fragrant perfume as the ritual slaughter of animals was performed which recalled Horus's immortal battle with Seth. Bulls, gazelles and ducks were

[16]

sacrificed. By virtue of this magical ritual, Tutankhamun now represented Osiris; the sacrificial killing symbolized a sacred rite as well as providing more food for Tutankhamun's journey and the feasting of the mourners.

According to the ritual, Muu dancers, who greeted the corpse at the entrance to the tomb, performed their dance to the music of harpists, whilst attendant priests incensed the air. The most important ceremony, the Opening of the Mouth, finally took place: the officiating Sem priest would lead the rite. The mummy would be daubed with milk and embraced three times, then the mouth of the mummy would be touched with the haunch of a slaughtered bull and the sacred instrument. The mouth and eyes were symbolically opened and Horus was invoked so that the deceased could walk and speak, and his body join the Great Company. Of course, whilst this ceremony was being carried out, Tutankhamun's corpse would be resting upright inside its shrine on the sledge so one of the guardian statues would be used instead. After being assured that the young king would breathe in the next world, the coffin was taken down the sixteen steps into the tomb, through the antechamber and into the place of burial where a rectangular stone sarcophagus containing three coffins, to be placed one inside the other, were waiting. Everything else was ready: the gold sides of four shrines would house, one inside the other, the golden-yellow sarcophagus; the four canopic jars inside their small shrines held the entrails and viscera of the dead Pharaoh.

The chamber would be crowded, the smell of incense, burning oil and freshly spilt blood pungently strong. The oil lamps in their alabaster jars glowed so the priest could recite the prayers and then the body was lowered into its lasting resting place. After the sarcophagus was closed and the treasures placed in the different chambers, this House of Eternity was sealed by the swift construction of plaster walls and makeshift doors. The rite would finish with a meal consumed at the entrance to the tomb by the principal mourners, all garbed in flower garlands. Afterwards the entrance would be finally closed and the ceremony completed . . .

This is how it should have been and, for most Pharaohs, perhaps it was. However, the death and burial of Tutankhamun conceals a dark and sinister mystery and his tomb and corpse bear eloquent testimony to this. The discovery of Tutankhamun's tomb and mummy by Howard Carter in the 1920s, as well as the more focused scholarship of modern Egyptologists, have ripped away a veil of secrecy and posed questions about Tutankhamun's death and burial which echo those awesome protestations from the Book of the Dead.

Was Tutankhamun's corpse prepared properly in the Wabet and later in the House of Beautification, or somewhere else? In 1907 the archaeologist Theodore Davis discovered a site now known as Pit 54 (sometimes designated Valley of the Kings Tomb No. 54 or KV54 for short). Davis actually thought it was a tomb but the curator of the Metropolitan Museum, New York's Egyptian Department, Herbert Winlock realized it was really a pit used by the embalmers to dump materials following the mummification of Tutankhamun's body. Pit 54 is only a short walk from KV62, Tutankhamun's tomb. Was Tutankhamun's body secretly dressed for burial at this lonely outpost in the Valley of the Kings?

Tutankhamun's tomb (KV62) may hold a treasure trove but

[18]

there was no mortuary temple, nor can the tomb be classed as truly worthy of a Pharaoh. Tutankhamun died before his mortuary temple or his proper tomb were finished; the one in which he was buried was selected by Ay: KV62 is hardly a fitting choice for an imperial prince with its narrow passages and dingy, small chambers.

Was Tutankhamun's corpse dressed for burial according to the proper ritual? It may be difficult to accept that it was not, bearing in mind the treasure hoard which filled his grave. Nevertheless, the embalming shows signs of an unholy haste. From the very beginning those who first inspected both Tutankhamun's tomb and his corpse have drawn attention to this haste. 'We found to our dismay that the mummy of Tutankhamun was in poor condition due, as is now clear, to the profuse anointings to which it had been been subjected,' Howard Carter reported.

Was this profusion the result of undue speed and poor light? An X-ray examination of Tutankhamun's skull by Professor Harrison of Liverpool University in 1968 indicated the head cavity was filled with unguents to keep the skull intact. However, this was done clumsily, the corpse being thrown about so that the substances introduced into his skull settled unevenly. Both Douglas Derry, who carried out a post-mortem in the 1920s, and Professor Harrison who repeated the process in the 1960s, commented on the ritual embalming incision along the left side. Derry talks of the cut being of 'ragged appearance', longer than it should have been, and somewhat different from that of other royal mummies which had been examined. Now this cut by the Ethiopian stone was an integral part of the ritual yet, according to the evidence, it was hurried and completed in a rather inexpert way.

[19]

Moreover, one of the aims of the embalmers, after the intestines etc. had been removed, was to restore the body to its normal shape. Derry, however, talks of a 'marked bulging on the right side . . . due to the forcing of the packing material across the abdominal cavity'.

Further evidence of haste is demonstrated in Derry's report when he talks of 'some whitish spots on the skin over the upper part of the back and shoulders'. These proved to be common salt mixed with sodium sulphate, the remains of the natron bath used in the embalming process. However, one of the principal functions of the embalmers in the House of Beautification was to remove all signs of the natron by careful cleansing and anointing, so why should so much natron be also seen all over the upper part of the back of the corpse? The limbs and head of Tutankhamun also became detached. To be sure, Howard Carter was not fully truthful in his description of how he actually handled the royal corpse (and sufficient proof exists of some rather rough handling) but he does admit that the corpse was virtually stuck in its tomb whilst the exquisite face mask was most difficult to remove. Carter and Derry also comment on how desiccated the head and limbs were:

> The cracked and brittle state of the skin of the head and face . . . was even more marked in the body and limbs . . . the skin of the legs, like the rest of the body, was a greyish-white colour, very brittle and exhibiting numerous cracks.

Derry then adds: 'The limbs appear very shrunken.' This begs the question of whether Tutankhamun's corpse was

[20]

given the full seventy days preparation or were the embalmers under strict orders to hasten the process? One way of doing this was to increase the strength of the natron solution used to remove moisture from the body. Was the natron so strong that the embalmers over-dried the mummy, and rendered it so stick-like and ingrained to the point of making it impossible to wash from the corpse? True, this could be said of other mummies. However, as Derry comments:

> With one or two exceptions, none of the Pharaohs have been found in his original tomb. Few in their coffins and none except Tutankhamun has ever been seen in the wrappings, coffins, sarcophagus and tomb in which he was originally laid to rest.

Carter's report also mentions a 'spontaneous combustion ... the result of some humidity at the time of interment as well as the decomposition of the unguents which generated a high temperature'. So, was Tutankhamun's mummy left in the open for some time? Was it taken into the tomb and laid elsewhere before being hermetically sealed inside its coffins? And why the delay?

Carter demonstrates that the mummy must have been placed in the tomb first and only then were the treasures brought in. Accordingly, we must revise the accepted story and ask: was Tutankhamun's body truly cleansed and purified according to the Osirian ritual in the Wabet and the House of Beautification? Or was it done clumsily and hastily in that lonely cave (KV54) with its bags of natron and rags of soiled resin?

Were the rites at the entrance to the tomb as lavish as they

[21]

should have been? Were all the priests present and the correct liturgy followed? The remains of the funeral feast found in KV54 indicate a meal for no more than eight people. Who were these? Why so meagre? Why so rushed that the remains were simply dumped in an adjoining pit? Was Tutankhamun seen to his House of Eternity with all the funeral pomp of an imperial state? Or hurried by a few into the sombre loneliness of the Valley of the Kings?

And the contents of the treasury annexe and store room? Time and again Carter's original report talks of undue haste, of an undignified chaos, of the materials simply being thrown in. Panels and lids being broken, shrines and caskets crudely trimmed to fit. Most of the wine was out of date, the food wrongly labelled, the sheets of the shrine hastily assembled and beaten together so forcefully they dented. The paintings on the tomb walls are unfinished and unaligned. The list of such discrepancies is long. Moreover, the suspicion surfaces that a great deal of the treasure was simply taken from somewhere else and that even includes the gorgeous face mask. The similarity between the corpse in nearby KV55 (Semenkhkare) and KV62 (Tutankhamun) has been clearly established. Was the latter's corpse taken secretly to the Valley of the Kings to be dressed and prepared for burial whilst the treasures, which Tutankhamun's tomb now holds, were removed from KV55? Some of the treasures bear Semenkhkare's titles, one of the beds definitely belonged to him. KV55 was apparently pillaged, on the orders of Ay, who wished to secretly supplement the meagre goods he had managed to smuggle from Tutankhamun's quarters at Malkata.

Why is Tutankhamun so often referred to as the child or boy Pharaoh? He was at least eighteen when he died, a good age for a country and culture where fifty per cent of the population never reached the age of thirty.

Why is Tutankhamun's tomb so empty of anything which tells us more about this Pharaoh – as a person in his own right – than that he cut a reed for a walking stick and collected some ostrich plumes for a fan? There are stylish portrayals of him riding a chariot, crushing enemies but Tutankhamun never went to war. He may have hunted but many portrayals of him, from his own tomb and elsewhere, depict him as indolent, sitting down – even when hunting.

Why did he have so many walking sticks, why over 400 shabtis to help in the after life? Was this Pharaoh a sickly man, in both mind and body?

These questions raise more vital ones. If the burial, despite all appearances, was unholy in its haste, were the perpetrators trying to hide something else? After Tutankhamun's skull was X-rayed by Harrison, Egyptologists quickly focused on one dramatic result of this X-ray, a definite swelling at the back of Tutankhamun's skull just behind the left ear. Was that, they asked, the result of a blow? If so, was it an accident or the bloody-handed work of some disciple of the red-haired god Seth? The head wound might be explained but why were his sternum and part of his rib cage missing?

If Tutankhamun was murdered, and the secrecy surrounding his death suggests he might have been, who was the assassin? One of the wall paintings from Tutankhamun's tomb provides an answer. It depicts the powerful Ay playing a leading role in the important ceremony of the Opening of the Mouth. However, Ay is not dressed as a vizier or a courtier but as Pharaoh! The sly old Chancellor had apparently usurped the double crown of Egypt, a clear violation of custom before the seventy-day period of mourning was finished. Moreover, what legitimate claim did Ay have to the throne? So was he the assassin? And the other seven his accomplices? Even Ankhesenamun? She was to prove before long that, despite her husband's death, she was determined to remain as a power in Egypt. Was she in collusion with Ay? Did she betray her young husband to her grandfather so as to share power? Some evidence exists to indicate this. A ring has been found which juxtaposes Ankhesenamun's cartouche (seal) alongside that of Ay. Finally, the evidence from the tomb and its contents betray one serious omission, the dark, brooding influence of General Horemheb, Egypt's Saviour, the Crusher of the People of the Nine Bows, Egypt's traditional enemies. Where was he when Tutankhamun was buried? What role, if any, did he play in those macabre events?

Tutankhamun undoubtedly was hurried to his grave, shrouded in secrecy. My analysis of his death and burial reveals a story of treason and treachery, of sacred rituals being ignored, of usurpation and intense political rivalry resulting in a bloody massacre at some lonely oasis on Egypt's borders. Out of the darkness of this mystery emerge men and women who lived over 3,000 years ago, who fought and struggled for power and, perhaps in some cases, paid the ultimate price. Tutankhamun's death and burial are like the gorgeous blue-gold mask which covered the young Pharaoh's face.

Its exquisite beauty fails to hide the sinister, hideous truth lurking beneath.

1

Pharaoh: the Glory of Egypt

I am a great one, the son of a great one.
I am a flame, the son of a flame.
Spell 43: *The Book of the Dead*

ANCIENT EGYPT'S FASCINATION IS EVERLASTING. Within or around its borders shoot long stems of culture, theology, philosophy, art and architecture which have had such a telling impact on succeeding civilizations. Ancient Egypt is an enigmatic paradox. The symbols and outward manifestations of its grandeur are obvious, yet there is much which is still hidden, which cannot be explained. This enigmatic paradox is reflected in the geographical structure of the country, a mixture of arid desert, the Red Lands or 'Des-hert' cut by the life-giving waters of the river Nile which rise deep in the south and flow into the broad seething Delta and on into the Great Green, the Middle Sea or Mediterranean. On either bank of the Nile stretch the Black Lands, the rich earth from which ancient Egypt drew its inspiration and wealth. The land itself was inhabited, as it is now, by a mixture of peoples: sand-dwellers and desert-wanderers, locked in their ancient rituals, together with the sophisticated inhabitants of sprawling cities, the grandeur of which rivalled the glories of Babylon, the magnificence of Persepolis or the majesty of ancient Athens; a country where poverty rubbed cheek by jowl with an opulent profusion of wealth which outshone

[27]

even the richness of Louis XIV's Versailles or the Ming dynasty of China.

Ancient Egypt was a mixture of stark simplicity and complex theology, art, architecture and craft work, a country of openness, with its vast deserts and fertile strips dominated by the persistent rhythms of nature, which contrasted sharply with the mystery of its soaring pyramids, hallowed temples, the ever brooding Sphinx and weather-beaten colossi. It was a kingdom of dusty trackways and barren wilderness, yet these held, and still hide, the secretive and sacred precincts of the Necropolis, the Valley of the Kings and Queens, which speaks so eloquently of another reality, another land, The Everlasting Far West, beyond the Far Horizon, where the Fields of the Blessed stretch eternally, the Kingdom of the Holy Osiris.

Historians debate the origins of ancient Egypt, its development from a collection of clans and petty kingdoms (later the nomes or provinces of Egypt) into the great divisions of the south (the Upper Kingdom) and the north (the Lower Kingdom) under their respective rulers, the kings wearing the white crown of Lower Egypt and the red of Upper Egypt. In about 3300 both kingdoms united under one clan and the double crown of Pharaoh. The title Pharaoh comes from the phrase 'God's House' or 'The Great House', illustrating how, from the very beginning, ancient Egypt's rulers enjoyed a semi-divine status. Following the writings of Manetho, the history of ancient Egypt has been rather arbitrarily divided into kingdoms, the Old, the Middle and the New, as well as by a succession of dynasties or ruling families which can be traced from about 3100 BC. The very length of ancient Egypt's history gives the illusion of development and tranquillity: the truth is very different. It is a story of violent warfare, bloodshed, conflict and ever-brooding tensions between Upper and Lower Egypt, between successive families and, above all, between Pharaohs and the various empires which grew up around Egypt's borders and threatened its security.

Each Pharaonic dynasty left its mark. The capital of Egypt was moved, according to the whims and religious ritual of its rulers, from Memphis in the north to what the Greeks called Thebes in the south. To ancient Egyptians, Thebes was simply known as Waset, the City, the Sceptre or Great City of the Gods, what Homer vividly described as 'Thebes of a Hundred Gates'. Succeeding dynasties expressed themselves in different funeral monuments, be it the pyramids of Giza or the great mortuary temples of Sakkara, near Memphis. Successive Pharaohs also tried to broaden and establish their kingdom in a search for security as well as hoards of wealth to fill their treasury, furnish their troops and fund their building programmes. Egypt's armies, according to the strength of different Pharaohs, marched east across Sinai, west against the warlike desert tribes and, most importantly, south past the First Cataract into the mysterious kingdom of Nubia which the ancient Egyptians called the Land of Kush. Kush was important to Egypt not only for timber but also for its rich mineral deposits and gold mines.

During the first seventeen dynasties, Egypt's fortunes fluctuated depending on the strength and military prowess of different Pharaohs. However, c.1650 BC, ancient Egypt faced one of its great crises, the season of the Hyena, when the Hyksos, foreign rulers of Semitic origin, invaded the Delta, conquered the north of Egypt and drove Pharaoh's power south so it could only be exercised in the area around Thebes. The Hyksos, a confederation of warlike tribes, set up their capital at Avaris in the Delta. Increasingly Hyksos rulers looked jealously south to the wealth and riches of Pharaoh. The Hyksos chariot squadrons, great four-wheeled war carts, edged further and further along the Nile, threatening to extinguish the power of Pharaoh for good. So confident did the Hyksos grow that one of its princes, or so legend has it, sent an impudent message south to Sekenenre-tao, the ruler of Thebes, complaining how the hippopotami in the royal pool there were disturbing his sleep and must be silenced or he would do it for him. Such a story cannot be verified but it reveals the Hyksos' desire to seek a *casus belli*, a reason to go to war against the rulers of Thebes and extinguish their power once and for all. Sekenenre resisted, his mummy has been found and the vicious wounds to his head, by an Asiatic war axe, illustrate how savage and fierce the Hyksos conflict became.

Eventually Sekenenre's second son, Ahmose, counter-attacked. The rulers of Thebes had studied the Hyksos very carefully and evolved their own war machine, including a swifter, lighter version of the chariot. It was all-out war, what the ancient consuls of Rome would call *bellum terra marique, igne gladioque* – 'war by land and sea with fire and sword'. Ahmose master-minded the campaign, sending his chariot squadrons 'like flames of fire before him' whilst he led a fleet of ships up the Nile. The Hyksos stubbornly resisted but Ahmose was successful, storming the city of Avaris. The Hyksos were expelled and Ahmose, founder of the eighteenth dynasty, began a systematic campaign of retrenchment followed by expansion.

A series of warlike and powerful successors cemented Ahmose's work. Amenhotep I confirmed Thebes as the capital of Egypt, founding the Necropolis, the City of the Dead, with its host of craftsmen involved in the making of funerary equipment, on the west bank of the Nile. Amenhotep also developed the temple complex at what is now called Karnak, the Most Perfect of Places, just to the north-west of Thebes. This became the home of the Theban god Amun, the Silent One, whose worship was developed so he rose in prominence amongst the gods of ancient Egypt. Amenhotep and his successors despatched their armies east, west and south, driving back the sand-dwellers and the Libyan tribes, and then east along the Horus Road which cut across Sinai into Canaan. Such ruthless aggression not only protected Egypt against foreign threat but also satisfied Egyptian hunger for gold, jewels, precious metals and wood. At the same time fresh armies under Tuthmosis I re-invaded the land of Kush, going beyond the Second and Third Cataracts, bringing the Nubians under the sway of Egypt and restoring the flow of precious tribute. So vital did Kush become that it had its own Viceroy, Pharaoh's direct representative, who consolidated Egyptian power by building magnificent fortresses protected by deep ditches and soaring mud-brick walls at least eight yards wide. Under the female Pharaoh Hatshepsut and her successors, Tuthmosis III and Tuthmosis IV, Egypt's foreign adventures continued. Its squadrons of war chariots reached the Euphrates, bringing under Egyptian rule the fertile coastline of Canaan with its rich deep-water ports of Tyre and Sidon. Time and again these Pharaohs proclaimed their greatness, boasting how they had driven back and conquered 'the vile Asiatic' or the 'rebels of Kush'.

The early Pharaohs of the Eighteenth Dynasty developed a

[31]

military machine which became feared throughout the Ancient Middle East: long lines of footmen, armed with spear, sword and shield in thick padded linen armour and striped headdresses. These were reinforced by hordes of mercenaries bought by Egyptian gold. However, the main part of this war machine was the war chariots of wood, leather and wicker-work embellished and embossed with electrum, a special alloy of gold and other metals. These two-wheeled chariots, six spokes to each wheel, carried two men: the charioteer, who managed the two-horse team and defended his companion with a large wooden shield. The latter was the 'fighting man', he was protected by body armour and carried a composite bow, a quiver of bronze-tipped arrows, as well as a sheath of javelins strapped to the side of the chariot. The purpose of this war machine was two-fold. A glance at the map shows how Egypt has few natural boundaries or fortifications. Sea-borne invaders from the Great Green could invade the Delta while the Nile, the life-blood of the kingdom, could be attacked and controlled by tribes living in the Red Lands, or any great power which rose across the Horus Road in Canaan. Egypt had not forgotten the Season of the Hyena. Its conquests and warlike stance were to ensure that it never occurred again. The second purpose of Egypt's foreign policy was its hunger, not only for treasure and bounty, but for essential goods and raw materials, such as wood, so lacking in its own country.

The constant flood of foreign tribute into Egypt trans-formed the country and nowhere better than at Thebes. Memphis, standing at the apex of the Delta in Lower Egypt, had been the traditional administrative capital. However, under the Eighteenth Dynasty, Thebes grew into the country's greatest city, its capital the home of the great God Amun-Re, and the site of the Necropolis and its rulers' Mansions of Eternity. However, Thebes' west bank not only housed the royal tombs, begun by Tuthmosis I in the Valley of the Kings, but also the burial place of the King's subjects. On the east bank the gorgeous city of the living, 'Thebes of a Hundred Gates', with the gold-capped temple cornices and silver-topped obelisks, became a thriving metropolis. To the north of the city stood the temple complex of Karnak and, at the centre of this, the shrine to Amun-Re. Once just a god of Thebes but now increasingly linked to the sun god Re, Amun-Re became the dominant god of Egypt. To this god and his priests, Pharaohs paid massive tribute and expressed their devotion in sophisticated building programmes which included statues, pylons (gateways), temples, stelae and obelisks of black granite, brown quartzite, white limestone and creamy alabaster. Pharaoh's power, and that of Amun-Re, was made manifest through papyrus proclamations, carvings and, especially, by paintings; these boasted of the exploits of Amun-Re and his beloved son Pharaoh, victorious and triumphant over a myriad of enemies. Such paintings were stylistic, often embellished with the ruler's personal seal or cartouche. Pharaoh would emphasize his power in more public displays by 'showing his face' to the people in the Hall of Audience, on the royal balcony, at the Window of Appearances or on ritual occasions such as the Festival of Opet. The latter took place in the second month of the yearly flood when the statue of the great god Amun-Re was moved, in a highly ornate ceremony and procession, along the Nile to the temple complex of Luxor so Pharaoh could, once again, commune with the divine and receive fresh power and glory.

By the time the great Amenhotep III was crowned Pharaoh

(c.1391 BC) Egypt was reaching its pinnacle of power, both at home and abroad. The kingdom was dominated by four elements. The first was Pharaoh, wearer of the crowns of Upper and Lower Egypt as well as the khepresh, the blue war crown. He was the Owner of the Great House who held the flail and the rod, the symbols of Egyptian justice, and rejoiced in his semi-divine titles. He was the living Son of the God where Heaven and Earth met. Statues of Amenhotep III found beneath the floor of the Luxor temple illustrate the status of Pharaoh in all his glory. Carved out of red quartzite, Pharaoh is wearing the Double Crown of Eqypt with its lunging uraeus (the Spitting Cobra), as well as a serpent collar, whilst a jewelled apron, decorated with uraei and embellished with solar discs, hangs over a beautifully pleated kilt of the finest linen. Amenhotep's 'Face of Power' was carved to shine down on his people as the sun did when it rose at dawn. Pharaoh's rule was absolute. He was both political and religious leader, his subjects were there to serve him. Pharaoh was their intermediary with the gods and his glory was manifest, not only in his palaces but in his magnificent building programmes across the Nile. The principal amongst these was the House of Eternity being redecorated for Amenhotep's journey to the Far Horizon to take his place in the Kingdom of the Blessed with the Divine Osiris.

The second dominant element of ancient Egypt was its pantheon of gods. Each city, each province or nomes, had its own god, or gods, often associated with the different functions of Nature as well as human activity. The growth and multiplicity of this pantheon eventually drew the mockery of the Latin poet Juvenal who exclaimed how the Egyptians would eventually turn anything into a god. Nevertheless, this fascination with the divine is evidence of ancient Egypt's awareness of another life. There was a consensus that the world had been created by a union between the sky goddess Nut and the earth god Geb under the protection and direction of the great Amun-Re. Nut and Geb had four children: Osiris, Seth, Isis and Nepthys. This sacred foursome gave rise to one of the most holy rituals of ancient Egypt. According to accepted belief, the red-haired Seth, consumed with envy, had caught and slaughtered his brother Osiris who was brought back to life by his sister and wife Isis, helped by Nepthys. Osiris and Isis had a child, the Hawk-Headed Horus who, armed with sacred powers, fought and struggled with his uncle Seth and eventually vindicated his sacred father Osiris. The Osirian ritual is closely associated with the seasons of Egypt, the rise and fall of the Nile, with death and rebirth. This, in turn, gave hope to the Egyptians that, provided they followed that ritual, both its physical as well as its spiritual tenets, immortality could be achieved. Other gods also ranked in the Egyptian pantheon, such as Anubis the Jackal-Headed Lord of the Mortuary, the overseer of funerary rites; Sekhmet, the Ravaging Lioness, the Bringer of Destruction; Hathor, the Goddess of Jubilation in human form, with a crown of cow horns around the sun disc on her head; Thoth, the Ibis-Headed scribe god, the recorder of men's deeds; Ma'at, daughter of Amun-Re, the goddess of truth and harmony, in whose scales of justice every soul would be placed for judgement. Different provinces, different cities favoured different gods; however, under the Eighteenth Dynasty, Amun-Re became paramount and his glory was manifest at Karnak.

The third important element was the army. Amenhotep III may have been the first Egyptian king to separate his chariot corps from the rest of the army, as well as deploy the first Egyptian mounted soldiers. Pharaoh was the army's commander-in-chief and sometimes led his troops into battle. More usually, however, Pharaoh's place on the field of battle was taken by his principal commander who rejoiced in the title of King's Son. The generals of Egypt led divisions of up to 5,000 men named after the leading gods of Egypt: Amun, Isis, Ptah, Osiris and Horus. The troops were commanded by officers known as standard-bearers. Their principal weaponry were the chariots, the sickle-shaped khopesh, swords, daggers, shields, the powerful composite bow, quivers of arrows and javelins; their body armour was usually of leather-covered padded linen. There was also the royal fleet made up of ships and barges with names like *The Glory of Aten*, *The Power of Amun*, *Our River Is Strong*, *The Star in Memphis*, *The Beloved of Amun* and *The Wild Bull* had masts and sails with added features such as cabins for officers. Wooden parapets along the decks, with gaps for oars, protected the rowers from arrows, whilst their prows had dramatic carvings, such as the head of the goddess Sekhmet devouring some 'vile' Asiatic. Egyptian troops and marines were a mixture of professionals, levies, as well as mercenaries from Kush and the various tribes of Canaan and Libya. Countless friezes of war paintings depict their victories, and captives of different nationalities, arms bound behind them, being led in triumph before Pharaoh or being crushed in battle by Pharaoh's troops. During peace time these troops, stationed in great garrisons at Memphis and Thebes, would also maintain public order, men such as Nebamun who, on Amenhotep's accession, was chief of police in western Thebes, whilst his brother Tury controlled eastern Thebes and, in Memphis, an ambitious military scribe

[36]

Horemheb would be promoted to be in charge of recruits, responsible for their life in barracks where they would await the pleasures of Pharaoh's will.

The fourth dominant element in ancient Egypt were the priests. Pharaoh might be the gods' regent on earth but, for practical purposes, many of his duties were delegated to the high priest of each deity, paramount amongst these being Amun-Re, the focus of the state religion. The leading high priest of Amun-Re was given the title of First Prophet and was supported in his role by other prophets. Priests were the servants of the gods. Amun-Re was worshipped by an army of different attendants, all of whom had to be ritually puri-fied: they bathed four times a day in the Pools of Purity, shaved all body hair and were garbed in robes of the purest linen. Each temple had its own hierarchy, such as lector priests, responsible for the sacred texts, or astronomer priests who studied the heavens in order to establish the correct time for certain rituals and performances. There were musicians and dancers. The Entertainers of Amun included high-ranking women. The temples had their own craftsmen, sculp-tors, overseers, architects and painters. Although established for religious purposes, the temples not only had their own workshops and long retinues of different flunkeys and servants but their own libraries and colleges – the Houses of Life. Temple priests owned vast estates in order to fund their building and festival programmes. They were directors of powerful corporations and, as the Greek historian Herodotus observed, lived a life of opulence and ease. 'They neither consume or spend anything of their own. Sacred food is cooked for them: to each is brought, every day, beef and geese in great abundance and the finest grape wines.' The priests married and enjoyed family life though, at certain times, they had to be chaste, free of any sexual contact. They were distinguished by their shaven heads, fine linen robes and white sandals. Lector priests often wore a ribbon across their chests, whilst leaders of the hierarchy wore leopard or panther skins across the shoulder or robes adorned with ritual necklaces and insignia.

The temples of Egypt were, therefore, not only places of worship and meditation but often the centre of civic activity, places of study, of medicine as well as the focus for pilgrims who wanted to cultivate their favourite god. Temple worship lay at the heart of Egyptian society, its economy as well as its theology, which accounts for the horror and chaos caused by Akhenaten's later attack on the gods of Egypt. Akhenaten's desire to create a new theology, a new reality, threatened to shatter all that had gone before.

The temples themselves were most impressive. There were cult temples to particular gods; smaller mortuary temples, set up like medieval chantries, to offer a litany of intercession for the dead; and sun temples, open to the sky with an obelisk to mark the centre of worship. The great temples of Karnak and Luxor were the most impressive. They were Pure Places and so ringed by great sloping walls intersected by gateways or pylons. These monumental gateways were approached by broad, basalt-stone avenues lined with ram sphinxes on either side. Above the gateway stood long poles sheathed in electrum, an alloy of gold, silver and copper, from which coloured pennants hung. The pylons, gatehouses and door-ways were decorated with evocative scenes glorifying the gods, Pharaoh or the achievements of the temple priests. Before the pylons stood soaring obelisks, capped in some special metal, on which were carved prayers, proclamations or the boastful achievements of Pharaoh.

The pylons at Karnak enclosed a small city in itself, the main building being the temple proper with steps sweeping up to the principal entrance, flanked by spacious courtyards. Beyond that lay the hypostyle, a hall of brightly-coloured columns. The tops of these pillars or columns were carved in the shape of lilies or acanthus leaves, painted to look as if they were twisting papyrus stems rising up from a floor, polished as smooth as glass, to look like water. This, in turn, would mirror a ceiling painted like the star-strewn sky. Deeper into the temple, in its darkest part, reached last by the rays of the rising sun, would stand the god's shrine, his naos or taber-nacle. This was served by the stolists, those priests who could enter the Holy of Holies every morning and at other prescribed times during the day. The stolist priests would open the doors of the naos, bring out the god's statue, embrace and anoint it, wrap it in pure white linen and lay before it baskets of choicest fruits, breads and meats as well as garlands of flowers.

The temple complexes also included libraries and schools, Lakes of Tranquillity, Pools of Purity, scriptoria and small side chapels. Gardens, enriched by black soil specially imported from Canaan, were freshly watered and tended, as well as sweeping lawns on which ibex, sheep and other animals grazed. The priests and their acolytes had other duties: they were business men as well as servants of the god. They were supposed to be 'pure' but they also had their fingers on the economic pulse of the country. Under Amenhotep III's reign the fourth prophet priest of the temple of Amun at Karnak was 'The sealer of every contract in

Karnak', apparently a cleric who was given a window of opportunity into most of the business dealings which took place in Pharaoh's thriving city. Whilst another, Pari, was 'overseer of the farms of Egypt', able to control the food supply. The power of the priests, particularly those of Amun, were a growing force to be reckoned with: they played, and would continue to play, a vital role in the politics of Egypt.

A further element in Egyptian life were a cluster of high-ranking court officials and senior scribes who formed Pharaoh's court and helped to run his empire. Many Theban relief scenes on the walls of palaces, temples or in the Houses of Eternity across the Nile, show these courtiers, high-ranking officials either displaying their glory or receiving the personal approbation of Pharaoh: being anointed or receiving the shebyu, the golden collar of honour, a sign of great trust at the imperial Egyptian court. These high-ranking courtiers lived in the palace but they also owned their own stately mansions and extensive estates. During their lives they built splendid tombs across the Nile in the Necropolis or, in singular cases, even in the Valley of the Kings itself; men such as Maya who rose to be State-Treasurer, serving Pharaohs Akhenaten, Tutankhamun, Ay and Horemheb. A Pharaoh's favourite such as Amenhotep III's cavalry commander Yuya, was allowed to carve his own tomb in the Valley of Kings. Many offices were hereditary, posts being handed down from father to son. The Sobek family in the south of Thebes, for example, held high-ranking posts in the Treasury. Nevertheless, other posts were open to men of great ability, irrespective of their origins. This reflects the biblical story of Joseph who fled from his brothers, was taken as a slave and rose high in Pharaoh's favour. Joseph's rise is mirrored by that of the great Pharaoh's namesake, Amenhotep, son of Hapu, who hailed from the Delta area.

A commoner, Amenhotep, son of Hapu, was educated at some temple school where his ability soon became known. As one of his statues proclaims, he was 'educated in the god's books [the temple library] and studied the words of Thoth' (the scribe god's hieroglyphs). Officials such as Amenhotep were not bashful, or modest, regarding their exploits: he describes himself as 'a truly excellent scribe, the first one to calculate anything'. He rose to become Scribe of Recruits, responsible for Egypt's manpower, and then held one of the most prestigious offices at court, the Overseer of All Works. Amenhotep played his prominent role in the Pharaoh's magnificent building campaign:

> I directed the King's likeness in every hard stone under Heaven, directing the works of his statues . . . I did not imitate what had gone before . . . There never has been anyone who has done the same since the founding of the Two Lands.

The rise of Amenhotep, son of Hapu, must have been noticed by another commoner, the future general and scribe of the army, Horemheb. Also a northerner of obscure origin, Horemheb served as a military officer under a succession of Pharaohs before achieving supreme office himself. Pharaoh's men were career administrators who belonged to a professional cadre, they worked hard for the ruler whilst gathering wealth, power and titles for themselves. Yuya rose to become chief minister under Amenhotep III and not only received the shebyu but forty other titles including Prince, Royal

Confidant, First Among the King's Companions, High Priest of Min, Lieutenant General of the King's Chariots. Such high-ranking officials can be described as viziers, Pharaoh's representatives. The duties of a vizier were laid down by Pharaoh Tuthmosis III who warned his first minister: 'Be vigilant regarding your office and all that is done within its name since it supports the whole land. In truth the office of vizier is not sweet but is, in fact, as bitter as gall.'

During Amenhotep III's reign these administrative offices were developed. There was a vizier for the north and south of the country, whilst the Viceroy of Kush had direct responsibility for one of the main sources of Egyptian wealth. To the north-east of Egypt, where Pharaoh's cartouche or seal held sway over the land of Canaan, that area was divided between the three Overseers of the Northern Countries. One of the most important court officials was the Overseer of Things which are Sealed, a post which approximates to that of our Chancellor of the Exchequer. He, like the others, was supported by a virtual army of royal scribes who held the most coveted posts. A Middle Kingdom text praises the office of scribe as, 'There is no job without an overseer except that of a scribe.' The ancient text 'The Teaching of Duat Khety' advises, 'Set your heart to writings . . . as for any scribe in any position . . . you shall not be wretched in this . . . he fills another's need. Shall not the scribe end up content? I cannot see another trade like it!'

These scribes were trained in local temple schools, a most rigorous education. The scribe would learn mathematics, accounting, history and geography but also the art of understanding and copying over 700 hieroglyphic symbols which represented sounds, objects and ideas, as well as the flowing

[42]

hieratic script and the plainer demotic writing. The scribe would be trained in the use of reed pens, his palette would contain pots of red and black ink, as well as the necessary knife for sharpening his pen tips. He would also become an expert in preparing the inner white pith of the papyrus reed: he would understand how it was laid out, intertwined, pounded out into a sticky sheet and dried under a weight until it became soft and pliable. After this the papyrus manuscript would be polished and cleaned with a piece of ivory or wood, ready for use and, when the document was completed, stored in the appropriate jar or basket.

The final element of ancient Egyptian life was the Osirian rite, the idea of rebirth and resurrection. Naturally this sprang from the Egyptian perception of nature, particularly the function of the Nile, the fundamental arbiter of Egyptian life. The Egyptian new year began when, after dropping behind the horizon for seventy days, the dog star Sirius or Sopet reappeared at sunrise. Egyptians, from long experience and careful observation, recognized this was a time for the level of the Nile to start rising, just as flocks of white ibises appeared in the fields on their migration to the south. Modern geographers explain how, in fact, the Nile's inundation is created by monsoons on the Ethiopian plateau, the source of the Nile, as well as to a lesser extent around Lake Victoria and its surrounding mountains where the White Nile originates. The Nile not only inundated the land but brought with it rich soil deposits. The ancient Egyptians regarded this as an annual miracle, for which they paid devout service, as well as the symbol of resurrection and rebirth in their own lives.

To the ancient Egyptians death was not an end, only a change, whilst the veil between life and death was very thin and could be parted. A red pottery bowl, forty centimetres in diameter, now in the Cairo Museum and dating from the early Twelfth Dynasty, contains a most singular letter written by Dedi to her husband Intef. Dedi complains how her serving maid is ill, she berates her husband for not doing more to help both herself and her maid. She warns Intef, 'Your house will be destroyed.' 'Fight for her,' Dedi adds, 'Watch over her.' The letter is significant because Intef is not away from home or some husband lost in his own pursuits of career or pleasure. Intef, in fact, is dead. Dedi is writing to him on a piece of pottery which was placed near his tomb asking him to intervene, very similar to a modern Catholic demanding the intercession of a favourite saint. Dedi's letter proves how ancient Egyptians, not only their Pharaohs and great lords but the ordinary people, believed they lived in a reality where life and death mingled, where the visible and invisible were closely connected.

One of the most telling characeristics of ancient Egypt is that culture's absorption not only with life around the Nile but life beyond death in the Kingdom of the Blessed West, across the Far Horizon, where Osiris and the other gods lived in glory. The early dynasties built their pyramids, mastabas and tombs at Giza and Sakkara in the north. Other towns had their own Cities of the Dead but the Pharaoh Tuthmosis I of the Eighteenth Dynasty was the first to use his builder Intef to exploit that lonely, rocky vein of valleys which are included in the majestic title Valley of the Kings across the Nile to the west of Thebes. Tuthmosis I's example was followed by his successors. The art of preparing for the after life not only led to those royal mausoleums of the Valley of the Kings and Valley of the Queens, but to myriad other tombs across the Nile. The

[44]

Necropolis of funerary craftsmen and artisans expanded, the specific task of these workers being the after life, the carving and painting of tombs, the preparation of burial chambers, the manufacture of coffins and caskets, as well as other funerary equipment and, above all, the skill of embalming and mummification.

The Egyptians viewed the centre of human activity as the heart and regarded the soul as taking three forms: the Ka, basically the life force, the Ba, how each individual characteristic manifested that life force, and the Akh, whereby the soul, after death, became an active spirit which could intervene in the affairs of the living. In her letter Dedi regarded her husband as an Akh, someone who could intercede, who could assist her mundane affairs as well as oppose the powers of any evil spirit, 'Out to the west', who also preyed in that twilight zone between life and death. The Egyptians regarded the after life in two phases. The first was a frightening journey to the Halls of Judgement of Osiris and the Fields of the Blessed. The soul would have to pass death-bearing snakes, punishing avengers, hunting demons, lakes of fire before it received judgement in the Halls of Osiris. Here the dead person's heart would be weighed in the scales of the Goddess of Truth, Ma'at; the heart would be weighed against the Feather of Truth. If judged pure, the soul would be allowed to dwell in the Fields of Eternity: if not, it would be seized by Amemet, the Bringer of the Second Death, a hybrid monster of crocodile and lion, which devoured the hearts of the damned. The Egyptians took this ritual very seriously. The entire funeral ceremony and the spiritual journey beyond the grave was dominated by coffin texts or the spells, prayers and curses from the Book of the Dead which described in heart-searing fashion the journey through the Underworld, the Tuat or Am-Duat. Nevertheless, such spells and prayers must also be accompanied by the second phase, the process of mummification where the body was ritually prepared for burial.

The rite of mummification was seen as one handed down by the Jackal-Headed God Anubis, Lord of the Mortuary, who had first assisted Isis and Nepthys in the preparation of Osiris's body after he had been slain by his red-haired brother Seth. The Egyptians regarded this whole ritual and rite with relish rather than apprehension. If the correct preparations were made, if the orthodox liturgy was followed, then all would be well. The Necropolis, the City of the Dead, was organized to achieve this. Tombs were carved out, furniture bought for future enjoyment in the after life, whilst the walls of these Houses of Eternity were decorated in vivid colours of black, white, yellow, blue and green ground from mineral deposits which gave the paintings an eye-catching glow and prevented them from fading.

These scenes provide a rich treasure house of knowledge about ancient Egypt; they also depict how the Egyptians regarded the after life, provided they entered the Fields of the Blessed, as a simple continuation of life on earth. Scenes of fishing, hunting, farming, personal triumphs and achievements, banquets and parties are vividly portrayed as joyous occasions where musicians and dancers plied their art and pretty girls, dressed in gorgeous robes and perfume-drenched wigs, sipped wine and nibbled at food amidst costly possessions which also filled the tomb. The latter included all the necessary items for life: beds, chairs, games, clothing, food and drink. Indeed, these tombs were not only a reflection of what life was like after death but, for those

[46]

who shared wealth and power, an eloquent means of reminding their families and everyone else of what they had achieved in this life.

Those who could afford such tombs would regard it as a holiday to go out and inspect how their last resting place was developing, as well as shop amongst the stalls of the artisans and craftsmen for any necessary funerary equipment. They would buy samples of coffins and caskets and, when they chose their own personal one, take it home to display it at banquets for their friends. After their deaths, relatives and friends would go out and visit the tomb. They'd feast in the small temple before it and read the coffin text or quotations from the Book of the Dead, as well as marvel at the dead person's virtues and achievements. Of course, as in life, so in death, everything has its price. Tombs, their paintings and contents, even the rite of mummification, could come as expensive as you wished, or as cheap. Nevertheless, it was the sacred duty of every Egyptian, every loyal subject of Pharaoh, to prepare for the journey across the Far Horizon.

All these elements came to full flower as Amenhotep III (his name means Amun is Satisfied), the glorious Sun King of Egypt, reached the thirty-eighth year of his reign, circa 1354 BC. Amenhotep, together with his Great Wife and Queen-in-Chief Tiye, had seen Egypt reach its apex of glory and power both at home and abroad. Amenhotep III had been a vigorous ruler, scarabs (pieces of rock carved in the likeness of a beetle and regarded as symbols of good luck) boast how this Pharaoh had personally killed 102 lions in the first ten years of his reign. Amenhotep saw himself as 'Neb-Maatra', the 'Beloved' of virtually every god in the Egyptian pantheon, and he expressed this belief in a range of sumptuous building programmes, be it the temple to Sobek the Crocodile God or to the Vulture Goddess Nekhbet at the entrance to the valley leading to the eastern desert gold mines. In such temples, the distinction between Amenhotep III and the individual god is deliberately blurred, his statue being placed next to that of the deity.

Nevertheless, it was at Karnak, 'Ipet-Sut' – 'the Most Pure of Places', where Amenhotep truly manifested his own glory and that of his god Amun-Re. He built a great pylon or gateway to the temple, the inscribed proclamation speaking for itself:

Another monument made for Amun, very great gate-ways before Amun-Re, Lord of the Thrones of the Two Lands, covered in gold throughout and carved with the God's image in the likeness of a ram, inlaid with real lapis-lazuli and worked with gold and costly stones. It is paved in pure silver and its outer gate set with stelae of lapis-lazuli on each side. Its two sides soar up to the sky like the four supports of heaven. Its flagpoles reach skyward worked in gold. His majesty brought the gold for it from the land of Karoy on his first campaign of victory, of slaying the vile Kushite.

Amenhotep also rebuilt on a site known as Southern Ipet, the Opet shrine where modern Luxor now stands. He developed this, renovating the shrine itself and surrounding it with sump-tuous quarters for the god, its crowning glory being a solar court of perfectly proportioned lotus columns fronted by a hypostyle hall over fifty-two yards long. He then linked this great temple with that of Amun at Karnak just over two miles away. Amenhotep added a viewing place where Pharaoh could stand, as well as an ornamental lake surrounded by exotic gardens. The whole scene was described on Amenhotep's funerary temple stela at Kom-El-Hetan: 'I made a viewing place facing Southern Ipet for my father Amun. A place of relaxation for him at his beautiful festival of Opet.' Opet was the festival in which Amun's statue, together with those of his wife and son, were brought from Karnak in sacred barges and, either taken by river or carried in procession along the sphinx route, to Southern Ipet at Luxor. The Egyptians believed that, during this festival, the king entered the sanctuary with the statue and emerged replenished and vibrant with divine power. The proclamation continues: 'It was planted with all kinds of flowers . . . it has more wine than water . . . it is rich in offerings, receiving tribute from every foreign land . . . gold, silver, cattle, all kinds of costly stones in their millions.'

Huge statues of Amenhotep III (later called the Colossi of Memnon) were also set up. If that wasn't enough Amenhotep built the sumptuous Malkata palace, the Palace of the Dazzling Aten on the west bank of the Nile directly opposite the king's new temple of Luxor. Pharaoh called it his House of Rejoicing. It included his own apartments and those of his Queen and family, 'villas of the west' for his officials, royal workshops and a small village for the craftsmen. It housed its own separate temple to Amun with a large court and processional way, whilst a harbour, over one and a half miles wide in front of the palace, linked the imperial quarters to the Nile. Malkata's walls were of mud-brick, plastered and painted white. Doors and window frames were of more hardy materials, acacia or sycamore wood, limestone and sandstone. There were drainage systems, bathrooms, as well as walled gardens and lotus-filled pools. The walls inside the palace were decorated in the most vivid colours possible, displaying scenes from the King's life, stories of the gods, inscriptions and triumphant proclamations. Ceilings and floors were tiled: these, in turn, were painted to depict a number of scenes, be it of Egypt's enemies being led in humiliation or the waters of the Nile with its rich bird and animal life. Furniture and ornaments from the best workshops in Egypt, executed by master craftsmen, filled the chambers, beds inlaid with ebony, gold and silver; caskets, vases, graceful pottery, precious objects, alabaster jars, wall hangings, flower baskets, all the luxury and pomp of an imperial residence.

Amenhotep had also achieved glory abroad. His Horus name, one of the five titles given to Pharaoh on his coronation was, 'Great of Strength, Smiter of the Asiatics'. In fact, Amenhotep rarely went to war. Apart from a punitive expedition into Kush, Amenhotep's cartouche held sway from Nubia in the south to Punt (Somalia) in the east, to the Delta and the Great Green and north-east along the Horus Road, past the diamond mines of Sinai into Canaan, what is now Palestine and Syria. The other major powers, Babylon and Syria, the Mitanni and the Hittites, regarded Amenhotep with awe and were flattered to call him brother.

Amenhotep's proclamations from his funerary temple quote from his prayer to his father Amun:

I did a wonder for your Majesty.
Turning my face to the south, I did a wonder for you . . .
Turning my face to the north, I did a wonder for you . . .
Turning my face to the west, I did a wonder for you . . .
Turning my face to the east and sunrise I did a wonder for you.

The message is very simple. Amenhotep saw himself, directly under the protection of Amun, as a world conqueror.

However, by the thirty-eighth year of his reign the great Pharaoh was fading. Amenhotep's earlier statues show a rounded face, large almond-shaped eyes, a retroussé nose and smiling mouth. Up until the end, the year of his death, (c.1354 BC), Amenhotep projected himself as young and vigorous. The reality, of course, was different. On a painted sandstone stela found at El-Amarna, the residence of his eccentric son Akhenaten, Amenhotep is depicted as decidedly corpulent, his face unhealthy. Moreover, if the mummified body discovered in his grandfather's tomb is indeed his, Amenhotep III's teeth were rotting, his gums scarred by painful abscesses. The pain in his mouth made him request Tushratta, King of the Mitanni, not only for the hand of his daughter in marriage but a sacred statue of the Babylonian Goddess of Love Ishtar from Nineveh to heal his pain. Tushratta lent it and found it very difficult to get it back. Nonetheless, Ishtar's help notwithstanding, Amenhotep III died and made his journey to the Far Horizon leaving his throne to his son, Neferkheperure, Beautiful are the Manifestations of Re, Amenhotep IV, who would soon change his name and bring it to the attention of all as Akhenaten.

Amenhotep IV's origins are obscure. He was not his father's heir-apparent but thrust into this position by the death of his elder brother the Crown Prince Tuthmosis. Now, as the Egyptologist Dobson has remarked, it was fashionable in paintings and carvings of the Tuthmosid dynasty for princes not to be shown. If that was the case, Tuthmosis, Amenhotep IV's elder brother, was an exception. He appears to have been the apple of his father's eye and was given a number of religious and civic titles with attendant functions to discharge. His death must have been the source of tragedy for the great Sun King and his wife Tiye, especially as their second son was eccentric, a young prince kept in the shadows, being over-looked, even positively ignored, because of his physical defor-mities.

Amenhotep IV was of singular appearance with his elon-gated skull, fleshy lips, slanting eyes, lengthened ear lobes, prominent jaw, narrow shoulders, pot belly, enormous hips and thighs and spindly legs. He may have suffered from Marfan's disorder, caused by a dominant abnormal gene which expresses itself in many of the physical attributes described above. Paintings of Amenhotep emphasize these physical aspects. True, the new Pharaoh's artists appear to have been under orders to shatter the artistic laws of the day and paint according to the truth, even if this meant exagger-ating it. Historians debate whether Amenhotep IV really had such an exceptional appearance, whether this was the work of the artists or whether he truly suffered from Marfan's. Whatever the answer to that question, Amenhotep IV was not only of exceptional appearance but displayed an individu-alism which he roughly brought to the attention of the Egyptian empire. Very little information exists about Amenhotep IV's boyhood, youth and early manhood. For a while he may have shared a co-regency with his father, even though he soon proved his determination not to follow in the footsteps of his illustrious parents.

By the middle of the fourteenth century BC, Egypt was a swollen empire with the priests of Amun-Re, in their temple complexes of Karnak and Luxor, exercising a power which any political leader would view as a potential threat. During the Eighteenth Dynasty, particularly under the reign of Amenhotep III, more prominence had been given to the worship of the Aten, the radiant sun god symbolized by the sun disc, an offshoot of the Egyptian worship of the sun. Akhenaten's cult, however, was a dramatic development of this. He not only emphasized the worship and devotion due to the Aten but sowed the seeds of a much more revolutionary dogma: that the Egyptian pantheon, with its accompanying Osirian rite, was superfluous, that the Aten was the one god, the Only One. Such a heresy, such dramatic unorthodoxy would have alarmed Egypt and, in particular, the priests of Amun, those power-brokers who controlled the temples and religious life and played such a major role in the economy of the country. Other Pharaohs had their chosen gods but the worship of one god to the total exclusion of any others would have a revolutionary impact upon Egyptian life. The change would be made all the more effective because Pharaoh combined the roles of ruler and supreme pontiff. Amenhotep III had spent his thirty-eight-year reign emphasizing how Pharaoh was not only one of the gods but their mouthpiece throughout the Two Kingdoms. True, Amenhotep III had paid devotion to the Aten, even built temples in its honour, but this could be discerned as a political move, an attempt to clip the wings of the priests of Amun, break their monopoly and demonstrate that, as a caste, they did not totally enjoy Pharaoh's pleasure. His son's devotion to the singular cult of the Aten certainly made itself manifest during the latter years of his father's reign. However, in the fifth year of his own, Amenhotep IV deliberately accelerated the process. He changed his name to Akhenaten, He Who Is Beneficial To The Aten, and expressed this devotion, this dedication to the

[53]

One God, in his elaborate hymn to the Aten which is striking for its extraordinary religious thinking as well as the quality of its poetry.

The Theban court and priesthood must have been disturbed by the changes which were coming. Akhenaten had begun his reign finishing off some of the building projects of his father at Karnak yet, even here, the Thebans must have been aware of the emphasis on the Sun Disc and the new king's singular mode of expression in name, face and form. The cause of such upheaval can only be speculated upon. Egyptologists still fiercely debate the true cause of Akhenaten's heresy. Some regarded him as a Christ-like figure, passionately devoted to his wife and daughters, who could not stand the corruption of the priests of Amun and so he and his family distanced themselves, both spiritually and physically, from what had gone on before. Others argued that Akhenaten's lonely childhood, his years of exclusion, of being overlooked, of possible ridicule, came to full flower in manhood. What most Egyptologists agree upon is the exclusivity of Akhenaten's belief, his ruthless determination to distance himself from Thebes and all it stood for, to devote himself to his own individual cult, whatever the consequences to himself, his country and empire. Akhenaten is described as a dreamer as well as a fanatic. Some of the stories which have grown up are mythical. He did not live the life of a holy hermit. He simply 'built his castles', the products of his own fantasy, and insisted that he and everyone around him should live in them.

Akhenaten's revulsion against the city, the teeming metropolis of Thebes, became apparent. By the time of his accession, Thebes had developed into a cosmopolitan, sophisticated city, the importer of exotic goods from abroad and a magnet for many nations. True, the poor might live in their fly-blown, mud-baked hovels but Thebes was also the centre of an empire where its court and priesthood enjoyed a life of opulent luxury in their multi-storeyed mansions and country estates, with their lush variegated gardens stocked with flowers and trees from every part of the empire. Thebes was a truly rich city, the houses of its courtiers, nobles and priests were painted and decorated with glazed tiles, perfumed with frankincense, incense, cassia and other fragrances. They were full of elaborately carved furniture, caskets, chairs, stools, beds and couches. Narrow windows high in the white painted walls caught the breezes which all the citizens could enjoy on their flat roofs in the evening. On such occasions they could feast on a wide range of meats, breads and wine and different kinds of barley meal in the light of oil-filled alabaster jars or the golden glow from coloured, scented candles.

In the morning they would return to these roofs to worship the rising sun and to catch the 'cooling breath' of Amun from the north. The Thebans dressed in the finest linen, beautiful gauze-like robes, quilted and pleated with coloured shawls and elaborately decorated sashes. They wore jewellery and precious stones of faience (a glazed ceramic substance) or glass, carved and sculpted in the forms of plants, flowers, animals or birds. Cornelian necklaces decorated their necks and chests, silver rings glinted on their fingers: highly decorated armlets, bracelets of precious metals with matching ear-studs shimmered in the light. Both male and female wore wigs or allowed their hair to grow long, enhanced with intricately entwined braids. Lips were carmined, eyes beautified with black kohl so as to give that almond-shaped effect so beloved of Egyptian artists. Their soft skins were protected by costly oils, such as sesame. They wore sandals of leather or papyrus, gilt-edged and decorated. When they left to visit each other's houses, the palace or temple, a horde of retainers surrounded them carrying expensive cosmetics and oils, as well as perfume-drenched ostrich fans to waft away the heat, dust and flies.

Akhenaten did not reject such luxury or finery, he simply wanted to display it in his own fashion, well away from that hated city. Accordingly, at about the same time he changed his name, Akhenaten pushed his revolution even further by openly proclaiming that he would no longer live in Thebes. Instead, he chose a place 240 miles to the north in the fifteenth nome of Egypt near the shrine of Thoth in the city of Hermopolis, a naturally formed amphitheatre protected by limestone cliffs. Akhenaten renamed this place Akhetaten, the Horizon of the Aten. So determined was Akhenaten to escape from Thebes and live in his new capital that he, his family, as well as those members of the court who followed him, lived under canvas whilst his beautiful new city was built. The site, known as El-Amarna, is now desolate, a place of hot winds and blinding sand. However, in his day, Akhenaten transformed it. He undoubtedly used all the power of a Pharaoh to make his dream a reality. The two essential building materials of Ancient Egypt were readily available: stone and the clay of the Nile. Thousands of workmen, labouring under a constant curtain of dust, made their Pharaoh's dream a reality. The new city was bounded by the Nile on the west and soaring cliffs to the east. A royal highway was built and Akhetaten, The Horizon of the Sun Disc, rose in three distinct sections: the central city, with suburbs to the north and south as well as attendant villages set aside for the workmen. The central city was where Pharaoh and his officials carried on what they thought to be the government of the empire. It was known as The Island Exalted in Jubilee. Nearby was a police station, training grounds and barracks. There was a House of Life, where the priests were taught the new religion under the aegis of their high priest Meri-Re. The focal point of the city was the Great House of Pharaoh with its maze of audience halls, courts, kitchens, gardens and royal balconies, the Window of Appearances where Pharaoh, his wife and family, would show their faces to assembled dignitaries and bestow their favour. Nearby stood the Castle of Aten, a temple where the royal family could worship privately and be reinvigorated by the glorious rays of their god. Other temples were built without the usual brooding statues or darkening corridors leading down to the Holy of Holies. Akhenaten's temples were to bask in the light of the sun, open to the sky.

Akhenaten saw his new creation as the direct work of god. He set up stelae on the boundaries of his new city proclaiming how Aten himself had led him to this spot. 'His Majesty appeared in his great chariot of electrum, like the Aten he rises in his city of the horizon . . . Now it is the Aten my father who advised me concerning it [the city] making Akhetaten . . . in this deserted place.' The proclamation concluded with a solemn vow that Akhenaten would stay in his new city: he would never move from it, not to the south, not to the east, not to the north, not to the west. It was a vow Akhenaten religiously kept.

One can only imagine the impact this had in Thebes and in other great cities like Memphis. For decades courtiers, career officials, diplomats, priests and army officers had basked in the smile of Pharaoh, ever ready to do his will. Now the will of Pharaoh had changed and they were caught in a cruel trap and, perhaps, one which Akhenaten maliciously plotted. Amenhotep III had proved that Pharaoh was Egypt and where Pharaoh went his power followed. So, what could the priests and the myriad courtiers and officials of Thebes do? If they followed Akhenaten to his new city they would be leaving their own livelihood and environment. If they refused to follow Pharaoh, then what advancement and further glories could they expect?

The dilemma is seen in the tomb of Rahmose, a nobleman of Thebes. Rahmose, like many of his kind, had built his sumptuous tomb across the Nile. Its paintings are typical of the period, showing this powerful courtier with his wife and family enjoying themselves as they would continue to do in eternity. However, before the tomb was completed, Akhenaten's revolution had made itself felt, leaving men like Rahmose caught in the middle of the turmoil. This is reflected in the art of the tomb where the style dramatically changes, featuring Akhenaten, with his misshapen body, giving audience to Rahmose and decorating him with honours.

If Akhenaten wished to have his revenge on Thebes then this must have been sweet indeed. Men like Rahmose were faced with a brutal choice: either accept the changes and win the favour of Pharaoh or walk out of public life for good. The fury and anger of the lords of Thebes can only be imagined. Little wonder that in the new city, a different breed of officials and courtiers emerged with a vested interest in the new regime.

However, the anger and hurt pride of the Theban court must have been nothing to the hatred and fury of the legion of priests of Amun and other temples. At a stroke Akhenaten had broken their power. He had withdrawn his face and favour from them. What were they to do? How could they react? They had little choice but to accept, seethe and watch their gorgeous world crumble and collapse around them.

Akhenaten's dramatic move to his new city not only sprang from his desire to cultivate and worship the Aten but, perhaps, to exercise his own vengeance on a powerful city and everything in it which he despised. His solemn oath, proclaimed boldly on the stelae along the perimeters of what he termed the Most Perfect Place, was also a warning to Thebes and to the rest of Egypt that he would not change his mind. Akhenaten's break with the past was probably more dramatic and startling in its effect than Henry VIII's rupture with Rome.

In the first instance, Akhenaten did not attack the established cults, he simply ignored them and moved away. This, in turn, emphasizes the main characteristic of Akhenaten's policy, a sacred exclusivity, of being alone accompanied only by those who had agreed that he should be alone. Akhenaten's principal supporter in this was his wife Nefertiti. Egyptologists still debate Nefertiti's true identity, her origins and family. However, there is an acceptable consensus that Nefertiti was Egyptian, that she had married the deformed Akhenaten long before his accession and that possibly she may have been the daughter of a man who was to become one of Akhenaten's leading courtiers, Ay, whose second wife Tey had been Nefertiti's nurse. In the first years of Akhenaten's reign Nefertiti's influence was all pervasive. A bust of her kept in the Berlin Museum reveals a truly beautiful woman and one can only reflect how the love and adoration of such a beauty thrilled and flattered Akhenaten's heart. He seemed totally obsessed with her, so infatuated that the boundary stelae set up around Akhenaten's new city include what is virtually a hymn or paean of praise to the virtues of his beloved, beautiful queen.

> The Heiress, Great in the Palace, Fair of Face, Adorned with the Double Plumes, Mistress of Happiness, Endowed with Favours, at hearing whose voice the King rejoices, the Chief Life of the King, his Beloved, the Lady of the Two Lands, Neferne-fruaten-Nefertiti [Good like the beauty of Aten – the Beautiful Woman Comes]. May she live forever and always.

Nefertiti emerges not only as the beautiful woman but a queen of great strength and vigour. There are carvings of her grasping the hair of a 'vile Asiatic', ready to smite him with a war club. This in itself is rather singular for that is the constant pose of many Pharaohs displaying their strength and power. Be that as it may, the carvings and paintings of El-Amarna constantly show Akhenaten and Nefertiti close together. Even across the centuries their love and affection for each other is obvious, and their devotion to their six daughters, one of whom Akhenaten is dangling on his knee or kissing tenderly. Akhenaten and Nefertiti emerge as a husband and wife completely absorbed with themselves and their family, united in their devotion to the Aten, to receive his rejuvenating rays. Yet such paintings also possess a chilling quality; Akhenaten, his wife and his family, seem to think that they are the only people alive, almost unaware of their public responsibilities and duties both to their country and to their empire.

2

The Power of the Aten

I am the Radiant One, the brother of the Radiant Goddess.
Spell 69 : *The Book of the Dead*

THE CITY OF THE ATEN FLOWERED LIKE SOME HARDY PLANT. The Pure Place prospered and developed, drawing in all strata of Egyptian society who were prepared to accept their Pharaoh's dreams. Temples and avenues were built, palaces, houses and gardens laid out. Canals and ornamental pools were drawn off the Nile. Much of the evidence from the city of the Aten has now disappeared. Akhenaten's successors saw to that. They literally levelled it to the ground, in that biblical phrase, 'leaving not a stone upon another'. A few walls survived for modern archaeologists, though their biggest find was the uncompleted tombs Akhenaten and his party built for themselves. The Pharaoh was determined not only to create his own city but his own Necropolis. His regime did not last long enough for us to study its full impact and development but there is no doubt that the Osirian method of embalming and mummification, the texts and verses from the Book of the Dead were no longer deemed necessary. Akhenaten's monotheism developed. The sun disc was simply a symbol. The Pharaoh taught that there was only One God, an invisible being who sustained all creation. Nevertheless, old habits die hard and fashion is difficult to change.

[63]

The nobles of Akhetaten had their tombs carved out and decorated with splendid drawings and paintings, which afforded an insight into the dreamlike existence of Akhenaten's new capital. One painting will suffice as an example. The steward Huya was a retainer of the Queen Tiye, Akhenaten's mother. She often visited her son and, indeed, had her own palace in the new city. Her arrival was marked by feasts and Huya's tomb possesses a painting depicting one of these. There is really very little difference between the painting on Huya's tomb and those of nobles in the Theban Necropolis. Food and drink had been served on flower-strewn tables. The ribbon-decked wine jars are obvious, as are the musicians and the Syrian dancing girls. Everyone is enjoying themselves. Many other tomb paintings convey the same message. The City of Aten was wonderful: in the presence of their Pharaoh life was enhanced not changed.

Nevertheless, Akhenaten and Nefertiti were living in a fool's paradise. The air of exclusivity, of self-absorption, is reminiscent of other noble families, at different times in history, totally unaware of the real-politik, the harsh facts of grinding politics both at home and abroad. Akhenaten's father, Amenhotep the Sun Pharaoh, had established a great empire. Egypt was feared and meant to be feared. There is no evidence that Egypt's enemies took advantage of Akhenaten's self-absorption to launch an all-out attack. However, sufficient evidence does exist to demonstrate that foreign rulers were aware that the flail and the rod were not held too securely. There was trouble in Nubia, nothing major but a minor revolt and disturbances which had to be put down. More serious trouble was brewing across Sinai in Canaan, the Northern territories of Egypt's empire.

Amenhotep III had brought such territories firmly under his rule, appointing governors or overseers to the northern provinces. Amenhotep had also established good relationships with the Mitanni king. Further to the north, however, a new power was beginning to emerge at the same time as Akhenaten was assuming sole rule over Egypt. The Hittites were a group of warring clans who could be divided and pitted against each other or simply cowed into compliance and submission: now they united under a veteran warrior, Suppiluliumas.

At first Akhenaten seemed unaware of the danger (and Hittite expansion is not an important part of this story) as Suppiluliumas began to imitate Egyptian policy in the area, undermining Pharaoh's influence, trying to subvert the local princelings from their allegiance. Minor disputes broke out. The roads became clogged with refugees and Egypt's client-rulers in the region began to send impassioned letters warning about what was happening, even naming the traitors responsible. Matters worsened when the Hittites dealt the Mitanni empire a crushing defeat and began to expand their influence south. Akhenaten's foreign minister in the City of the Aten received letter after letter describing the situation, begging that bowmen and chariots be sent to assist. Most of the letters were apparently filed and very rarely answered. Undoubtedly General Horemheb and others would have kept a wary eye on the border.

However, the Hittites showed no signs of sweeping south in an attempt to seize the Horus Road and threaten the Nile Delta. The real danger was psychological. Egypt's foreign policy was not being defended: its allies were being told to look to themselves and the impression of a serious weakness

[65]

at the heart of Egypt's empire was growing. Beyond Sinai a guerrilla war broke out. Pharaoh's allies either transferred their allegiance or those who stood firm were simply defeated and removed.

No real evidence exists about internal discontent in Egypt but, undoubtedly, Akhenaten's religious policies must have dealt a savage blow to Thebes of the Hundred Gates, the temple complexes of Karnak and Luxor and the economy so closely linked to them. The priests of Amun must not have taken too kindly to the new orthodoxy. Nevertheless, Akhenaten was protected not only by his own troops under General Nakhtmin (or Minnakht) but by the lasting reputation of his father who had enhanced the power of Pharaoh and rendered him godlike. Pharaoh was not a constitutional monarch, he could not be brought to book. True, in Egypt's history there were treasonable conspiracies, particularly in the harems of different rulers over the succession, but open regicide was, in the main, regarded as a direct attack upon the gods. Akhenaten, hidden away in his dreamlike city, could still count on being protected by his own father's legacy, if not his troops. Nevertheless, courtiers were removed and disgraced. There were examples from the tombs of the City of the Aten of officials' and courtiers' names being scratched out. The sentence of *damnatio memoriae* – any record of them being expunged – was passed against them. They were regarded as 'non-persons' whose existence became nothing more than sand in the wind.

Akhenaten's streak of despotism must have provoked resentment and violence. His chief of police was Mahu and in Mahu's tomb there is a singular painting. It shows Mahu bringing prisoners before Akhenaten's vizier for sentencing.

[66]

They appear to have been agents provocateurs. Mahu is shown running beside Pharaoh's chariot as Akenhaten and his family make triumphant progress through their city. The prisoners cannot be simply dismissed as thieves found with their hands in the apple barrel. These men must have posed a real threat to Pharaoh; Mahu must have gloried in their capture and conviction, basking in the triumph of apprehending such law-breakers. It is quite possible, though the evidence is not conclusive, that Mahu had uncovered an attempt to assassinate Pharaoh and the painting in his tomb celebrates this achievement.

Akhenaten's patience with the old gods of Egypt and their religious centres grew very thin: in the ninth year of his reign he counter-attacked, sending out soldiers and envoys with strict instructions to obliterate the sign of any other gods throughout Egypt. It was both tyrannical and petty. Even in one of his own father's inscriptions, the prefix Amun was chiselled out whilst in the glorious tomb of Rahmose the goose sacred to Amun was erased, a pathetic attempt by Rahmose's family to comply with Pharaoh's decree and appear loyal to the throne. Nevertheless, Akhenaten's actions were both malicious and intolerant and would do little to placate the nobles, generals and priests.

Akhenaten's religious dreams turned into mania. Perhaps his mind was unhinged but the halcyon existence in the City of Aten was drawing to a close as tragedy bit deeper and deeper into the royal family's sun-filled fragrant existence. Queen Tiye, widow of Amenhotep III, died. Tiye was level-headed, experienced and a sure hand in guiding Egypt's foreign policy. Tushratta the Mitanni king often wrote to her, his respect for her status and influence more than obvious.

[67]

Other tragedies followed. Akhenaten reigned for seventeen years and, sometime between Year 12 and Year 15 'the Beautiful Woman', his beloved wife Nefertiti simply disappeared from the political scene. Some historians argue she may have died, others speculate that her inability to produce a male heir lowered her status in Akhenaten's eyes and that she was exiled to a palace in the north of the City of Aten. Others argue that Nefertiti and Akhenaten clashed over Pharaoh's religious revolution or the effect it was having on the Country of the Two Crowns as well as beyond its borders. Nefertiti's disappearance is as mysterious as the woman herself. It has recently led to another more startling theory, according to which she simply re-invented herself, was reincarnated as the mysterious Pharaoh Semenkhkare (the Spirit of Re was Ennobled) who took the throne name Ankhkheperure (Living are the Manifestations of Re). What historians do agree on is that the 'beautiful woman', always at Akhenaten's side, simply disappeared. The Great Queen certainly had her rivals. According to the evidence, Akhenaten had other wives; one was Kiya, probably a Mitanni princess, who may have died in childbirth providing Akhenaten with the male heir he so desperately needed. Kiya's death occurred before Nefertiti's disappearance and the position of both was usurped by Meritaten, one of Akhenaten's own daughters who was 'consort' to both her own father and, later, the mysterious Semenkhkare.

The evidence about the end of Akhenaten's reign is scarce, clouded in mystery and fiercely-debated amongst Egyptologists. It was customary among Pharaohs of the Eighteenth Dynasty to keep their young sons in the background. Only when they came of age or Pharaoh's powers began to weaken, were they taken into government and a co-regency established. Such an arrangement existed between Amenhotep III and Akhenaten. In the latter's case, as his reign drew to an end, this mysterious Semenkhkare, whose origins and identity still continue to mystify historians, emerged as co-regent. Evidence suggests that Semenkhkare, who married Meritaten and died at the very most within eighteen months of Akhenaten, is also the occupant of the mysterious tomb KV55.

This tomb in the Valley of the Kings figures prominently in the debate amongst Egyptologists regarding the close of the Akhenaten era. At first the archaeologist who discovered it believed the remains found in KV55 (King's Valley Tomb No. 55) belonged to a noble lady, perhaps one of Egypt's queens, but forensic evidence proves this wrong, demonstrating the human remains in Tomb 55 are those of a man in his early twenties with a striking physical resemblance to Tutankhamun. The true identity of Semenkhkare, the occupant of Tomb 55 and the fate of Nefertiti do not concern the present argument, except for the extraordinary events which occurred after Tutankhamun's death. However, it is important to note, what most Egyptologists have agreed, that Tomb 55 was the temporary sepulchre of a prince of the Tuthmosid line, associated with the Aten cult and linked closely by blood to Tutankhamun. Moreover, it was used not only as a tomb but as a storage place for objects associated with the Aten cult.

On Semenkhkare the arguments twist and turn. Was Semenkhkare Akhenaten's homosexual lover? Was Semenkhkare Queen Nefertiti in a new incarnation? Was Semenkhkare a half-brother of Akhenaten or even a son? My own view is that Semenkhkare – Ankhkheperure – a name

[69]

and title which does not include an open reference to the Aten, was Akhenaten's half-brother, brought into the co-regency as Akhenaten's health declined as well as a sop to the growing opposition to Akhenaten's monotheism. It is difficult to reach any firm conclusion except to note that by the year of Akhenaten's death the Tuthmosid line had been greatly depleted. Amenhotep III had begotten at least four daughters and two sons. Akhenaten himself is seen in a number of paintings with at least six daughters. However, the dynasty may not have been physically strong and there is considerable evidence of plague raging in the Middle East at the time. At all events, by 1334 BC, Akhenaten, Semenkhkare and Nefertiti, not to mention five of Akhenaten's daughters, had disappeared from the political scene. The Tuthmosid line could only boast of one of Akhenaten's daughters, Ankhesenpaaten (who later took the name Ankhesenamun), about ten or eleven years old, and the young boy Tutankhaten, later known as Tutankhamun, who in 1334 BC must have been no older than seven or eight. (Ankhesenpaaten and Tutankhaten will, for the sake of clarity, be referred to by their 'Amun' names, Ankhesenamun and Tutankhamun.)

Ankhesenamun's parentage is quite clear but Tutankhamun's origins, indeed, the entire chronology around his life, is still a matter of debate. A block of stone from Akhenaten's reign, now in the Brooklyn Museum, New York, bears a reference to Tutankhamun as a child, calling him 'The King's son of his body, his beloved Tutankhaten', whilst the famous Restoration Stela, the official proclamation issued during Tutankhamun's reign that the Aten cult was to be abandoned, described Tutankhamun as 'His Majesty who came to the throne of his father'. The mysterious Semenkhkare might have been Tutankhamun's father: the remains found in Tomb 55 are closely related both in physical appearance and blood group to Tutankhamun. Nevertheless, we can estimate that Tutankhamun was born around the ninth year of Akhenaten's reign. Semenkhkare outlived Akhenaten by no more than eighteen months at the very most. The remains from Tomb 55 belong to a young man of about twenty: that would have made him scarcely in his teens when he could possibly have fathered Tutankhamun, whilst his wife Meritaten must have been even younger. It is, therefore, difficult to conclude that they were Tutankhamun's parents. True, the word father in ancient Egypt could refer to anyone of the elder generation and, in this context, it could be synonomous with predecessor. However, Akhenaten always referred to his daughters as 'the beloved of his body', the same phrase used to describe Tutankhamun.

In fact, Tutankhamun was probably Akhenaten's son by another wife, the elusive Kiya. When his mother died in childbirth Tutankhamun was then raised by a wet nurse, Maia. It has already been pointed out how the Tuthmosids in the main, kept their young male heirs if not out of mind, then certainly out of sight. The presence of the powerful Nefertiti, with her brood of daughters, would also ensure Tutankhamun was kept very much in the shadows, whilst his weak health would have kept him hidden from the public eye. Nonetheless, by about 1334 BC Tutankhamun and his half-sister Ankhesenamun were thrust into the limelight. They were the only surviving members of the Tuthmosid line, yet they were mere children. So who would control Egypt?

A great deal of speculation exists pointing out how Akhenaten, his mysterious co-regent and successor

Semenkhkare, together with Meritaten, Akhenaten's daughter who was married both to her father and then to Semenkhkare, all disappeared in a very short time. The question has been posed whether they were murdered. If they were, why didn't this mysterious assassin, the regicide, make a clean sweep of the family and ensure that a very vulnerable young boy, and his equally vulnerable half-sister, also made their final journey to the Far Horizon and into the Blessed West?

The fact is that Tutankhamun and Ankhesenamun were of sacred blood, the imperial line. They belonged to the Tuthmosid clan, whose name was sacred. Their great ancestor Ahmose had driven the hated Hyksos out of Egypt and their warlike ancestors had created an empire the like of which had never been seen before. The reign of their grandfather Amenhotep III had been a glorious pinnacle in Egyptian history. Accordingly, these two children, whatever the reservations of individuals, would have been regarded as sacred. True, their father Akhenaten had displayed destructive, idiosyncratic beliefs but those could not be viewed as a reason for the deposition and murder of his children.

Some evidence exists that the mysterious Semenkhkare had already begun to put out peace feelers towards the cult of Amun and the Theban hierarchy. This would not have been difficult. Considerable evidence indicates how, as Akhenaten's reign drew to an end, many were having second thoughts. Redford has pointed out that the priesthood of Aten was actually drawn from other cults: it borrowed a great deal of its organization from the worship of Amun and other gods like Ptah.

A good example of growing doubts about the Aten is the abandoned tomb of the priest Pawah at El-Amarna. In the

[72]

furthest recesses of his mausoleum, Pawah has written a prayer to the God Amun, a petition to regain his sight. It included a confession of guilt for Pawah's former apostasy as well as a plea for help. It should have been inscribed on a stone plinth and placed near a statue of the god but Pawah's prayer is hidden away: it demonstrates that, at least for this once important priest, the glory of the Aten was fading and it was time to return to the old gods. Such an attitude must have been representative of many of the leading courtiers, officials and generals of the time. Once Akhenaten and Semenkhkare died, there was a very strong desire to return to the old ways. However, many of Pharaoh's subjects were extremely cautious. This demonstrates the power of the office of Pharaoh and there was no open attack upon the cult of Aten, at least not yet, whilst Akhenaten's city continued to function for a number of years after his death.

At the beginning of Tutankhamun's reign a consensus emerged amongst the power-brokers that, under Akhenaten, Egypt had not prospered either at home or abroad, whilst the attack upon other gods in Year 9 of Akhenaten's reign had been unforgiveable. The proof of this consensus on what constituted Egypt's ills at the beginning of Tutankhamun's reign is the Restoration Stela. The Stela's basic tenet is that the Aten cult would not be persecuted, it would simply be ignored whilst the old orthodoxy would be renewed. Aten would be regarded as one god amongst many and the monotheism of Akhenaten would be allowed to wither on the branch.

These power-brokers behind the stela can be divided into two groups, each with their interests regarding the future course of Egypt and the policies Tutankhamun should follow. The first group is the Aten or Amarna faction. The second is the military high command under General Horemheb. The former group would include Pharaoh himself and his ten-year-old half-sister. The old Jesuit adage 'Give me the boy and I'll give you the man' can certainly be applied to these two. They had been raised by Akhenaten himself who, whatever his faults, displayed great interest in his family. Pharaoh had been Aten's representative on earth and the art of Amarna clearly illustrates how the royal family were closely associated with the Aten cult. Akhenaten's offspring must have eaten and drunk the worship of Aten, been instructed in its tenets and hymns, and participated in its divine liturgy during the formative years of their lives. This upbringing precluded any real persecution of the Aten cult as any outright attack would have included the last of the royal family. A different approach was decided on: the royal couple were to be gently weaned and led back to the old ways, a simple enough task for the powerful men who now surrounded this precious pair.

Some of those who had been closely associated with Akhenaten were not extended the same privilege and favour. Men such as Tutu, Akhenaten's chamberlain, and Panehsy, first servant of the Aten, had lavish tombs prepared at El Amarna and received many titles from Akhenaten but both quietly disappeared after Pharaoh's death. No evidence indicates they were executed but they may well have been banished, their estates forfeited. The distinct impression is given that, although the young royal couple were cherished and favoured, certain of Akhenaten's ministers and leading priests were quietly and surreptitiously removed by the other power-brokers.

And who were these? It is fashionable amongst Egyptologists to talk of rivalry from the very start between the rising star General Horemheb, based at the great garrison city of Memphis, and Ay who emerged as Tutankhamun's first minister. Historians seize on the fact that both Ay and Horemheb eventually succeeded to the throne of Pharaoh: consequently, from the start, they must have been enemies and rivals. This is incorrect. Akhenaten had been a tyrant. He and his wife Nefertiti had displayed an imperiousness and dedication to themselves which was breath-taking. One can safely assume that any person left in power at the end of Akhenaten's reign must have been an Atenist who, whatever his or her reservations, had paid lip service to the cult of the Aten and been favoured by Akhenaten. This is true of Ay and it applies equally to Horemheb.

My second point is a corollary to this: those who were in power at the end of the Amarna era, or at least those who were most powerful in that group, would do everything to ensure their survival, to cling to power, to develop that power and so ward off any criticism or attack from political opponents. If such an attack emerged it would have a twofold source, the cities of Memphis and Thebes. Both, before the reign of Akhenaten, had served as capitals and royal centres of government. Both were the centres of temple worship: Memphis's principal deity was Ptah, whilst Thebes could boast of the temple complex of Karnak and Luxor dedicated to Amun-Re. Both had powerful priesthoods and, just as importantly, served as major garrison cities for the Egyptian army. Memphis and Thebes, and the vested interests they represented, would have to be addressed by those power-brokers who survived the post-Akhenaten crash. Accordingly, it is wrong to talk of distinct groups or factions but of one which operated in a way very similiar to our modern Mafia: a faction, closely bound by blood ties, with direct access into the House of Pharaoh, the source of all power in Egypt. Such a group did exist, the Akhmim party.

The town of Akhmim, where there was a flourishing cult to the fertility god Min, lies on the east bank of the Nile between El-Amarna and Thebes, opposite the modern town of Sohag. It was the birthplace of Queen Tiye, wife of the magnificent Amenhotep III, who enjoyed her husband's favour throughout his reign, despite his many marriage alliances to other younger princesses. Tiye exercised considerable influence both at home and abroad. Political circles in Egypt had, since the reign of the female Pharaoh Hatshepsut, been wary of the influence of women. Tiye broke this tradition. A woman of considerable ability, she came from a provincial noble family. Her marriage to Amenhotep also broke the tradition of previous Pharaohs choosing their princesses either from the immediate royal family or from abroad. Amenhotep's infatuation with Tiye is reflected in the buildings and pleasure parks he built for her, as well as the many proclamations issued throughout his kingdom extolling his Great Queen's virtues. Tiye was the daughter of Amenhotep III's favoured courtiers Yuya and Thuya, both of whom were from Akhmim where Yuya was prophet of Min, 'in charge of the oxen of Min'. His wife Thuya was 'in charge of the harem of Min'. Both rose to the highest rank at the imperial court thanks to their daughter's favoured position with Pharaoh. Yuya won the title of Divine Father, a great honour, and served in the army as Overseer of the King's Horses and Lieutenant-General of the King's Chariots. Thuya also enjoyed high status and titles, in particular, 'Royal Mother of the Chief Wife of the King'.

This noble, but provincial, couple from Akhmim won high

favour with Amenhotep III through the influence of Queen Tiye and they were joined by others. Tiye's brother Anen served as a priest in the important post as Second Prophet of Amun. All three, Yuya, Thuya and Anen were granted the privilege of securing burial places in the royal Necropolis. More importantly, a considerable amount of evidence indicates that Queen Tiye had a second brother Ay. As the Egyptologist Aldred has pointed out, the names Yuya and Ay sound very similar, and Yuya's mummy is one of the best preserved to be discovered. A comparison between the head of a statue in the Cairo Museum, thought to be that of Ay when Pharaoh, with Yuya's mummy, does show a very close family resemblance: clever, shrewd faces displaying large noses, receding foreheads, high cheek bones, prominent lips and a deep jaw. Ay was also involved in the Akhmim cult of Min; he certainly dedicated a chapel to that god at Akhmim, and Ay followed his father's policy of growing close to the imperial throne through marriage. The Akhmim clan owed their initial supremacy to Tiye's marriage to Amenhotep III. Ay then cemented it by a second such marriage alliance. Considerable proof exists that Ay was the father of Nefertiti, his first wife was her mother, his second, Tey, was Nefertiti's nurse, a word which in ancient Egypt can also stand for foster mother.

Ay was, therefore, well placed for a position of great power. He never took the title of vizier, that was too lowly an honour for the likes of him. Indeed, as I shall prove, Ay saw himself as wielding supreme power over Egypt and Pharaoh Tutankhamun, the fruit of years of scheming and plotting. Ay probably began his public career during the reign of Amenhotep III, both in the army and in the civil service. A member of the powerful Akhmim clan, he would owe his rise not only to family connections but to his own innate ability and skill. Ay also proved to be a man who could swim with the tide and trim his sails to whatever wind blew. He rose to foremost prominence at Akhenaten's court at El-Amarna. He built and decorated a tomb there which includes magnificent pictures of the heretic Pharaoh and his family, as well as a copy of Pharaoh's famous hymn to the Aten. If Akhenaten was the founder of the Atenism, Ay, for his own secret purposes, proved to be one of that cult's most fervent supporters. He makes this very clear in a proclamation from that same tomb:

> I was one favoured by his lord daily. My favours increased year by year inasmuch as I was extremely competent in His Majesty's opinion: so he doubled my perquisites for me, like the number of the sands. I was at the head of both the princes and the common people . . . I was a truly correct person, one in whom there was no greed. My name [i.e. reputation] reached the place because I was useful to the king and obeyed his teaching, and performed his laws . . . I was competent and a man of good character . . . contented and patient . . . who followed the will of His Majesty as he had commanded, as I listened unceasing to his voice.

Petrie describes Ay's tomb as one of the most magnificent at Amarna and Ay, following in the footsteps of his father, collected the noblest and most prestigious titles in Egypt which display his service in both the military and civil administration. He was Commander of the King's Horse and

[78]

Lieutenant-General of Pharaoh's chariots, so Ay would be known to the officer corps of the Egyptian army. He was personal scribe to Pharaoh and would therefore be privy to all public and secret documents. He was the Royal Fan-Bearer who stood at Pharaoh's right hand and, above all, he was Divine Father or Father of the God, which illustrates a close personal relationship with the Pharaohs.

Ay was the head of the Akhmim Mafia. In this case the word Mafia most accurately describes his spider-like power and influence. Ay's parents were the father and mother-in-law of the great Amenhotep III, his sister that magnificent Pharaoh's Chief Wife and Great Queen and his own daughter Akhenaten's wife. Ay could boast of powerful connections in the priestly caste of Amun through his brother Anen and be on speaking terms with all the great and good in Pharaoh's court, as well as the civil and military administration. Ay had shown himself indispensable to Akhenaten, whilst at the same time feathering his own nest with promotions and honours. Ay is portrayed as a sly old man. The evidence however indicates a Mafia chief of personal charisma, power and cunning, a man to be feared, a tough former soldier, a skilled administrator, held in awe for his talents by all at Pharaoh's court. Ay was not some sly Polonius hiding behind the arras but rather the Metternich or Bismarck of post-Amarna Egypt. Yet he also made his mistakes for it must have been Ay who first spotted and promoted the talented military scribe Horemheb, who was later to prove to be Ay's nemesis.

Horemheb came from the city of Henes in the Delta; a commoner, Horemheb has not had a good press. He is often depicted as an inveterate red-neck, a man of peasant stock who had nothing to do with the cult of the Aten, hated everything it stood for and was only too ready to launch the most savage persecution against it. This is more fiction than fact. Horemheb served Akhenaten; he must, therefore have paid lip service to the Aten, whatever his private beliefs. One of Horemheb's regiments was named after the Aten, whilst the statue of Horemheb in the Metropolitan Museum of New York bears the carved inscription: 'May your Ba come forth each day to see the Aten.' A stela of Horemheb (British Museum No. 551) reads: 'The Hereditary Prince Horemheb says, "Hail to you One who is splendid and skilled, Atum-Horakhte, You the risen on the Horizon of the Sky . . ."'

Horemheb must have won the favour and attention of both Akhenaten and Ay: a career soldier who demonstrated both courtly skills and military prowess. One further statue of Horemheb depicts him in a rather remarkable pose, that of royal scribe. He sits cross-legged in the classic scribal position, a papyrus across his lap, a linen shawl about his shoulders, a well oiled wig falling down below his neck. The statue displays a strong but sensitive face. The inscription on the base of this statue (in the Metropolitan Museum of Art, New York) boasts of Horemheb's campaign against crime and lawlessness. Horemheb was not only a general and a scribe but also a chief of police, a man who carried the double responsibility of defending Egypt's borders against foreign incursion and enforcing Pharaoh's peace within those frontiers. Horemheb was based at Memphis where he began a splendid tomb, the most gorgeous and ornate in the nearby Necropolis of Sakkara. The tomb boasts of his titles, Overseer of the Army, Royal Scribe, Overseer of the Royal Works.

It would be easy to regard Horemheb as just a rank outsider. He was certainly not of the Theban aristocracy; he gained promotion through sheer merit but, importantly, that was not unknown in ancient Egypt. What is significant is that Horemheb was a leading light in the Egyptian military at the time of Akhenaten's death. He must, therefore, have owed some of his fortune and favour to the heretic Pharaoh. Some Egyptologists claim that Horemheb spent some time at Amarna, the City of the Aten. They argue that Tomb 24 in the El-Amarna Necropolis may have belonged to him under an earlier name, Paatenemheb. Redford rejects this but Paatenemheb could have changed his name to introduce the Horus prefix. He was certainly devoted to the Horus cult of his native town and Tomb 24 does hold an inscription about its intended owner as Overseer of the Soldiers of the Lord of the Two Lands.

Others dismiss this evidence but where else would Horemheb have gained Pharaoh's favour? Horemheb's first wife, Amenia, was buried in Horemheb's tomb in Sakkara, near Memphis; his second wife Mutnejdmet was sister to the powerful Queen Nefertiti and another daughter of Ay. Mutnejdmet is depicted in some of the Amarna paintings where she is always accompanied by two dwarfs. One painting in particular shows her standing slightly distant with a considerable gap between her and Akhenaten's first three daughters. Mutnejdmet apparently disappeared from Akhenaten's court around Year 8 of that Pharaoh's reign. I consider this to be the year she married Horemheb, a political marriage alliance arranged by Ay. At the same time all building work on Ay's tomb at Amarna ceased. Did Ay, cunning as a mongoose, already see which way the wind was blowing, that the Amarna age would not last? Ay, in view of his policies under Tutankhamun, must have prepared the ground for a return to the old ways. A marriage alliance with

[81]

the rising military star Horemheb, followed by that soldier's posting to Memphis, would control one important area, whilst Thebes could be managed by the likes of Ay's close ally General Nakhtmin and Mahu, Akhenaten's chief of police.

Ay, of course, would also take others with him. Some of Akhenaten's old ministers disappeared. Men like Tutu took the blame for what had happened, whilst others attached themselves to Ay's rising star. Some who had served Akhenaten, rose to prominence during the reign of Tutankhamun and the stewardship of Ay, officials such as Pentju, Royal Scribe, King's Chief, First Servant of the Aten in the Mansion, Chief of Chiefs, Noble of the First Rank. More importantly, Pentju was Chief Physician, One Who Approaches the Person of the King. There is every likelihood that this Pentju is the same Pentju who became a vizier, under Tutankhamun. He was present at that Pharaoh's funeral and, as Chief Physician, undoubtedly played a prominent part in the mysterious events leading up to Tutankhamun's death. Another who served Akhenaten and survived the political crash was Maya, who may have crossed swords with Akhenaten and suffered a temporary disgrace, even though he was General of the Lord of The Two Lands, Overseer of the House, Pacifying the Aten, Royal Scribe, Overseer of All Works of the King. A consummate politician, Maya was allied with Ay, yet he managed to survive the collapse of Akhenaten's dream, the death of Tutankhamun, as well as the usurpation of Ay, to continue his work as chief treasurer under Horemheb.

All these men clustered round Ay, leader of the Akhmim clan. They would conciliate the priests of Amun and other temples: the nobles and officials who had lost favour under Akhenaten, not to mention the craftsmen and merchants of

Thebes and Memphis. Maya would re-invigorate the royal revenues and be responsible for an extensive building programme. Maya would set the lead for the scribes and careerists of the Egyptian court, able men who saw their own promotion and enrichment as identical with the advancement of Egypt's interests both at home and abroad.

Another careerist was Nakhtmin, a leading member of the officer corps at the Amarna court. Nakhtmin set up a stela on which Akhenaten was called 'The Ruler of Happy Hearts who Curbed All Lands', 'The Mighty King Lord of Every Foreign Land'. He was closely associated with Ay, probably linked by blood, though their precise relationship is uncertain, be it cousin, son or brother; I suspect the latter. Nakhtmin was, according to Redford, a member of Amenhotep III's cabinet, so he must have been quite old by the time of Tutankhamun's accession. A statue of Nakhtmin in the Cairo Museum describes him as 'The Hereditary Prince, Noble, Seal-Bearer of the King of Lower Egypt, Great of Praises in the Royal Palace, the Royal Scribe, Commander of the Army, Nakhtmin . . . for the Ka of his Mother, the Servant of Min, the Musician of Isis, Yuy.' The latter phrase links Nakhtmin with the town of Akhmin and, possibly, he might have been another son of Yuya, Ay's mother. If Horemheb was in charge of the army command at Memphis, Nakhtmin would certainly have been responsible for the garrisons around Thebes, as well as the international bodyguard which patrolled the streets of Amarna, pictures of whom decorate the tombs at Amarna.

The generals and standard-bearers, that powerful officer corps, who'd seen Egypt's interests abroad suffer under Akhenaten, also represented a powerful pressure group. A fair reflection of Egypt's foreign prestige at the time of Akhenaten's death are the Amarna Letters. These are clay tablets, usually written in the Akkadian script, dealing with Egyptian interests across Sinai during the Aten ascendancy. They were filed in the 'Foreign Office' archives at Amarna and, when the city was abandoned, left there. A good number of them come from a ruler called Rib-Addi, Prince of Byblos in what is now Lebanon. Rib-Addi sent letter after letter to Akhenaten pointing out how he and others of Pharaoh's allies were now being discomfited and even threatened by interests hostile to Egypt. These letters, over 3,000 years old, reveal Rib-Addi as a loyal and brave man at the end of his tether. Rib-Addi asks for a small chariot squadron, a few hundred of Egypt's crack infantry to save the situation but he didn't even receive a reply. In despair Rib-Addi directed letters to Akhenaten's generals but they, too, showed that, whilst Akhenaten held the flail and the rod, Rib-Addi was not to place his trust in princes or his confidence in the war chariots of Egypt. The Prince of Byblos received no squadrons of war chariots, no bowmen from Nubia, no troop of foot soldiers, not even skilled advisers. He didn't even receive a reply worthy of mention. Akhenaten's foreign policy can be summed up in that he did nothing wrong but, there again, he did nothing right.

Under the Tuthmosids, Egypt had evolved a highly efficient and effective war machine with troops based along the frontiers, their headquarters being at Memphis and Thebes. During the reign of Akhenaten this war machine ground to a halt. Akhenaten had himself depicted in certain warlike poses. He did receive prisoners and treasure in the Hall of Foreign Tribute at his City of the Sun Disc but these were minor affairs. Akhenaten may have signed a peace treaty with the Hittites but he does not appear to have been aware of the

The Luxor Temple dedicated to Amun – the earliest parts date
from the reign of Amenhotep III

Statue of Amenhotep III

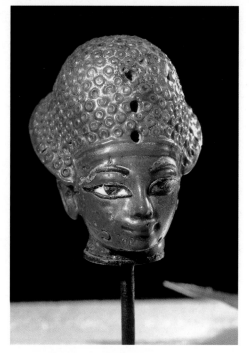

Miniature blue glass paste head
of the pharaoh Amenhotep III,
wearing the blue or war crown

The head of Queen Tiye, wife of Amenhotep III
and mother of Akhenaten

Left: The God Amun from the temple complex of Karnak – the reign of Tutankhamun

Below: Relief from the processional colonnade of Amenhotep III at Luxor depicting a scene from the Opet festival

Akhenaten – a classical depiction of the Amarna era

The famous crowned head of Queen Nefertiti – found at Amarna

Right: A relief from a stela depicting the close family ties of Akhenaten, Nefertiti and three of their daughters, all basking under the rays of the Aten

Below: A classic Amarna relief showing Nefertiti worshipping the Aten

Left: A relief from an Amarnan tomb – soldiers in a war chariot

Middle left: Scribes rendering their accounts

Below: A sandstone relief of Amarna period depicting chariots

An intriguing sculpture, thought to be the mysterious
Semenkhkare – or Nefertiti

Once thought to be the mysterious Semenkhkare, this is
certainly Tutankhamun and his wife-queen Ankhesenamun

The lid of a casket of Tutankhamun. The King is in a garden with Queen Ankhesenamun and is leaning on a staff

growing threat from under their new, warlike King
Suppiluliumas and the real danger the Hittites posed to
Egyptian interests across Sinai.

The generals must have been displeased but their growing
disquiet sprang not merely from a love of fighting or a desire
for glory. Egypt's armies depended heavily on foreign tribute,
as well as precious metals and wood for their weapons. The
officer corps must have chafed at the bit and wondered, if
Akhenaten's policies were continued, whether the tide of
troubles, the Season of the Hyena, would return. If the
kingdom of Kush, held down by troops and powerful
fortresses, staged a successful revolution then the political and
economic consequences for Egypt would be dire. The other
nightmares were a possible Hittite advance across Sinai, invasion by land or indeed even from the sea. Egypt's life-line was
the Delta and the Nile. If any hostile power advanced its
standards, as the Hyksos did, and seized cities in the Delta, or
along the great river, Egypt would be divided, its power
broken, the glories and prestige gained by the Tuthmosid
Pharaohs would be lost.

Accordingly, all these power-brokers came together in 1334
BC and a decision was made on the governance of Egypt
during the minority of the royal children. These powerful
men, pragmatists with long service in the civil and military
administration, decided on what was good for the country
and planned for the future. The politicians decided on two
things, first, that the Aten cult be left to wither and, secondly,
that Egypt's return to the old ways should be implemented as
quickly as possible. Their policies are best described on the
Restoration Stela set up under Tutankhamun's name, during
the opening years of his reign, in the temple complex of

Karnak. It is a profound political statement which pithily describes Egypt at the end of the Aten age with an action plan for what was to be done to rectify the situation. Of course it was issued in Tutankhamun's name but it represents the policies of the power-brokers behind the throne rather than the occupant of the throne itself. This important message was proclaimed in the first year of Tutankhamun's reign, in the fourth month of Akhet, Day 19. At the top of the stela, quite appropriately, is a carving of the young Tutankhamun paying service to Amun, a clear indication of what was coming next. The wording of the stela is as follows:

Year 1, fourth month of Akhet, Day 19, under the Majesty of Horus: Strong Bull, Pleasing of Births to the Two Ladies, Effective of Laws, who Placates the Two Lands, Golden Horus, Young of Appearance, who Pleases the Gods.

Son of Re: [Horemheb, Beloved of Amun, carved over Tutankhamun], Ruler of Southern Heliopolis. This is followed by Tutankhamun's titles, [to be later crudely deleted and Horemheb's titles carved over them.] May he be given Life, like Re forever and ever, Beloved of Amun Lord of the Two Lands, Foremost in Karnak [Ipet-sut], Beloved of Atum, Lord of the Two Lands of Heliopolis; of Re-Horakhte and Ptah-south-of-his-wall, Lord of Memphis: and of Thoth, Lord of Hieroglyphs [literally speech of the gods] the One who appeared upon the throne of the living Horus, like his father Re.

The good god, son of Amun, son of Kamutef [literally, Bull-of-his-Mother, a title of Horus], the good son, the holy egg whom Amun created, father of the Two Lands, the one who makes the one who made him, the Bas of Heliopolis united in order to form him, to be King forever and ever, as Horus, living immortally. He is the effective King who did what was good for his father and all the gods. He restored everything that was ruined, to be his monument forever and ever. He has vanquished chaos from the whole land and has restored Ma'at to her place. He has made lying a crime, the whole land being made as it was at the time of Creation.

Now when His Majesty was crowned King, the temples and the estates of the gods and goddesses from Elephantine as far as the marshes of Lower Egypt had fallen into decay. Their shrines had tumbled down, turned into piles of rubble and overgrown with weeds. Their sanctuaries were as if they had never existed at all, their temples had become footpaths. The world was chaotic and the gods had turned their backs on this land. If an army was sent to Djahy [Canaan] to extend the boundaries of Egypt, it would have no success. If you asked a god for advice, he would not attend; and if one spoke to a goddess likewise she would not attend. Hearts were faint in bodies because everything that had been was destroyed.

Now some days after this, His Majesty appeared upon the throne of his father and he ruled the Two Banks of Horus [Egypt], the Black Land and the Red Land being under his authority and every land bowed down before his might. Now His Majesty was in his palace which was in the House of Aakheperkare [Memphis], being like the Sun in the sky, and His Majesty carried out the works of this land and everything the Two Lands required every

[87]

day. Then His Majesty considered in his heart and looked for something which would be effective for his father Amun. He made the holy statue out of genuine electrum, giving to it more than had been done before. He made his father Amun 13 poles long, the holy statue being made of electrum, lapis-lazuli, turquoise and every noble and precious stone, although the Majesty of this holy god had only been 11 poles long before. He also made Ptah-south-of-his wall, Lord of Memphis, his holy statue of electrum, 11 poles long, the holy statue being made of electrum, lapis-lazuli, turquoise and every noble and precious stone, when the Majesty of this noble god had been only 7 poles long before. His Majesty made monuments for the gods, making their statues from electrum from the tribute of the foreign lands. He restored them forever, endowing them with offerings forever, laying aside for them divine offerings daily, laying aside bread from the earth. He added great wealth on top of that which existed before, achieving more than his predecessors had ever done. He allocated waab-priests, God's Servants whose reputation is established. He has enriched their tables with gold and silver, bronze and copper without limit. He has filled their store-houses with male and female workers and with His Majesty's booty. He has added to the wealth of every temple, doubling, trebling and quadrupling the silver, gold, lapis-lazuli, turquoise and every noble and precious stone, together with byssus, white linen, ordinary linen, oil, fat, resin, perfumes and myrrh without limit.

His Majesty, Life, Prosperity, Health, has made quays for the river from new wood from the hill-slopes from the pick of Negau, inlaid with gold, the tribute of foreign countries, so that they might decorate the river. His Majesty, Life, Prosperity, Health, picked male and female servants, musicians and dancers who had been women of the palace, their cost being charged to the palace and to the treasury of the Two Lands. I shall have them protected and guarded for my ancestors, the gods, in the hope that they will be contented, by doing what their kas wish while they protect Egypt.

Now the gods and goddesses of this land are rejoicing in their hearts, the Lords of the temples are in joy, the provinces all rejoice and celebrate throughout this whole land because good has come back into existence. The Ennead in the temple, their arms are raised in adoration, their hands are filled with jubilees for ever and ever. All life and might is with them, and it is for the name of the mighty King Horus, repeater of births, beloved son of his father Amun, Lord of the gods, who made the one who made him, the King of Upper and Lower Egypt, his eldest son, the true and beloved one who protects his father who begot him. His Kingship is that of his father Osiris, son of Re, the son who is good to the one who begot him, plentiful in monuments, rich in wonders, the one who makes an accurate monument for his father Amun, fair of births, the King who has established Egypt.

The Restoration Stela is a manifesto, a royal proclamation describing briefly what had happened and should not have, and how matters were to be put right. These are the words of Pharaoh which 'jumped down from his lips and would run the entire length of the Kingdom of the Two Lands'. The

Restoration Stela is, perhaps, an imitation of the famous Dream Stela set up by Tutankhamun's ancestor Tuthmosis IV in which he justified his claim to the throne. The text of the stela is very important, not only because of its message but because it symbolizes the contract between the power-brokers. No reference is made to monotheism, or the over-riding cult of the Aten. Great emphasis is laid on Amun and, although there is mention of the Aten, Pharaoh is still 'beloved of Amun'. The past is quickly dismissed. Tutankhamun did 'What was good for his father and all the Gods'. This is the nearest the Stela comes to apologizing for what has happened during Akhenaten's reign. Tutankhamun's actions are described as if he had already achieved them. 'He restored everything that was ruined . . . He has vanquished chaos' and, above all, 'restored Ma'at to her place . . . He has made lying a crime'. In other words Tutankhamun has re-established the truth, the way things should be. The Stela then goes on to describe how the shrines and temples throughout the kingdom have been thrown into chaos, deserted, pillaged and overgrown with weeds, as if the gods themselves had been driven from Egypt. It is significant that in the second part the Stela goes on to describe how Tutankhamun has paid special devotion to Amun and to the god Ptah, the latter (depicted as a light-skinned man, clothed in mummy wrappings with a heavy ornamental collar) is closely associated with the city of Memphis. Apparently under Akhenaten's supremacy the priesthood of other cults had been disbanded, Tutankhamun had to choose new priests and open the treasuries to re-establish their temples, Houses of Life and workshops.

Now this proclamation may have been published outside Karnak but it was drawn up in Memphis. The stela actually says Tutankhamun was in 'The House of Aakheperkare' which is in Memphis. Some Egyptologists believe Tutankhamun was taken to Karnak for his coronation but I think otherwise. The temple complexes of Luxor and Karnak, after years of neglect, must have been in some state of disrepair, whilst the royal council would regard Thebes as an unsafe place for the immediate appearance of Akhenaten's heirs. Resentment would be running high against the Akhenaten clan and there may not have even been the priests or the facilities available for the elaborate coronation to be carried out. It would be best if Thebes saw its Pharaoh crowned elsewhere.

Memphis would be a perfect choice for such a ceremony. It had been under the direct control of General Horemheb who was not as zealous as he should have been in the persecution of the other cults. Memphis was Horemheb's power base, the home of royal troops, a garrison town where Tutankhamun would be protected. Moreover, Memphis itself had been the place where Horemheb's ideal Pharaoh, Amenhotep III, had also been crowned as a boy: Horemheb, as Pharaoh, would later date his reign from the end of Amenhotep III's rule.

Horemheb undoubtedly played a powerful role in the wording and publication of the Restoration Stela. Tutankhamun is depicted as having a revelation whilst in the sacred city so closely associated with the General. The Stela gives the impression that the young Pharaoh had woken from a bad dream and could now see the way forward under the wise guidance of others. It is interesting to note that, although precedence is given to the God Amun, great emphasis is also laid on the cult of Ptah of Memphis. When Memphis was a royal capital, during the early dynasties of Egypt's history, Ptah's cult grew accordingly. Indeed, the Memphis priesthood claimed Ptah was the oldest god and had created Re-Aten out of pure thought. This was a clever jibe at Akhenaten's monotheism. The Memphis priesthood taught that Horus was the heart of Ptah and Thoth his tongue. The hidden messages of this Restoration Stela would not be lost on its readers. Aten was not the sole god of Egypt.

Indeed, it could be argued that Aten was only the product of a more ancient, wiser deity. The emphasis on Ptah was also a veiled rebuff to the cult of Amun. Men like Ay and Horemheb, astute, skilled politicians, must have realized that one of the causes for Akhenaten's religious revolution was a revulsion at the growing power of the Amun priests at Luxor and Karnak. Amenhotep III had done a great deal to diminish their power and Horemheb and Ay were quietly pointing out that, if the old days returned, it would not be a case of jumping from the pot into the fire: Egypt had many gods, no one cult should dominate.

The influence of Horemheb can also be seen in the many references to Osiris's son Horus. True, Horus was often associated with Pharaoh and his coronation ceremonies. However, in Horemheb's description of his own coronation a few years later, he reveals he has a special devotion to the Horus cult of his native town in the Delta. There are other allusions to Horemheb's grievances about how the military had suffered under Akhenaten, such as the need to rebuild quaysides and secure fresh imports of timber. The Nile was essential to Egypt's trade, any decline in its riverside cities and commercial centres would have been felt, particularly by the army, which depended on a constant stream of raw materials for its armouries. There is also a patent reference to Egypt's military strategy: 'If an army was sent to Djahy [Canaan] to

extend the boundaries of Egypt, it would have no success.'
Horemheb is describing Akhenaten's foreign policy. It doesn't
say Egypt suffered reversal or defeats but, although nothing
wrong happened, little good was achieved. The growing
power of the Hittites over Canaan must have been a matter of
great concern and something which had to be addressed
sooner rather than later. Horemheb must have been very
proud of the Restoration Stela, for when he later succeeded to
the throne, he did not destroy it but simply carved his name
over that of Tutankhamun's. In other words, it was his party
manifesto. He was only too willing to take it over himself as
well as let everyone know that it had been his idea in the first
place.

Tutankhamun may have been crowned at Memphis and
then returned to display his crown to the people of Thebes.
Nor can we rule out that a coronation or Crown-Wearing
Ceremony took place at both cities. Tutankhamun's tomb
contains pendants and pectorals displaying the Vulture
Goddess of the south, Nekhbet, as well as the Vulture
Goddess of Upper Egypt, beautiful blue and dark-red
jewellery in a gold cloisonné effect. The Metropolitan
Museum of Art in New York contains a carving of
Tutankhamun's head showing the God Amun touching him
in approbation and confirmation. Undoubtedly much would
have been made of the new Pharaoh's coronation as the
priests, masked as the gods they impersonated, came to greet
him and accept him into the Divine House. He would be
purified, then dressed in the garb of Pharaoh: the white mitre
and red mortar-shaped cap, the Atef crown of the god Re, the
blue crown or khepresh, the Diadem of the Two Tall Plumes.
He would hold the flail and the rod and assume his Great

[93]

Name consisting of five titles selected by the scribes from the House of Life. The first would be his Horus title which represented the earthly incarnation of the God; his second would be based on the image of the two great goddesses of Egypt, the Vulture and the Cobra, whose constant appearance invoked eternity. The third name was the Golden Falcon which represented the principle of good and eternal life being victorious over evil and annihilation. He also became King of the South and the North, taking the glorified title of Nebkheperure (The Lordly Manifestation of Re) and his fifth title, the one probably given to him at Amarna, Tutankhaten, Living Image of the Aten – later changed to Tutankhamun – Living Image of Amun.

The newly crowned Pharaoh would journey up and down the Nile in his royal barge accompanied by incense-waving priests, a royal progress displaying the might and power of Pharaoh; it also emphasized how the errors of the last few years were now to be quietly forgotten. For a while Tutankhamun was allowed to keep the El-Amarna suffix af Aten. There would be no persecution of the Aten cult, no military attack on the city of Akhenaten. Nevertheless, in that first year of the new Pharaoh's reign, the battle lines were drawn. Ay thought he controlled everything but, perhaps, he had under-estimated Horemheb's rise to power during the last years of the Aten cult. Horemheb was a power to be reckoned with but there would be no open breach. Egypt had a Pharaoh, the way forward had been proclaimed and that was the end of the matter. Nevertheless, the seeds of future conflict had been sown. Horemheb would not trust Ay and the 'Divine Father' would keep more than a watching brief on the ambitious general at his headquarters in Memphis: it was a time for military campaigns in Kush and elsewhere to keep the army happy and Horemheb busy.

Nevertheless, some uncertainty would exist. All parties would wonder if the Restoration Stela was a wishful dream or a harsh political reality. After all, Ay had been a leading supporter of Akhenaten. Would he have second thoughts? Would there be a second revolution? The city of El-Amarna still stood, whilst there was the question of the new Pharaoh, as well as the Princess Ankhesenamun. In the early years of the new reign both were just bewildered children, snatched from their family home and paraded through the great cities and temples of Egypt. The rule of the Kingdom of the Two Lands would be left to surer, wiser hands. But the years would pass. Tutankhamun and Ankhesenamun would grow older and mature. Perhaps they would think back to the glory days of the Sun Disc and what guarantee did Horemheb, or even Ay, have that Tutankhamun was not an Atenist through and through? When he reached the age of a young warrior, would he follow the path of his grandfather Amenhotep III or invoke the visions and dreams of Akhenaten? If that happened, would Ay, growing old, probably a man in his late fifties, once again support a cult which had cost Egypt so much? Would Horemheb accept any reversion? What role would he play? And, if the young king failed to produce a living heir, be it male or female, what then? Who would decide on the next Pharaoh?

Both Horemheb and Ay were climbing the greasy pole of royal preferment but Akhenaten's reign had proved how men who had risen high could also fall very low. It was a time of waiting. Such problems would have to be left to the future. The Kingdom of the Two Lands had to be replenished and reinvigorated, its enemies beyond its borders taught a lesson. Now the coronation and triumphant parades were over, the proclamations issued, it was best if the young Pharaoh and his royal half-sister disappeared whilst the wounds of the country were cleaned and healed. Tutankhamun and Ankhesenamun returned to El-Amarna where they married and played in its empty halls and gardens, no longer lovingly tended as they once had been. And, as for the future? Both Ay and Horemheb were born pragmatists, perhaps future problems would be addressed with more radical solutions.

3

Tutankhamun: the Living Image of Amun

No place of slaughter belongs to him:
he will go to the place of sacrifice.
Spell 70: *The Book of the Dead*

THE SETTLEMENT OF POWER HAD TAKEN PLACE. Tutankhamun had been proclaimed to the people and his coronation publicized. The religious processions at Memphis and Thebes were viewed in all their glory amidst the chanting of priests, gusts of incense, the hymns of the temple choirs, the carrying of shrines and the honouring of gods: a public testimony to the restoration of what had been. Egypt's gods had returned. Pharaoh had reissued his laws and Ma'at would bring harmony to all the people of Egypt. It was pure propaganda, so beloved of politicians of every age and every culture. The real power lay in Memphis and Thebes. General Horemheb could now refurbish the army, move troops and foot soldiers up towards Sinai. In Thebes Ay could issue his proclamations, restore confidence amongst the nobility and the priests. Tutankhamun and his wife Ankhesenamun were best kept in the shadows. We can only speculate on their mental state. In Egypt children grew up fast. The ten-year-old Ramesses II was associated with his father's military preparations, whilst Amenhotep III's elder son Tuthmosis had been given political and religious offices to discharge. But these were different times.

Harmony had to be restored. Pharaoh was only nine or ten years old and, as we shall see, there must have been speculation aboul his general health. It was best if both members of the royal family were withdrawn from the public eye. Evidence indicates that Tutankhamun and his half-sister were returned to the palace of El-Amarna, probably living in the northern section where archaeologists have found dockets and inscriptions referring to Tutankhamun. Some historians claim Nefertiti was still alive but there is very little evidence to support this. The city of El-Amarna was being deserted, though it would take at least another ten years before it became a ghost town. Undoubtedly during Tutankhamun's minority the City of the Aten was methodically pillaged by the authorities; furniture and treasures here moved back to the royal residences at Memphis, Thebes and elsewhere. Moreover, during Akhenaten's rather long exile from Thebes, the royal residences there must have fallen into disrepair. They would need to be replenished and refurbished, courts and chambers repainted, pools freshened and revitalized. The minority of Tutankhamun gave Ay and Horemheb a free hand. They would act on Pharaoh's behalf. They would wield real political power. El Amarna would be allowed to bleed to death, though as a royal residence it was a good compromise, situated between Thebes and Memphis; both Ay and Horemheb would have access to the young prince.

During their stay at the City of the Aten, Tutankhamun and Ankhesenamun were married and, when the time was ripe according to Ay, returned to Thebes. This took place some two years after the young Pharaoh's coronation. Tutankhamun and his new wife would process in to the Malkata, Amenhotep's gorgeous palace, making it easier for the nobles and priests of Thebes to accept him. A sufficient time had

[100]

elapsed for Ay and Horemheb to demonstrate their promises were good and the Restoration Stela indicates the frenetic activity which had taken place during the opening years of the reign. The stela had promised three crucial reforms, a return to the old gods of Egypt, a massive building programme to reflect this, and the re-establishment and extension of Egypt's imperial foreign policy. It would seem that the first two were the responsibility of Ay, whilst Horemheb and his generals would accomplish the third.

A great deal of what Tutankhamun built was later usurped by succeeding Pharaohs, some of it was destroyed, yet the building programme which took place during his ten-year reign, in a country recovering from upheaval, appears most impressive. Ay would have direct responsibility for this but the king's chief adviser was Maya who bore the titles, Overseer of the Building Works in the Place of Eternity, Overseer of the Building Works in the West, Overseer of the Treasury, the King's Scribe. Maya was responsible for raising the money and spending it on behalf of Egypt. If Ay was cunning, Maya was also a man to watch. He had undoubtedly experienced the years of Akhenaten and survived. He would serve Tutankhamun well and perhaps, even his successor, whilst he managed to survive the swift accession to power of General Horemheb where, for services rendered, he was given further dignities: Fan-Bearer on the Left of the King, Leader of the Festival of Amun in Karnak. Maya was a man with a foot in either camp. He had links with Horemheb, building a tomb for himself next to that of the general in the Necropolis at Sakkara, near Memphis.

Maya may have been the link between the two parties but, as Tutankhamun's reign progressed, the two major political groups would have developed, strengthened and absorbed others. The Aten group was finished in everything but name. All they had were memories and a crumbling city beside the Nile. Akhenaten was dead, his principal councillors had either disappeared or, having seen the light, were converted. The only danger was that the young Pharaoh, who now proclaimed himself Tutankhamun in loyalty to the old gods, together with his wife, might, when he reached manhood, have a change of heart, being unable to escape the influence of Akhenaten and the dream of Aten. Undoubtedly both Tutankhamun and Ankhesenamun must have undergone a period of re-education during their two years at El-Amarna. It was a suitable location, as those in charge clearly pointed out, to demonstrate how the glories of yesterday were fading and would be best soon forgotten.

Ay, Nakhtmin and the Akhmim clan would now closely identify themselves with the city of Thebes, the nobles, the powerful merchants and the influential priestly caste. This left Horemheb and his supporters at Memphis with their own views and policies which Ay had been willing to support, removing any sense of grievance. Horemheb could be assured that the building programme promised by the Restoration Stela would take place under Maya who would also ensure that the general received the human and material resources the army high command needed. Nevertheless, the honeymoon period which marked the coronation of Tutankhamun and proclamations such as the Restoration Stela would begin to fade though, as yet, there would be little reason for confrontation or a power struggle: Egypt had its Pharaoh and certain tasks had to be done. The building work would continue.

Whilst Tutankhamun was at El-Amarna he would have

been allowed to play the role of Pharaoh and permitted to choose to build a tomb there. The abandoned workings in the royal Necropolis at El-Amarna show such a tomb was begun but never completed. This may have been part of the process of giving lip-service to the heretical cult and avoiding serious confrontation. The real work would have continued of restoring the old status quo. A fragment of stela from El-Amarna, now in Berlin, represents Tutankhamun making offerings to the gods, not to the Sun Disc but to the gods of Thebes and Luxor, Amun and Mut. The Theban priests must have been delighted by this, to see the position reversed and their gods being worshipped at the very heart of the heretical cult. They would make other demands. Tutankhamun's figure was added to the decoration of the third pylon at Karnak, a powerful testimony to where the young Pharaoh's religious allegiances really lay. The destruction of Akhenaten's temples was begun, probably at the same time as Tutankhamun and Ankhesenamun left El-Amarna. After all, the priests would argue, such building materials could well be used elsewhere, whilst the damage wrought by the Atenists to the east face of the pylon of Karnak was also repaired. A broad, basalt-paved avenue lined by ram-headed sphinxes (the ram's head was a symbol of Amun) was built linking the tenth pylon at Karnak with the precinct of Amun's wife the Goddess Mut at Luxor. Small mansions were also built there in Tutankhamun's name. Only a few blocks of these remain. One was called the 'Mansion-of-Nebkheperure-in-Thebes,' the other, the 'Mansion of the Beloved-of-Amun-Who-Sets-Thebes-in Order'.

The message is very clear. Karnak and Luxor were being restored, the power of the city enhanced and this was the divine ordained duty of Pharaoh. A seated colossus identified as Tutankhamun was placed in the court of Mut's temple, together with a beautifully carved sphinx inlaid with calcite. Other fragments, showing Tutankhamun seated between Amun and Mut, indicate how this propaganda work was carried apace. A black granite pair-statue of Tutankhamun standing with Amun is now in the British Museum which also holds a statue of similar design including the Nile god Hapi. Statues with the same motif, kept in the museum at Turin, and carvings promulgating the same message can be seen in Cairo and Copenhagen. The conclusion reached is that the architects, sculptors and carvers were under orders to produce almost a factory-line list of statues to be placed in the great temple complexes of Karnak and Luxor. Their theme was constant: Tutankhamun with Amun; Tutankhamun with Amun and Mut; Tutankhamun with Mut; Tutankhamun with other gods of Egypt adorned with the features of Tutankhamun. The range and number of these relics indicate that, virtually every year, the temples of Karnak and Luxor were not only being refurbished and enhanced but that this was due to the direct influence of Pharaoh with whom these gods were closely associated.

Ay also worked hard to placate the priests of Amun, to satisfy their demands, as well as to win their favour, both for the present and to plan against whatever the future might hold. Such a building programme is even more remarkable when one reflects that the flow of tribute from beyond Egypt's borders must have been impaired by Akhenaten's rule. Foreign princes were not as quick as they had once been to respond to Pharaoh's demands. Indeed, as shall be shown later, the situation in Kush, the treasury of Egypt, had become so precarious that a major expedition was necessary, the new Viceroy Huy, one of Ay's close lieutenants, had to be sent south to firmly re-establish Egyptian rule and restore the flow of tribute.

Other building programmes continued at Thebes and elsewhere. The majestic processional colonnade of Amenhotep III at Luxor was gorgeously decorated with portraits of Tutankhamun being painted on the door jambs of the north wall. Sphinxes, carved out of blue-painted calcite, were also commissioned for the colonnaded court. Of course, Ay would have to be wary of Horemheb in Memphis. If Karnak and Thebes were to be objects of Pharaoh's favour so was the important temple complex of Egypt's former ancient capital. The temple of Ptah was also refurbished in Tutankhamun's name but this was later usurped by Horemheb. In the Cairo Museum there are fragments which bear testimony to building work by Tutankhamun at Giza, as well as at the ancient Necropolis of Sakkara. Similar building work was carried out in Nubia. Naturally, it was important to show that the new Pharaoh had returned to the traditions and customs of the Tuthmosid clan who had first exploited the Valley of the Kings and led to the thriving trade of the Necropolis.

Every Pharaoh chose his tomb in the valley as well as the place for his mortuary temple. It would be important for Thebans to realize Tutankhamun also intended this and that there would be no more desertions, no more forsaking of Karnak, Luxor and the Valley of the Kings for madcap schemes in some city hundreds of mile to the north. Under Ay's direction Maya selected a tomb for Tutankhamun, possibly the one now known as KV25, later usurped by Ay, as well as a mortuary temple to be erected on the spot occupied by Ramses III's funerary monument at Medinet Habu. At the same time the two colossal portrait statues which were intended to decorate its entrance were ordered, though these were later usurped by Tutankhamun's immediate successors.

The fragmentary evidence available illustrates a wide-sweeping construction programme which would have convinced the people of Egypt that, once again, Pharaoh had come into his own. The traders, craftsmen and artisans who profited from this programme of increased public spending, would also broadcast the news. Once again the imperial work-shops with their sculptors, carvers, craftsmen and builders would be aware of the changes proclaimed by the Restoration Stela. Every stratum of the population would feel the effects. Horemheb would have little to complain about whilst, for the powerful priests of Karnak, Luxor and elsewhere, revenge and retribution must have tasted exceedingly sweet. Of course, this begs the question, was this radical programme of public works done to enhance the name of Tutankhamun or that of Ay? In all fairness, according to the evidence available, it would seem that at the time the main beneficiary was Tutankhamun. Only after his mysterious death and swift burial did others try to usurp this for their own particular purposes.

Accordingly, within three years of Tutankhamun's acces-sion, the radical and swift change of imperial policy in domestic and religious matters must have been known from the Delta to beyond the Third Cataract. Tutankhamun had been crowned but hidden away at El-Amarna for two years. Now it was time for him to re-emerge and it seems that this return from El-Amarna coincided with the reconsecration of the temple complex at Karnak and Luxor during the great

Opet Festival. The Opet Festival, which always took place in the second month of Paophi, was a religious event which celebrated the power of Pharaoh, the cult of Amun and Mut and the religious supremacy of the priests who serve them. At the same time it was an occasion for public rejoicing with meat, bread, wine and beer being distributed to the citizens of Thebes. Such a festival, neglected during Akhenaten's reign, was not immediately restored. The temples of Karnak and Luxor were in no fit condition for such an ornate ceremony, whilst the temper of the priests and crowds of Thebes may not have been amenable. Everything had to be prepared and, I suggest, this was done during Pharaoh's two-year stay at El-Amarna.

Only when everything was ready was the Festival of Opet revived in all its glory during the third year of Tutankhamun's reign. So important and triumphant was this festival, in which Tutankhamun participated, that it was a subject of glorious paintings on the east and west walls of the processional colonnade at Luxor, though, like the Restoration Stela, these were later usurped by Horemheb. The west wall describes how Tutankhamun processed from Karnak to Luxor, whilst the east wall celebrates his return. The journey was along the Nile in a splendid flotilla of boats, including the royal barge, escorted by the sacred barges of the Theban gods Amun, his wife Mut and their son Khonsu. All three images were carried down in sacred barques to the riverside but only after Pharaoh himself had performed the important rites of decorating them with flowers and other offerings, as well as blessing them in clouds of incense.

The paintings describe how the priests, escorted by acolytes and others, carried the sacred boats containing the tabernacles of the gods shoulder-high. Once they had reached the river-side, the sacred burdens were carefully placed in their barges. The entire flotilla was gently towed southwards by sailors along the tow path, escorted by musicians and singers, dancers, priests and all the temple retinues. Members of the royal bodyguard would keep order as the banks on both sides of the Nile would be crowded with onlookers and well-wishers. During the voyage Tutankhamun, with great pomp and ceremony, would symbolically seize an oar to manifest that he took full responsibility for this sacred journey: a telling proclamation of how the words of the Restoration Stela were facts not empty phrases. Once they had arrived at Luxor, the naos of each god would be lifted up and carried into the sanctuary. After this had taken place the public festivities would begin, feasting and dancing, songs, popular shows and concerts, as vivid and as exciting as any modern carnival in the cities of Spain or South America. The celebrations would last at least eleven days: the imperial and temple treasuries would be open to furnish all the necessities for this public holiday. At the end of this sacred time, Pharaoh, re-invigorated by meeting his divine father and mother, would escort the statues of their gods back up the Nile to Karnak. Of course, it was all good publicity, skilful propaganda and Ay would take the credit. Tutankhamun was not only a crowned Pharaoh but also first priest of Amun: the god's temples were restored, reparation was being made.

Tutankhamun and his young wife, about this time aged eleven and thirteen respectively, would be bewildered though, like children of any age, happy to be the centre of attention and eager to participate in the rejoicing. Ay would have certainly made his power felt. One interesting part of the

Restoration Stela is the promise, 'He allocated priests, God's servants, whose reputation is established.' In other words the priesthood of Thebes, decimated by Akhenaten's heresy, was brought up to strength by Ay. He would have the power to allow those who had deserted Amun back into the fold, as well as appoint new nominees to positions of influence. There was more: 'He has enriched their tables with gold and silver, bronze and copper without limit. He has filled their store-houses with male and female workers and with His Majesty's booty . . .' The message is clear enough. The priests were not just reappointed and told to work but received lavish rewards in their new office. If this wasn't enough, 'He has added to the wealth of every temple'. The priests were appointed, rewarded and promoted by Ay but also given every guar-antee that their places of work would be restored to their former glory.

This great Festival of Opet, the first of Tutankhamun's reign, must have been a manifestation of Ay's patronage and power, an occasion to demonstrate to all what he had done and achieved. If Tutankhamun was hailed as glorious, 'Fair of births, the King who has established Egypt', then Ay was the power behind the throne who would take the credit. One of the most telling phrases in the Restoration Stela are the words, 'and with His Majesty's booty'; the temple priests were being lavishly rewarded, and bought, from Pharaoh's own revenues, particularly the fruits of foreign tribute. There is not a shred of proof that during his life Tutankhamun faced any opposition from a city and a priesthood which had every cause to hate his name and that of his family. This must have been Ay's achievement, who was soon to prove, even during Pharaoh's life, that he held absolute power, whilst after

Tutankhamun's death Ay was able to reap the harvest he had sown.

One problem, however, which was not a matter for publication or glory, was Akhenaten's City of the Sun Disc. Ay and the rest of the Akhmim clan had been an important part of the Atenist cult. They may have been pragmatists and seen it as a way of advancement. However, Ay was the brother of Queen Tiye, the father of Nefertiti, and the crumbling city of El-Amarna posed one serious problem. When Akhenaten had moved to El-Amarna, the Valley of the Kings and the Theban City of the Dead were neglected. A new Necropolis was founded at what is now known as Wadi Abu Hasah El Sahari which opens out amongst the eastern cliffs opposite the central city of the Aten capital. Akhenaten himself chose his own tomb there, No. 26 in the El-Amarna series, and plans were laid for himself and his family to be buried there. Of course, the Aten dream collapsed. El-Amarna became a ghost city. All those who wished for advancement shook its dust from their sandals but what once had been a dream for them now became a nightmare. Akhenaten's corpse, together with those of Nefertiti and at least five of their children, not to mention Tutankhamun's mother Kiya and the mysterious Pharaoh Semenkhkare, had been buried in its Necropolis. Ay, for all his cynicism, would have known he had a duty to the dead, whilst Tutankhamun and Ankhesenamun must have also been aware of their solemn responsibilities to their family and blood relations. The honouring of the dead was an essential part of Egyptian thinking. Ay must have known that if the royal corpses were neglected, grave robbers would break in, the mummies would be desecrated and their treasures broken up to be sold in the market places and cities along the Nile.

[110]

The problem must have taxed Ay's wily brain. The royal corpses had to be preserved and protected. A solution would be demanded. Royal burials were always elaborate ceremonial occasions but, in the new reality, in Ay's desperate attempt to restore Ma'at and harmony, how could the royal mummies be removed and re-interred without alienating the powerful priesthood of Amun and the scores of other groups with grievances against the Aten cult? True, public re-interment would not be necessary but, if they were moved, where in the Valley of the Kings could they be placed? Egyptian rulers of every dynasty demonstrated that they took their responsibilities as Guardians of the Royal Necropolis very seriously. The burial places of rivals might suffer desecration, nevertheless, the tombs of kinsfolk and innocents had to be protected. Time and again in Egyptian history there is evidence of royal burial places being opened and their mummies removed to other more secretive tombs where they could be kept safe. There was the additional problem that, in the heyday of Amun's reinstatement, memories of Akhenaten and his kin would not be pleasant. Many in Thebes, and especially its Necropolis, would only be too willing to execrate his memory through desecration of his corpse and tomb. Of course, the pillaging of royal graves was also very lucrative. No official text or inscription exists proving that Ay ordered the removal of the royal corpses from El-Amarna but it must have taken place and under the greatest secrecy. Logic would dictate that. The places where the royal corpses were moved to, or at least one of them, the mysterious Tomb 55 in the Valley of the Kings, still exists.

Tomb 55 was discovered by the English Egyptologist Edward Ayrton, working for the wealthy American Theodore

Davis. He stumbled on a small, unfinished one-roomed crypt not very far from where Carter would find KV62, the tomb of Tutankhamun. The tomb contained a coffin of an anonymous mummy and burial equipment belonging to Akhenaten, his mother Queen Tiye and other members of Akhenaten's family. Amongst these objects was a naos of gessoed and gilded wood especially made for Tiye by her son Akhenaten, together with a set of four beautifully sculptured calcite canopic jars with their usual portrait headstoppers. Finally, a mixed bag of small objects inscribed with other names was found, amongst these seals of Pharaoh Tutankhamun.

The coffin in KV55 had suffered from humidity as well as a rock fall but there was also evidence of deliberate damage carried out in antiquity. Wherever possible in the tomb, royal names and inscriptions had been hacked out. The mummy inside the coffin has also suffered due to the passage of time, as well as the lack of effective techniques in 1907 to preserve it. Davis truly believed that he had found the tomb of Queen Tiye, wife of Amenhotep III, mother of Akhenaten, grandmother of Tutankhamun. However, when Professor Elliot Smith, the anatomist, examined the skeleton in Tomb 55, he established it was that of a male in his mid-twenties. This led to further debate, with some Egyptologists claiming the skeleton from Tomb 55 was that of the heretical Pharaoh Akhenaten himself. A few years later Dr Douglas Derry, who carried out the study of Tutankhamun's skeleton, confirmed Smith's findings. The skeleton from Tomb 55 was a male though Derry claimed it belonged to a younger man, not in his mid-twenties but aged twenty or twenty-one. Derry also confirmed, which later research proved, that there is a strong physical similarity between Tutankhamun and the skeleton found in Tomb KV55. Accordingly, most Egyptologists came round to the belief that the mysterious occupant of KV55 must have been Semenkhkare, Akhenaten's mysterious co-regent.

Some Egyptologists have tried to argue that the remains in KV55 are those of the Great Royal Wife Nefertiti but this side-steps the findings of the medical experts. The debate still goes on. The mysterious human remains in KV55 have been hailed as belonging to Tiye, Nefertiti, Akhenaten, Semenkhkare and, in the next few years, someone else's name may well be put forward. I, however, agree with the findings of the specialists that the skeleton in KV55 is that of a young man no more than twenty-one years of age, very closely related to Tutankhamun and, in all probability, Tutankhamun's immediate prede-cessor, the elusive Semenkhkare.

The debate has not been helped by other findings in the tomb. The reconstructed coffin lid found in KV55 is now on display in Cairo Museum. When Davis found it, the lid had been broken into three parts due to a rock fall. Egyptologists who have studied this have found that the lid, and the entire wooden coffin it covered, had first been made and carved for a royal female but were later modified to receive the body of a royal prince. The stoppers on the canopic jars have also been carved in the likeness of a royal female of the El-Amarna group. Accordingly, we have the male corpse of a Tuthmosid prince in a coffin probably made for a princess, with canopic jars which should have had a likeness of the dead prince but, instead, display those of a royal princess. In the same tomb we also have what can only be called the battered shrine of Queen Tiye's sepulchre. There is the additional problem of the royal inscriptions and names being gouged out and, of course, Tutankhamun's seals being found amongst the debris. The problem is even more complicated for, when Carter began to sift through the vast treasures found in Tutankhamun's tomb, a number of objects, including wine jars, writing palettes and other items, were found not to belong to Tutankhamun but to a wide range of Akhenaten's family.

Akhenaten had made it very clear in one of the stelae set up around his royal city that he and his family would never move from the sacred City of the Sun Disc. One stela, which stands not far from the entrance to the royal Necropolis at El-Amarna, bears an inscription which demonstrates that, after death, Akhenaten decreed that his body and that of his family were to be buried there. The inscription reads:

> May a tomb be made for me in the eastern mountains of Akhetaten: may my burial be made in it, in the Millions of Jubilees which my father the Aten has decreed for me. May the burial of Queen Nefertiti be made in it, in the Millions of Years that my father the Aten decreed for her. May the burial of Princess Meritaten be made in it, in these Millions of Years. If I die in any town in the north, south, west or east in these Millions of Years, let me be returned, so that I may be buried in Akhetaten. If Princess Meritaten dies in any town in the north, south, west or east in these Millions of Years, let her be returned so that she may be buried in Akhetaten.

So, what did happen to the El-Amarna corpses? I suggest the following took place. Ay would be deeply concerned by the increasingly deserted royal tombs at El-Amarna. The ties of kinship, not to mention the demands of religion, would require something be done. At the same time Ay did not wish

[114]

to upset the priests of Amun or, indeed, draw attention to where the El-Amarna royal corpses would be buried. I doubt very much whether Tutankhamun or his first minister would be involved in the execration of the memories of their close kin. Aten worship had not yet been proscribed. The attack on Akhenaten's memory would begin late in Horemheb's reign and be pursued with a vengeance by Horemheb's own successors. Ay's problem was proper care for the royal corpses, so he looked round the Valley of the Kings for possible hiding places. Ideally he would choose deserted tombs or caverns built specially for the purpose of housing the remains from El-Amarna. One of these could have been what is now known as KV54, the burial pit found not far from Tutankhamun's own tomb. Others more suitable would include the burial place of Amenhotep II and what we now know as KV55 and KV62, very close to each other. The coffins would be taken from El-Amarna and either transported by river or land to the Valley of the Kings and distributed in various resting places, KV65, the tomb of Amenhotep II, KV35 and KV62 which later served as Tutankhamun's tomb. There is every likelihood that this transportation was carried out in great secrecy by Ay and trusted members of the Akhmim group. Any damage or desecration was not the work of Ay but later rulers and, most propbably, the passage of time.

There is considerable proof to justify this interpretation. Susan James in her study of the mummy K61070 which was discovered in the tomb of Amenhotep II, has argued, quite convincingly, that this mummy dubbed 'The Elder Woman' by Elliot Smith could well be the mortal remains of Akhenaten's beloved wife, the 'Beautiful Woman' Nefertiti. James argues that both this mummy, as well as K61072,

[115]

entitled 'The Younger Woman', in the same cache, have the characteristic features very close to those associated with the extended Egyptian royal family in the latter half of the 18th dynasty. The breadth of each skull is less than four-fifths of its length, giving them an 'egg-head' appearance, a physical characteristic which can be seen in the mummy of Yuya, father of Queen Tiye, as well as those of Tuthmosis IV and, of course, both Semenkhkare and Tutankhamun. If the removal of these mummies, together with that of the occupant of KV55, were the work of hostile forces, it poses the question 'Why remove them in the first place? Why not destroy them utterly where they were?' Coffins can be smashed, mummies broken up and turned to dust, yet, according to the evidence, mummy K61070 and K61072, as well as the occupant of KV55, were moved quite tenderly and gently. Those mummies deposited in Amenhotep II's tomb were hidden carefully and secretly, whilst that of KV55 was also treated with dignity until much later in Egyptian history.

I suspect KV55, together with KV62, were used as storage rooms which explains the confusion there, with a myriad remains belonging to other individuals. When the removal from El-Amarna first took place, KV55 and other caches would have been nothing more than warehouses packed with a hoard of possessions. However, because KV55 and KV62 were small, tombs such as KV65, and possibly others, were used for the overflow. Many of the items found in Tutankhamun's own tomb belonged to the other members of the Akhenaten clan, even the gold bands around his corpse. Although on certain items royal titles have been gouged out and replaced with Tutankhamun's name and titles, there is no evidence that any of these goods had been abused or ill-

[116]

treated. The royal tombs at El-Amarna were methodically and reverentially cleared and cleaned, their contents removed to the Valley of the Kings and hidden away in secret caches, one of which, KV55, was actually sealed by Tutankhamun, or at least by his ministers acting on his behalf. When Tutankhamun mysteriously died, and Ay wished to hurry him to his grave, KV62 and the nearby treasure hoards of KV55 came in very useful indeed. I suggest the transfer of goods from El-Amarna to the Valley of the Kings was the direct responsibility of Ay and his immediate entourage and carried out during Tutankhamun's reign. Horemheb may have known but not been party to the details or the secrecy involved.

The Restoration Stela committed Egypt to re-establishing its power abroad and this was Horemheb's duty. Yet, even here there is evidence that, if Horemheb did the hard work, Ay and his associates were more than prepared to take the glory. In ancient Egypt the army had three functions: to maintain law and order at home, to defend Egypt's borders and, when ordered, to cross those borders to strengthen and expand Egyptian influence. The maintenance of law and order could warrant the use of regular troops but usually each city had its own mayor and police. The palace would have its own praetorian guard of foot soldiers and chariot squadrons. During Tutankhamun's reign, as with everything else, Ay would keep the palace guard under his control or that of his kinsman General Nakhtmin, a powerful member of the Akhmim clan and, judging from Tutankhamun's tomb, a close confidant of the young Pharaoh.

The second and third functions, defending Egypt's interests abroad, would require regular troops. Succeeding Pharaohs were always keen to tighten their control over what they regarded as their own province, the kingdom of Kush. One of Amenhotep III's first duties as Pharaoh, when he was no more than fifteen years of age, was to show the 'vile Nubians', the inhabitants of Kush, that he truly was 'Horus in the South'. Kush was a treasure source, possessing rich gold mines lying between the Second and Third Cataracts, as well as out in the east Nubian Desert. Other minerals would also be mined there: malachite, copper carbonate, together with galena, both of which were essential to Egyptian industry as malachite was used in the smelting of copper, whilst galena was a source of lead.

Amenhotep, together with his faithful Viceroy Merymose, had swept south to crush opposition, defeating the rebels and taking almost 30,000 prisoners. We know this from the great Victory Stela set up in Nubia which declared:

Someone came to tell His Majesty that . . . the Vile of Kush had plotted rebellion . . . His Majesty led on to victory . . . His Majesty reached them like the wing stroke of a falcon. Like Montu [The Egyptian God of War] in his transformations . . . [Amenhotep] the fierce eyed lion, whose claws seized the Vile Kush, who trampled down all its Chieftains in their valleys and threw them down in their blood, one on top of the other.

Even the so-called peaceful Akhenaten, as Redford points out, had displayed his power and majesty in Kush, crushing opposition, taking prisoners and impaling others.

During Tutankhamun's reign the situation was no different. The tribesmen of Nubia were always ready to rebel, fiercely resenting the tribute which flowed down the Nile to Thebes, Pharaoh's demands for hostages and the ransacking of the wealth of their country. There is no evidence to show Tutankhamun led his armies south. True, there are paintings from his tomb showing a warlike Pharaoh in his splendid war chariot, body rigid, bow pulled back, ready to loose another arrow, as his horses and the wheels of his majestic chariot, together with his war dogs running alongside, trample down what looks like fleeing Nubian tribesmen: this was more colourful propaganda than reality. It was conventional to depict Pharaohs in warlike poses and bellicose, triumphant moods. There is even a painting of Tutankhamun, with the head of a sphinx, crushing the heads of hapless Nubians but this is sycophantic praise. Tutankhamun's courtiers were just flattering the memory of their dead prince. They are borrowing an image from the Victory Stela of Amenhotep, Tutankhamun's grandfather, who described himself as a raging, roaring lion tearing down his opponents.

If Tutankhamun was not the leader in the projected campaign against Kush then who was? General Horemheb must have played a part: paintings from his tomb at Sakkara portray the general bringing Nubian captives before Pharaoh and receiving the approval and approbation of his prince. Horemheb was involved in the Nubian campaign and displayed his exploits both in his tomb at Sakkara and on the stela describing the events which led to his own coronation as Pharaoh. Nevertheless, his nose may have been put out of joint, for the real star of Tutankhamun's Nubian campaign was that close member of Ay's circle, the court official and former soldier Huy. He was Tutankhamun's Viceroy of Nubia and Huy un-ashamedly described his achievements in his own tomb paintings which have been analysed by the historians Davis and Gardiner.

These paintings place Huy very much at the heart of affairs. After all, Huy was an old Nubian hand. He had served as Scribe of the Correspondence under Amenhotep III's Viceroy Merymose, so Huy was well placed to know the country. Huy, who was also present at Tutankhamun's mysterious burial, rejoiced in some of the highest titles in the land. He was not only Viceroy of Nubia but 'Divine Father', one of the 'Fan-Bearers on the King's Right Hand', 'Supervisor of the Amun's Cattle in the Land of Kush', 'Supervisor of the Land of Gold of the Lord of the Two Countries'. Huy's military exploits had earned him the title of His Majesty's Brave in the Cavalry. Very little if any mention is made of General Horemheb's role. Huy's tomb paintings lavishly describe how he was installed as Viceroy. Tutankhamun is formally dressed in a swirling robe of pleated linen, wearing the khepresh crown and enthroned under a canopy, in one hand the crook and flail and in the other the ankh or sign of life. Huy is brought before him, garbed in formal robes and carrying the flail of office, to be greeted by Maya, the Head of Treasury, who declares the terms of office. Huy accepts these whilst the courtiers chant to Pharaoh: 'You are the son of Amun . . . may He send you the chiefs of all lands bearing choice goods from all their countries.' Huy is then invested with the gold ring of office, together with the seal by Ay, Pharaoh's right-hand man. Huy and his retinue leave to the acclamations of the court and immediately sets sail to Nubia whilst, on the quayside, his wife and family unite in a paean of praise.

Huy fully justified the confidence placed in him, establishing law and order, enforcing Pharaoh's writ and ensuring a rich flow of tribute north. Huy's tomb paintings then describe the Viceroy's victorious return to Thebes with barges loaded with tribute, as well as hostages who would reside at Pharaoh's court. This motley gorgeous procession, led by the victorious Viceroy, carries baskets of food and gold in many forms, as it goes forward to meet Pharaoh, once more sitting under a canopy in one of the palace courtyards. Huy, holding his emblems of office, introduces the nobles of Kush in person so they can make obeisance and offer the tribute: finely carved furniture, armchairs, beds, shields, bows and arrows, baskets of gold rings, bags of gold dust, cornelian and jasper heaped up in bowls, ivory tusks, ebony boomerangs, gold-plated chariots and animal skins. All this is followed by a beautiful woman, probably intended for Tutankhamun's harem, as well as slaves loaded with manacles.

In fact, we have three versions of the Nubian campaign. The first, according to paintings found in Tutankhamun's tomb, depicts Pharaoh in warlike mode, riding down scores of Nubians: this was merely a pictorial representation. In theory Pharaoh was commander-in-chief and, like the Caesars of Rome, the victories of Pharaoh's generals were really the work of Pharaoh. Tutankhamun could be painted as a warrior but the paintings in Huy's tomb depict a different scenario. Tutankhamun, and this is an issue to be discussed later, is not depicted as a warrior like his grandfather, a raging lion charging south to tear his enemy to pieces. On both Huy's departure to Nubia and his return, Tutankhamun is simply sitting down, commissioning the Viceroy to go south and receiving the tribute on his return.

Huy's tomb also gives an insight into the power structure at Thebes. He is not bashful in viewing himself as Viceroy, or even more. One scene from his tomb depicts Huy's return almost as a Pharaoh holding the flail as well as the crook. He may pay homage to Tutankhamun but Huy's tomb pictures also illustrate Nubian tributes being presented directly to the Viceroy. One in particular graphically describes Hiknefer, the Prince of Aniba in Nubia, accompanied by two colleagues in feathered headdresses, nosing the ground, or about to do so, in front of the Viceroy. The inescapable conclusion drawn from a close study of these pictures is that Huy saw himself very much in charge. He is active whilst the Pharaoh is passive. He does not receive the seal of office directly from the Pharaoh but from another powerful official which can only be Ay. Tutankhamun can be depicted as a warlike chieftain in the pictures on the fan found in his tomb. He may have had body armour buried with him but, as far as Huy was concerned, Huy was the victor of Nubia and, rather than Huy basking in Pharaoh's glory, the positions are reversed.

The third version of this Nubian expedition is that of General Horemheb. Scenes from the east wall of the second courtyard on his Memphis tomb depict Horemheb leading Nubian captives into the presence of his prince. On one level these different versions can be amusing but they do betray the tensions at Tutankhamun's court. Huy, in his paintings, claims the credit, whilst General Horemheb presents an alternative version. There is no evidence of two Nubian campaigns. Horemheb may have gone ahead to prepare the ground for Huy or may have acted in concert with him. Nevertheless, the inescapable conclusion is that both men claimed the glory for what can only be termed a victorious campaign. Little wonder that, when Horemheb came to power, he never forgot Huy's slight.

The other area of foreign policy concern to Egypt was across Sinai. A new power had arisen in what is now the province of Anatolia in modern Turkey. The Hittites had united under their King Suppiluliumas and, in a brilliant and bloody campaign, utterly crushed Egypt's old ally the Mitanni. During Akhenaten's reign the princes of what is now Syria and Palestine began to feel the winds of unrest. Egypt's client states begged their overlords to send help but little was offered. Akhenaten is always depicted as the villain of the piece, though Amenhotep III had also been neglectful of his northern allies. The El-Amarna Letters describe the confusion which reigned in the area of Palestine and Syria during the latter part of Amenhotep III's long reign.

It is easy to condemn Akhenaten for his vacillation but a close study of any map illustrates the daunting logistics of organizing an army and either marching it across Sinai or organizing a sea-borne invasion through one of the great ports along the Canaan coastline. The personnel and material resources would have been immense, as the great Ramesses II later discovered when he launched his all-out attack on the Hittites in 1274 BC . Even he, with all his military prowess and the full resources of Egypt behind him, could only achieve a pyrrhic victory. The distance between Thebes and the potential battle ground was some 1,000 miles and victory was not assured.

To be fair, Akhenaten followed the usual conventions of Egyptian foreign policy; he sealed treaties with the great princes of the Mitanni or Babylon, whilst managing to control the local chieftains and potentates, setting one off against the other or, more usually, educating them at the Egyptian court, then sending them home with heavy bribes. The Hittite victory against the Mitanni naturally upset the balance; this, coupled with Akhenaten's inaction, heightened the tension, Egypt's ally Rib-Addi, Prince of Byblos, had to face the opposition of wily Aziru of Amurru who had allied himself to the Bedouins and other gangs of cut-throats. The Hittites watched this confusion with interest but never really intervened. Indeed, as Redford points out, Akhenaten sealed a peace treaty with the Hittites and allowed Aziru enough rope to hang himself. Rib-Addi was eventually driven from his throne, hunted down and killed. Only then was Aziru forced to come to the Egyptian court where he was held hostage for a number of years, perhaps even blinded, before being allowed to return home.

During Tutankhamun's reign the unrest and chaos in Palestine and Syria had its effect. We know from Horemheb's tomb that refugees crossed into Egypt, begging for protection and help. They complain, according to these inscriptions from Horemheb's Memphis tomb, how their dwellings have been destroyed, their towns devastated, their crops burnt. They ask for asylum and that Pharaoh do something to bring peace to their war-torn country. Horemheb, based in Memphis and now free of his Nubian commitments, must have urged Tutankhamun's court that action had to be taken. Horemheb's tomb boasts that he accumulated titles such as the 'King's Deputy in All Countries', 'King's Elect', 'The Greatest Amongst the Favourites of the Lord of the Two Countries', 'The True Scribe Well Beloved of the King'.

Whatever he trumpeted, Horemheb was committed to a restoration of Egypt's fortunes across the Sinai peninsula. The Restoration Stela quite clearly states: 'The World was chaotic and the Gods had turned their backs on this Kingdom. If an

[124]

army was sent to Djahy [Canaan], to extend the boundaries of Egypt it would have no success.' Now, the wording of the stela must be examined very carefully. It doesn't say an army was sent but if an army had been sent by Akhenaten it would have achieved very little. What seems to have happened during Akhenaten's reign is that the Foreign Office at El-Amarna fell back on the usual strategy of maintaining peace treaties with the great powers and bribing the minor princes across Sinai. This policy appears not to have had much success. Egypt was faced with refugees, a dimunition of its influence in the area and the ever-brooding presence of the Hittites. Horemheb and his standard-bearers must have itched to do something but what? The logistics of sending an army across Sinai would have been formidable and would have required a build-up of troops and resources. However, as the Restoration Stela points out, Egypt was in no position to launch an all-out offensive at the beginning of Tutankhamun's reign. Nevertheless, as the years progressed and normality returned, Horemheb must have seized his opportunity. The temple worship was restored. Nubia was brought firmly under Egyptian control; this would not only boost Tutan-khamun's building projects but fill the war chests. Even so it would take time and planning for an offensive. It would also mean finding new allies.

Evidence from the El-Amarna letters demonstrate that the King of Babylon grew alarmed at how Tutankhamun's ministers were extending peace feelers to Babylon's subjects, the Assyrians. The King of Babylon asks Tutankhamun: 'Why have they [the Assyrians] gone to your country? . . . Let them return here empty-handed.' There seems to be considerable evidence to justify Redford's view that, by the closing years of

Tutankhamun's reign, Horemheb and his generals were having their way. Egypt would no longer depend on its allies in Canaan but launch an attack, with its allies, including the Assyrians, against Hittite influence. This must have taken place in the last two years of Tutankhamun's reign. Until then Pharaoh and his advisers had little to fight with. Horemheb's tomb in Memphis, together with the inscriptions the general-turned-Pharaoh published, hint that some offensive took place. The south wall of the second courtyard of Horemheb's Memphis tomb depicts Syrians, even occasional Hittites, being led as prisoners into Tutankhamun's presence. Horemheb may have been rather economical with the truth. He does not boast of an outright victory but lets the spectators of his paintings and the readers of his inscriptions draw their own conclusions.

Horemheb's expedition would have had a two-fold purpose. First, it dealt out justice to those minor princelings in Syria and Palestine, to demonstrate that the power of Egypt was not to be ignored. Prisoners and hostages must have been taken for, in one painting from Horemheb's tomb, a very angry-looking Syrian prince is being held amongst the captives. The second purpose of such a campaign would be to check the power of the Hittites, to curb their influence and to take the standards of Egypt's regiments as far north as possible.

In fact, Horemheb began a campaign that was to last for years and continue well after his death. We have very few details of it which implies that Horemheb was not as successful as he would have liked. Many years later the great Ramesses II decided on an all-out offensive against the Hittites. The imperial regiments were mustered and, from the

[126]

Nile Delta, Ramesses led his forces into Canaan. I doubt if Horemheb launched a similar blitzkrieg against the Hittites. Such an all-out attack, whatever the outcome, would have been recorded elsewhere.

Egyptian interference across Sinai usually took the form of sending troops and officers, what we would now call advisers, to raise local levies and so go to war. Rib-Addi, Prince of Byblos, who wrote so many importunate letters to Akhenaten, did not demand an all-out invasion; he asked for fifty pairs of horses, probably a chariot squadron, reinforced by 200 infantry. Other requests ask for archers. Horemheb followed such a policy, moving north from Memphis to a strategic listening post in the Delta. From here, he supervised the despatch of infantry and chariot squadrons, either across the Horus Road or by sea to some friendly port. Mercenaries may also have been hired, as the Egyptians recruited from many nations, be it Libya or even the desert-dwellers and sand-wanderers. It is no coincidence that in the eighth year of Tutankhamun's reign, Maya the treasurer was instructed to levy a tax across Egypt and institute offerings to all the gods of Egypt. This would have just been in time for military activity across Sinai, where Egypt's armies would need treasure as well as the protection of the gods. However, Tutankhamun never completed the tenth year of his reign. This military campaign is significant not so much because of what was achieved but for what happened during this time and the political consequences for Egypt.

Horemheb may have sent more than Rib-Addi had ever asked and, according to Redford, the campaign was closely co-ordinated with the Assyrians. This followed the usual pattern of Egyptian foreign policy, to be allied with another power and, if necessary use their force to achieve mutually beneficial aims. The Hittites would be vulnerable to an Assyrian assault across the Euphrates, whilst Egypt's attack would come from the south across the Orontes river. If successful, the area which is now modern Syria could be detached from the Hittites. The Assyrians attacked, they crossed the great river whilst the Egyptian forces marched on Kadesh, a strategic city which the Egyptians had always coveted and would do so during succeeding reigns.

However, Suppiluliumas was able to deal with both attacks. The Assyrians were driven back across the Euphrates and the Egyptians had no choice but to break off their siege and retreat south. According to Hittite records, Suppiluliumas followed them crossing the frontier and attacked the cities of the Amki, the most northern part of Egypt's empire around Antioch. So the campaign was not something to boast about. True, the south face of the great pylon at Karnak (Horemheb's work) displays the usual head-bashing scene of captive prisoners of war with a list of conquered places and a line of bound Asiatic captives. Redford points out that one place-name in particular, Tachkisi, was a district just north of Damascus and possibly part of Egypt's abortive campaign against Kadesh. Horemheb's Memphis tomb paintings depict groups of Asiatic captives, yet Horemheb's lack of real success echoes the Duke of York of the popular nursery rhyme, marching his soldiers here and there without actually achieving much. He was a general who helped quell Nubia, though the glory was taken by Huy, and who played an important role in the first great Egyptian counter-attack against the power of the Hittites, only to achieve very little to boast about. Horemheb was pleased to confine himself to

[128]

generalities and bombastic phrases in his proclamations, stating how, 'He was henchman at the feet of his lord on this day of slaughtering Asiatics.' But which lord? Which day? Which Asiatics? Where and when? All these questions are never answered: I believe Horemheb is referring to the Amki campaign, and, perhaps, its sinister, bloody aftermath.

Nevertheless, this attack, late in Tutankhamun's reign, upon the Hittites and their inevitable counter-attack on the province of Amki is significant, not because of Egyptian with-drawals, or whatever prisoners they took. During that attack news arrived of how Tutankhamun the 'Strong Bull of Creative Forms', the 'Dynamic of Laws Who Ruled the Two Lands, who Propriates all the Gods', 'King of Upper and Lower Egypt', 'The Lordly Manifestation of Ra', the Living Image of Amun was no more. Tutankhamun had died, gone to the Far Horizon and the Fields of the Blessed Osiris.

4

A Most Secret Death

You shall possess your body.
You shall not become corrupt.
You shall not have worms.
You shall not be distended.
You shall not stink.
You shall not become putrid.
You shall not become worms.

Spell 154: *The Book of the Dead*

APART FROM THE HITTITE RECORD AND PHARAOH'S OWN TOMB, there is surprising little evidence that Tutankhamun's death was marked or noted. His throne was usurped by Ay, whilst his young wife, after a brief period in the political sunlight, disappears for ever. Nevertheless, Tutankhamun was a Pharaoh who reigned nine years, he brought Egypt back from a heretical cult to its old religion and ways. Yet it was almost as if he had never lived. If we compare Tutankhamun's death with that of his grandfather Amenhotep III, the latter's death caused grief even as far as the Mitanni court from where its King, Tushratta, wrote:

> When my brother Nimmuwareya [Mitanni for Amen-hotep] went to his fate . . . Nothing was allowed to be cooked in a pot. On that day I myself wept . . . On that day I took neither food or water. I grieved saying, 'Let even me be dead or let ten thousand be dead in my country and, in my brother's country, ten thousand as well but let my brother whom I love and who loves me be alive as long as heaven and earth: that was the love in our hearts.'

[133]

There is no record of such outpouring of grief at Tutankhamun's death. Instead, he was hurried to an unmarked grave, not the one chosen for him; he was buried in secret, the doors of his tomb sealed, all but forgotten. Indeed, the total sum of Tutankhamun's reign can be summed up by his second coronation name, he who 'Propriates All the Gods', or by the inscriptions on the ornate cabinet found in his tomb, Son of Amun, Begotten of the Bull of his Mother. He, whom Mut Mistress of Heaven and Earth Suckled with her own Milk. He whom the Lord of the Throne of Two Lands Created to be Ruler, and Maker of Monuments so that They Came into Existence at Once to his Father and All the Gods. 'He Built their Temples Anew, he Made their Statues of Fine Gold. He Provided their Offerings on Earth.' In other words, Tutankhamun was a devout Pharaoh who built and enhanced the temples of the gods. He published the Restoration Stela. He was crowned, stayed at El-Amarna but emerged to lead the extravagant and gorgeous Opet Festival. What more can be said?

First, during his reign a successful expedition into Nubia restored Egyptian rule, whilst there is considerable evidence of increased Egyptian military activity across Sinai. Secondly, his court and policies were dominated by members of a very powerful council and, by the time of his death, these councillors belonged to two rival factions. One faction was led by Horemheb and his military council in Memphis: when Tutankhamun died Horemheb was absent in the Nile Delta enhancing his reputation whilst defending Egypt's interests against the Hittites. The second faction was the Akhmim clan led by Ay: the latter never assumed the title of vizier but appears to have acted as the Pharaoh's Vice-Regent and was supported by powerful courtiers such as Huy and General

Nakhtmin. These two factions governed Egypt and dictated policy. Finally, during Tutankhamun's reign, the desertion of El-Amarna accelerated and the coffins of the Akhenaten clan were brought into the Valley of the Kings to be hidden away in KV55 and elsewhere. But what else can be said? Here is a Pharaoh who reigned nine years, whose tomb was found virtually intact, whose corpse has been the subject of at least two scientific surveys and yet he still remains a shadowy mystery.

The scientific surveys provide a very accurate physical description of Tutankhamun for his body was examined by pathologists, Professor Derry in 1929 and, some forty years later, by Professor Harrison of Liverpool University, whilst the dentist Filce Leek examined Tutankhamun's teeth. Admittedly all these post-mortem examinations, particularly Derry's, were not carried out in the most scientific fashion. The restrictions imposed by the Egyptian authorities, the lack of proper equipment, not to mention that the most thorough examination took place in the 1920s when the study of mummies was still in its relative infancy, have not helped. Nevertheless, certain conclusions were reached. Tutankhamun was about eighteen or nineteen years of age when he died. In height he was five foot six and a half inches. He had the elongated head, like many of the late Eighteenth-Dynasty rulers, his eyes were sloe-shaped, his features were in proportion, with generous lips, he had slightly protruding front teeth and high cheek bones. Tutankhamun was of slender build with what Carter called 'a refined and cultured face . . . a serene and placid countenance.' More importantly, Tutankhamun appeared not to have died from any serious sickness. There was no evidence from his bones of the myriad infections which plagued the lives of the ancient Egyptians.

[135]

Of course, it can be argued that Tutankhamun's tomb might tell us a great deal about the Prince but, as shall be shown, the ownership of a great deal of the contents in his tomb is highly questionable. To all appearances Tutankhamun was an active young man: his tomb contained chariots, weapons, a corselet of armour, throwing-sticks, boomerangs, daggers and ceremonial shields. One of the latter depicts Tutankhamun as a sphinx trampling hapless Nubians. Of course, we know that in truth the Nubians were trampled by Huy and Horemheb whilst Tutankhamun remained in his palace. There are inscriptions to Tutankhamun being a 'smiter of vile Kushites and Asiatics'. The second state chariot found in the tomb displays a frieze of bound Nubians and Asiatics, whilst a captive of each nation adorns one of his many walking sticks.

According to the contents of his tomb, Tutankhamun was also a keen hunter, thundering out in his chariot across the eastern desert near Heliopolis. One of the ostrich-feather fans carries the inscription that it was made out of 'feathers obtained by His Majesty when hunting in the desert'. On each face of the palm of the fan are embossed vivid scenes of Tutankhamun hunting the huge birds whose plumage will be stripped from their carcases, treated and coated in perfume so as to provide cool fragrance either in the heat of the desert or the warmth of his palaces. Tutankhamun is shown riding his chariot and shooting arrows whilst, alongside, a saluki hound rushes up to finish off the bird. The King is dressed like a god. He wears a short wig with two streamers, a decorated leopard skin corselet and a kilt with an ornate apron. A bowman's leather bracelet protects his left wrist whilst, to free his hands, the reins of the chariot are wrapped round his body. Two horses, gorgeously caparisoned, pull the chariot, their manes are trimmed, ostrich plumes dance in the head stalls of their bridles, whilst sun discs decorate both harness and chariot. Two cases are strapped to the chariot for bows and small javelins, a quiver of arrows is suspended from the back of the King's girdle.

On the reverse side of the ostrich plume the King is shown returning from the hunt, reins in hands, together with his bow and whip. He has donned a long pleated garment with a shoulder wrap of feathered fringes. Two attendants carry the ostriches killed by the King. An inscription reads:

> The good god who secures his quarry in hunting, who engages in combat in every desert, who shoots to kill like the goddess Bastet. His horses are like bulls when they convey the King of Upper and Lower Egypt, the Lord of the Two Lands. Possessor of a strong arm, Nebkheperure, given life for ever like Ra.

According to both the hunting scenes and inscriptions, Tutankhamun was a most vigorous young man who, when he wasn't hunting, played senet with its checker board or other games of chance.

Tutankhamun was married to Ankhesenamun and the scenes displayed on the golden shrine found in his tomb, together with those on the ornamental chest, are highly reminiscent of the affectionate scenes from El Amarna showing Akhenaten and Nefertiti in connubial bliss. There is a tenderness about these images which, accepted at face value, would indicate a very happy marriage. The outer faces of the door to the golden shrine display incidents from the daily life of Tutankhamun and his Queen. In one Ankhesenamun, in a plumed headdress, stands with her hands raised in praise before Pharaoh who grasps in his right hand the crook and sceptre and, in his left, a lapwing. Another panel on the door describes the Queen holding out a bunch of flowers towards Pharaoh. Similar scenes from the same shrine have Ankhesenamun grasping her husband's arm or hand whilst offering him flowers.

The other side of the shrine provides different views. In one, Pharaoh stands in a papyrus boat throwing a boomerang. His Queen stands behind him watching him hunt, in her left hand she holds a fly whisk. A second fowling scene has Pharaoh sitting on the edge of a papyrus thicket. He is seated on a stool with a thick cushion, his pet lion cub by his side, whilst the Queen squats on a cushion at his feet. Pharaoh has his bow drawn and is about to shoot an arrow at a flock of birds rising from the papyrus thicket, one of which he has already brought down. A further scene has Pharaoh, again on a cushioned chair, holding a vase containing flowers while the Queen pours water into it with her right hand, whilst flowers are grasped in her left. A more intimate scene displays Pharaoh seated on a stool, holding a bouquet of flowers and poppies, the Queen before him, her left elbow resting on his knee whilst her right hand is cupped to receive the water, or perfume, her husband is pouring.

Similar images decorate the beautiful ornamental chest from the tomb, showing Tutankhamun and Ankhesenamun intimately together. Pharaoh, again, is seated on a cushion, the Queen squatting at his feet. Tutankhamun is shooting with his bow, his aim directed at wild fowl and fish in a rectangular pool, possibly one of those constructed by Amenhotep III's architects at the Malkata palace. Ankhesenamun, as she is

[138]

often depicted, squats on a cushion, a flower in one hand, an arrow in the other, ready for her husband to grasp.

Consequently, it seems that Tutankhamun and Ankhesenamun had a happy marriage and that his Queen even conceived two children who unfortunately never survived. When Carter opened Tutankhamun's tomb, he found an undecorated wooden box which contained two miniature anthropoid coffins. The first was fifty centimetres, the second about fifty-eight centimetres long. They contained two foetuses both female, one of five months, the other of about eight months gestation, both the result of miscarriages. The second and larger foetus was examined by Professor Harrison who suggested that the baby had a condition known as Sprengel's Deformity, Spina Bifida and Scoliosis. Were these two infants the children of Tutankhamun and Ankhesenamun? Most Egyptologists claim they were yet, like a great deal of what's contained in Tutankhamun's tomb, they remain a mystery.

Does the tomb represent the life of a vigorous, eighteen-year-old Pharaoh who loved hunting and fishing? Many of the scenes depict the Pharaoh, bow in hand, arrow notched. Yet, if that was the case, why couldn't those who buried him arrange to have the King's own bow of honour buried with him? The tomb does contain such a bow which Carter described as 'A work of almost inconceivable fineness'. Yet on this bow the name Ankhkheperure (one of the titles of the mysterious Semenkhkare) has been clumsily altered to that of Tutankhamun.

Egyptologists have always been fascinated by Tutan-khamun's mummy and the contents of his tomb. The rumours about a curse have been debunked more often than not, yet speculation about some 'dark deed' has run high, particularly since Derry's autopsy. For why should a handsome and vigorous young Pharaoh have died so unexpectedly? In view of Ay's usurpation of Pharaoh's crown, was Tutankhamun the victim of a palace intrigue, foully murdered by his successor? Tutankhamun's tomb contains many references to the Aten. Did he and his wife, as they grew to maturity, demonstrate sympathies for their dead father's heretical cult? Did Tutankhamun threaten to leave Thebes, put the clock back once again and return to El Amarna? Was that why he was murdered? Did he represent a threat to Ay who had worked so long and so hard, together with people such as Horemheb and Maya to restore Egypt's fortunes? Or did Ay, aided and abetted by others, including Horemheb, have delusions of grandeur? Was Ay tired of playing the bridesmaid, of being just the eyes and ears of Pharaoh? Did he wish to be Pharaoh himself? The murderer certainly seems to be Ay. He directly profited from Tutankhamun's death. Did he plan it, with malice aforethought, during the Amki campaign when General Horemheb was busy in the north with affairs across Sinai?

Derry's autopsy did not reveal any signs of foul play but, of course, murder, like charity, comes dressed in many forms. In 1968 Professor Harrison carried out his autopsy. The x-rays taken showed a thinning of the bone behind the left ear, though there was no fracture involved. Harrison did find a small fragment of bone in the skull but this had nothing to do with the thinning behind the left ear. Most pathologists now conclude the bone fragment had nothing to do with the mummification process or, indeed, any trauma to the skull but was due to post-mortem damage. Harrison also

[140]

established that the sternum and part of the rib cage had been removed, probably during mummification. However, these findings were seized upon by Egyptologists such as Brier, Aldred and Dodson. Brier maintains that there is every possibility that the thinning of the skull behind Tutankhamun's left ear was the result of a blow. Aldred argues, without giving evidence, that it could have been the work of an arrow.

Dodson wonders whether the missing sternum and ribs was due to an accident, a fall from a chariot? Professor Brier, in particular, builds up a case for murder. He immediately seizes on the fact that Tutankhamun's predecessors, Semenkhkare and his wife Meritaten, only reigned for a short while after Akhenaten and disappeared very quickly and quietly. He argues that the deaths of a young Pharaoh and his Queen together indicate foul play. However, at about the time Semenkhkare and his wife died, plague was raging in the Middle East and both Pharaoh and his Queen could have been casualties of this. Indeed, if Semenkhkare and Meritaten were murdered, why not include Akhenaten, Nefertiti and their other daughters?

Of course, we do not know how virulent, this plague was and ancient Egyptians, be they Pharaoh or pauper, did not have the life expectancy of modern man. One Egyptologist has argued that only fifty per cent of Egyptians who survived childhood reached the age of thirty. Elliot Smith, in his analysis of other royal mummies, demonstrated how Tuthmosis IV, Tutankhamun's great-grandfather, may have been as young as twenty-five when he died. Amenhotep III did not reach fifty, whilst Akhenaten was, at the very most, in his early thirties when he journeyed to the Far Horizon.

The Wisdom text known as the Papyrus Insignia in the

[141]

Leyden Museum has a line which talks of 'man spending another ten years to old age', and this was reckoned to be forty! Men such as Ay, Maya, Horemheb, as well as later Pharaohs like Ramesses II might live well past the biblical three score years and ten but they must be regarded as exceptions rather than the rule. Moreover, the Tuthmosid line does not appear to have been a healthy one: Tuthmosis IV was dead by his mid-twenties; Amenhotep III was dead by his fiftieth birthday; Amenhotep III's Crown Prince, Tuthmosis, dead by his mid-teens; Akhenaten dead by his early thirties; Semenkhkare dead by his early twenties.

According to the evidence, Akhenaten and Nefertiti had six daughters but perhaps only one, Ankhesenamun, survived into full adulthood. Finally, in the absence of any real clinical autopsy on Tutankhamun's skeleton, we cannot reach an irrefutable conclusion that he did not harbour some potentially dangerous disease. Indeed, Tutankhamun's tomb does hint at some possible physical weakness. True, we have Pharaoh hunting in his chariot out in the desert but one scene shows Tutankhamun gently leaning on a staff, holding out his hand towards his wife. Another painting, now held in the State Museum, Berlin, shows the Queen offering Pharaoh a flower. Reeves attributes these figures to Akhenaten and Nefertiti, others claim they are Semenkhkare and Meritaten, whilst I agree with El-Mahdy that they represent Tutankhamun and Ankhesenamun. What is significant is that Pharaoh is, once again, leaning on a staff. A close study indicates he is experiencing difficulties, ill at ease in standing. Was a staff, a walking stick, essential for Tutankhamun? Is that why his tomb contained so many? Carter wryly observed that Tutankhamun may have been an amateur collector of walking sticks. Egyptologists have also been amazed by the number of shabtis, statues representing those servants who would help Pharaoh with his work in the after life, found in Tutankhamun's tomb, 413 in all! Does this betray an anxiety by those who buried Tutankhamun that this energetic young Pharaoh would need extra help in the after life? The above-mentioned scenes of Tutankhamun and Ankhesenamun do tend to show the King in a seated position, even when hunting. Was there something seriously wrong with him? Some physical weakness? Or are these just tender intimate scenes of Pharaoh sitting 'shooting fish in the barrel'?

I would like to develop this theme further. Did Tutankhamun suffer some form of mental weakness as well as a physical handicap? True, Derry and Harrison talk of a 'serene' and 'placid countenance'. There are hunting scenes on the objects from his tomb. Another has him as a sphinx trampling enemies but these were the work of craftsmen, gifts from courtiers. We have no real evidence that Tutankhamun went to war or even that he went hunting in the deserts around Heliopolis. Such depictions are ritual and, in Tutankhamun's case, not all that many. There are a few inscriptions describing him as a 'smiter' of Egypt's enemies but another corpus of evidence, as shall be shown, presents a different version.

It is remarkable how Egyptologists constantly talk of Tutankhamun as a 'child', a 'boy Pharaoh', a 'young man' but this is an inaccuracy. Only fifty per cent of ancient Egyptians were fortunate enough to survive to the age of thirty. Tutankhamun reached the age of eighteen. Even in our century, with our *jeunesse dorée*, eighteen is regarded as maturity. A young man of eighteen in the UK in the twenty-first century can vote, buy alcohol, drive a car, be in full time employment, be called up for military service, etc. In ancient Egypt eighteen would be regarded as full maturity. After all, there is evidence that boys as young as ten were included in the armies of Pharaoh. Prince Ramesses, later to be the magnificent Ramesses II, was taken on campaign at about the age of ten or eleven; he was certainly on active military service by his mid-teens. Tutankhamun's grandfather Amenhotep III succeeded to the throne at an early age but, again, in his mid-teens participated in a fire and sword campaign in Nubia which he boasted about in a series of proclamations. Does the constant epithet of 'child' or 'boy Pharaoh', as applied to Tutankhamun, betray a subconscious attitude to this enigmatic Pharaoh? Is there something about Tutankhamun which remains childlike?

The contents of his tomb certainly demonstrate this. We are not too sure about what really did belong to him. Tutankhamun was of warrior age and yet the list of weapons is relatively short: a cluster of bows and arrows, the best of which, the Bow of Honour, belonged to someone else. Other bows are child-size. There were two slings, some leather scale armour and a few ornately carved boomerangs or throwing-sticks. Eight shields were found, of which at least four were ceremonial, two khepesh (curved swords) and two daggers, one of which was certainly a gift from the Mitanni court to the Egyptian royal family. It is hardly an armoury, whilst the chariots were either ceremonial or of the wickerwork type used for hunting. Was Tutankhamun mentally and physically active? Or a simple-minded child who grew to maturity? If one surveys Tutankhamun's inscriptions it is very hard to find the boasting so common among ancient Egyptian rulers and their leading lords and officials. Treasurer Maya represents this style. An inscription in his tomb sums up his view of his glorious career in one telling phrase: 'In the beginning I was very good, at the end I was brilliant!' Akhenaten must have been about eighteen when he distanced himself from the temple worship of Amun. The stelae he set up around his new city are full of the 'I' and the 'me', what he wants and how it is to be done. 'I shall make Akhenaten for the Aten my father, in this place. I shall not make Akhetaten for him south of it.' Inscriptions from Amenhotep III's reign carry the same bombastic boastful vein, where the imperial 'I' and 'me' are again emphasized. In Amenhotep's case a series of scarabs exist boasting how, aged only thirteen or fourteen, he went on a very dangerous wild bull hunt around the Wadi Natrun.

The inscriptions about Tutankhamun are always passive, in the main in the third person, and usually limited to his building programmes. Of course, it could be argued that this was the work of Ay, that he kept Tutankhamun in the shadows while he acted as the King's eyes, ears and mouth. This could be understood for the opening years of Tutankhamun's reign, but for a fully grown man of eighteen? A prince who had reigned for nine years? A Pharaoh who had spent his formative years at the court of Akhenaten whose inscriptions and drawings constantly emphasize his sacredness, his uniqueness, the all importance of Pharaoh's words and deeds? There is a passivity about Tutankhamun which is quite chilling. It provokes the questions:What did he actually do? What did he actually achieve?

In the glorious campaign against Nubia, in both the despatch of Viceroy Huy and the latter's return, Tutankhamun is represented as seated, lolling on a throne, even the commissioning of Huy into his high office was carried out by

[145]

the omnipotent Ay. The same is true of the family depictions discussed above. Pharaoh is not only seated or resting on a staff, both he and his wife are garbed rather incongruously. On the scenes from the ornamental chest, Tutankhamun is sitting on a curved-back, well-cushioned chair with a footstool. He is wearing the Blue Crown, whilst Ankhesenamun, squatting at his feet, is dressed in all the queenly regalia of Egypt. It's almost as if they had come from some official reception and wandered out into one of the gardens still garbed in their finery. The King, tired and distracted, sits on a stool, picks up his bow and begins to shoot at the wild fowl nestling in the thickets, whilst his wife, seated on a cushion at his feet, hands him the arrows. Of course, one could argue that perhaps this is the truth, Pharaoh and his Queen being packed off by Ay once the official reception was finished. Nevertheless, the figure depicted in these scenes is of a young man who had been raised in a despotic Pharaoh's court and who would know the sacredness of his own person. Was this Pharaoh simply the rubber stamp of Ay? Was he feckless and weak? Or was the condition more serious – a frail, young man, weak in both body and mind and therefore completely under Ay's thumb?

The contents of Tutankhamun's tomb seem to prove this: the lack of the bombastic boasting found in Horemheb's and Ay's tomb is significant. True, Tutankhamun was buried in a hurry but there is a lack of any wall painting, or scarab emphasizing any great achievement by Tutankhamun in his own right, as his own person, except for two rather pathetic references to 'a reed cut by His Majesty's own hands' and feathers collected whilst hunting, as if these in themselves were great achievements. There is a patronizing tone about these references, arrogant adults dealing with a child or condescending teachers praising a not-so-bright pupil. Would the same have been written of Akhenaten, Tuthmosis III or Ramesses II? The presence of so many shabtis and walking sticks also indicate a frailty, whilst Ankhesenamun's constant presence may not only be as a Queen and wife but nurse, possible assistant for this Pharaoh who is, so often, portrayed as sitting down – even when he went hunting. Tutankhamun may have had dress armour, state chariots and a few pieces of weaponry. Inscriptions may credit him with the achievements of his ministers and generals and images be painted of what he may have done when hunting near Heliopolis, but the truth is that Tutankhamun was frail, either from the start or progressively so. It is significant that Patrick Cave-Brown has pointed out how the fire-making equipment from Tutan-khamun's tomb is that of a child which would not require the same strength as that for a fully grown man. But was this frailty only physical?

One particular piece of evidence has survived which clearly demonstrates the relationship between Tutankhamun and his first minister. It is a fragment of a sheet of gold depicting Tutankhamun, escorted by his wife, performing the ritual smiting of a captive in the presence of 'Divine Father', Ay. The depiction of Pharaoh smiting Egypt's enemies is a common theme. Pharaoh, one hand grasping a weapon, the other the hair of some hapless captive, is about to inflict the blow in the presence of a god, usually Amun-Re or Montu. In this piece of evidence, however, according to its inscription, the place of the god has been taken, by Ay. This fragment, possibly more than any other piece of evidence, clearly demonstrates how far Ay had risen and how he must have won over the

[147]

allegiance of the Amun priesthood for the Pharaoh's first minister to assume such a role. More importantly, it demonstrates Ay's influence over Tutankhamun.

Too much play has been given to the notion of Tutankhamun as a child: it is a legend which permeates the scholarship on his reign as well as the popular books bought by schools. Margaret Oliphant's very readable account of Ancient Egypt published by Kingfisher calls Tutankhamun the 'boy King' whilst the Time/Life book, beautifully written and exquisitely presented with photographs, diagrams, etc., has two chapters on Tutankhamun; one is entitled 'The Child King, At Study and Work' and the other 'The Sporting Achievements of an Adolescent Pharaoh'. It is remarkable how this legend has persisted and, as has been noted, perhaps it's a subconscious reaction by students of the period to Tutankhamun's passivity, his total acquiescence with his ministers. Would Akhenaten have adopted such an attitude who, as early as the sixth year of his reign, set up stela defining the limits of El-Amarna with the following drastic, egocentric decree.

> There shall be made for me a sepulchre in the Orient Mountain: my burial shall be [made] therein in the multitude of Jubilees which Aten my father hath ordained for me, and the burial of the chief wife of the King, Nefertiti, shall be made therein in that multitude of years . . . [and the burial of] the King's daughter Meritaten shall be made in it in that multitude of years . . .

Whatever one's opinion of Akhenaten, this decree is permeated with arrogance, the vibrancy of his convictions, the

[148]

passion of his belief, against which Tutankhamun's stereo-typed inscriptions are only a pale imitation. Akhenaten would never have bowed before any man, nor would Amenhotep III or Tutankhamun's successors such as Horemheb, Seti I or the Ramessid Pharaohs.

The overall impression is that Tutankhamun was weak and frail both physically and mentally, very dependent on Ay and his Queen Ankhesenamun. The actual details of this fraility will be analysed later. It may have been there from the start or the result of some degenerative process. Whatever, the political consequences are clear: Tutankhamun was Pharaoh but the true power at court was Ay and probably Ankhesenamun who played a more powerful role than the depleted evidence suggests. It is no coincidence that on the piece of gold foil discussed above, Ay takes the place of the god. In a similar scene from the arm-brace of Tuthmosis IV, Pharaoh performs the smiting before Montu, his back guarded by the goddess Wadjet the Cobra. Behind Tutankhamun, however, stands the ever protective Ankhesenamun.

Accordingly, if Ay was the king-maker, the overlord, why kill the very source of his power, a Tuthmosid prince who was so pliable and so ready to acknowledge Ay's authority? Moreover, if Ay was so keen to seize power, why did he wait until this pliable prince had reached eighteen? Ay had held the reins of government long before Tutankhamun's ascendancy to the throne, his sycophantic attitude to Akhenaten is a matter of record. If Ay was some power-mad politician it would have been much easier to make a clean sweep when Tutankhamun and Ankhesenamun were mere children. As it was, Ankhesenamun survived her husband to play a role which has muddied the water and deepened the mystery surrounding her husband's early death. Ankhesen-amun was a princess of the blood royal, very much in the mode of those women who played such a prominent part at the courts of the rulers of the late Eighteenth Dynasty, Yuya, Tiye and Nefertiti. She might not claim the throne in her own right but she would, at least, have a say in who should and Ankhesenamun did exactly this. Of course she could be depicted as Ay's fellow conspirator, a double-dealing, cold-blooded husband-killer. However, there is no evidence to support this.

The same is true of other leading ministers of Tutankhamun's court. In his description of the opening of the tomb Carter talks of haste, an unholy haste: nevertheless, Carter also comments on the care and the affection which attended Tutankhamun's funerary arrangements. If Ay was an assassin, then he would have had to buy the support of Maya, Nakhtmin and Huy. Maya's affection for the King is apparent in the gifts he made to Tutankhamun's tomb: 'Made by the servant who is beneficial to his Lord Nebkheperure, the overseer of the treasury, Maya.' Or the five shabtis donated by Nakhtmin (Minnakht): 'Made by the true servant who is bene-ficial to his Lord. The King's scribe Minnakht, for his Lord Osiris, Lord of the Two Lands, Nebkheperure justified'. Or again in his military capacity: 'Made by his servant the beloved of his Lord, the General Minnakht, for his Lord, the Osiris, the King Nebkheperure justified.' These men may have supported Ay but that does not mean they embraced regicide and treason. Indeed, Ay may have been able to count on General Nakhtmin and others but, after Ay's death and the triumphant accession of Horemheb, Maya emerged as one of the general-turned-Pharaoh's favourites. Imperial titles were bestowed on him: 'The Fan-Bearer on the left of the King', the 'Leader of the Festival of Amun and Karnak'.

Of course one name is missing from Tutankhamun's funeral and the gifts which adorned his tomb. There is no trace of General Horemheb. One Egyptologist has wondered whether one of the royal pall-bearers, depicted in the painting in Tutankhamun's burial chamber pulling the royal coffin, is the good general. There is no real proof of this: Tutankhamun's tomb bears not the slightest trace of General Horemheb. Of course, much play has been made of Horemheb's hostility to the Aten cult, his attack on the memory of Ay, the appropriation of the monuments of Tutankhamun and Ay for his own use. Yet, as has been noted, Horemheb, whatever his reservations, had been an Atenist and owed his power to that cult: his attack on the Aten cult, and his two predecessors on Pharaoh's throne, came much later. Horemheb certainly settled any grievance he had with Ay and men like Huy but, in his tomb at Memphis, Horemheb did not have the memory of Tutankhamun defaced. Paintings still exist in that tomb where Horemheb is receiving the acclamation of Tutankhamun or displaying the spoils of victory before him.

More importantly, after Horemheb came to the throne, Maya became one of his principal ministers. Maya knew where Tutankhamun's tomb lay. Indeed, he would have reported that it had twice been violated by robbers. Horemheb had the opportunity to clear the tomb, desecrate it and expunge Tutankhamun's memory for good. He did not do this. In fact, Maya was sent in to make good any damage, re-seal the tomb and allow Tutankhamun to lie in peace for the next 3,000 years. Horemheb's attitude is understandable. He was a general and a successful soldier but also a politician. He would usurp the most public monuments such as the Restoration Stela but not the private memories of Tutankhamun. Horemheb apparently did not see Tutankhamun as an enemy or as a rival but as a legitimate Pharaoh; Perhaps he also felt a deep compassion for this retiring young man, handicapped perhaps both physically and mentally.

Egyptologists argue that Maya's restoration of Tutankhamun's tomb was a personal act of compassion, a matter he kept to himself. I doubt this. The seals used show that Maya was acting in an official capacity, assisted by his chief scribe. Moreover, if Horemheb wanted to know where Tutankhamun's corpse lay, and he must have done, Maya would have only been too willing to supply the information. To conclude, Horemheb had nothing to do with Tutankhamun's interment but I doubt if he would have sat on the side lines and allowed a regicide to succeed to the throne.

Naturally, Horemheb must have been furious at Ay's usurpation. There is strong evidence of a deep mutual antipathy between the two. Horemheb's tolerance towards Tutankhamun's tomb is even more surprising when one studies the provocative painting which would have angered Horemheb beyond all measure. Only one chamber of Tutankhamun's tomb possesses any wall paintings. One in particular, as described by Carter, is very striking:

On the north wall, east corner, we find the scene of historical importance of Ay as King with royal insignia, clad in the leopard's skin of the Sem priest. Here King Ay officiates at the funeral ceremony of 'The Opening of the

Mouth' of the dead Tutankhamun represented as Osiris. Between the living and the dead monarchs are the objects connected with the ceremony laid out upon a table, which are the adze, the hind limb of an ox, the fan of a single ostrich feather, and a double plume-like object: these are surmounted by a row of graven gold and silver cups containing what may be balls of incense such as we found in the antechamber.

The conspiracy theorists have been quick to fasten on this painting and the reasons are obvious. When a Pharaoh died, his successor often fulfilled the role of the Sem priest and carried out the important ritual of the Opening of the Mouth which symbolized the beginning of a series of mystical events which would take the soul of the dead Pharaoh into the Field of the Blessed. What is singular about this painting is that not only does Ay perform the ceremony but does so as Crowned Pharaoh. The ritual demanded that the coronation of Pharaoh's successor should only take place after the solemn seventy days required by the funeral ceremony and after Pharaoh was sealed in his tomb.

Several theories could explain this painting. First, the remote possibility exists that Ay became Tutankhamun's co-regent, a fairly common practice during the Eighteenth and Nineteenth Dynasties. Akhenaten was co-regent with his father and, during the Ramesses period, it became part of official policy, initiating the co-regent into the responsibilities of office to both deepen and widen his experience. Ay wouldn't need such experience, whilst the Egyptologist W. J. Murnane's scholarly investigation of co-regencies in Ancient Egypt has found little evidence that Ay ever acted as

Tutankhamun's co-regent. True, he may have seized such a position during Tuankhamun's final days but, if that was the case, why the unholy haste? Perhaps it was because Ay knew his position as the self- proclaimed heir of Pharaoh was tenuous and wished to beat off any challenge.

The second explanation could be more brutal and stark: Tutankhamun died and Ay had himself proclaimed and crowned as Pharaoh. However, to do this, Ay would have to publicly violate ritual, have the complete support of the Theban court, not to mention the priests of Amun. Of course he may have won this but, there again, Ay acted so hastily in burying Tutankhamun that such a public ceremony would defeat the object of secrecy and so provoke the very crisis he was so desperately trying to avoid.

The third explanation is to examine the purpose of tomb wall paintings. The particular one in question is definitely of the El-Amarna style, though done in haste. Ay would summon craftsmen and artists who had served in Akhenaten's court. Nevertheless, the style of the painting is irrelevant to its true purpose. Wall paintings in Theban tombs were three-dimensional in time. They represented the past, the present and the future. In Tutankhamun's case, the past was totally ignored. The few paintings in the tomb depict the ceremony of The Opening of the Mouth, whilst others show Tutankhamun wearing a wig, filet and white kilt, standing before the goddess Nut, 'Lady of Heaven, Mistress of the Gods, who gives health and life to his nostrils'. Other scenes show Tutankhamun embracing Osiris or between Anubis and Isis, together with quotations from the Book of the Dead.

In other words, all the paintings of Tutankhamun's tomb are concerned with the future, on earth and across the Far

Horizon in the Kingdom of Osiris. Tutankhamun would be accepted amongst the blessed whilst, on earth, Ay would be honoured as Pharaoh. The painting of the Opening of the Mouth ceremony is not just a description of what has happened but what is, and will, happen once Tutankhamun's funeral rites are completed. This would accord with Ay's arrogance, so marked in the scrap of gold discussed above where he has himself appearing in the role of Amun. A similar arrogance is manifest in his own tomb where, unlike Horemheb, Ay virtually makes no reference to Tutankhamun; the Pharaoh he had served for almost ten years.

Indeed, Ay was acting in such haste that he wanted this painting to be a proclamation to those around him of what was happening. It is interesting to note that when Carter examined the seals he'd found both on goods in the tomb and on their doors, there is no reference to a seal by Ay as Pharaoh. Indeed, Carter points out, for example, that the seal on the doors of the second shrine 'bore impressions of two distinct seals, one bearing Tutankhamun's pre-nomen [one of his coronation titles] . . . The second bore the device of the royal Necropolis seal without other distinguishing marks or royal insignia. The doorway to the annexe of the tomb had also been sealed hastily, the plaster . . . still wet.' All four seals are those of Tutankhamun whilst, 'when the tomb was eventually closed and sealed, the seals of the dead King were used instead of those of his successor.'

Tutankhamun's seals were used because Ay's were not yet fashioned. It was early days and Tutankhamun's successor was still in a terrible hurry. To conclude, the painting of Ay conducting the Opening of the Mouth ceremony is very significant. It provides, as shall be shown, an insight into the time-line Ay followed and the audience he was addressing.

Tutankhamun's tomb and its contents do point to undue haste, a conspiracy to hurry the King to his grave and have done with it. Admittedly the tomb was robbed at least twice but Carter remarks that not even those violations explained the chaos within. Here the conspiracy theorists are on firmer ground. The tomb, its contents and the mummy all show that the sacred rites of burying the Pharaoh was hasty and very haphazard. Supported by officials such as Maya, Ay appears to have had one objective, to pay honour to the dead Pharaoh but to have him buried as quickly as possible. Isn't this, the conspiracy theorists argue, further proof of some dark deed and a sinister haste to hide it? To provide a clear answer, Tutankhamun's tomb and its contents must be analysed.

Tutankhamun's tomb is cut into the bed rock of the valley, overshadowed by a slope rising directly above it. The limestone has been dug away to create an entrance stairway with sixteen steps. The tomb itself lies about thirteen feet beneath ground level. The last six steps of the staircase, together with the lintel and jambs of the entrance door, have been cut away to enable the larger pieces of Tutankhamun's grave goods, such as the quartzite sarcophagus and its shrines, to be passed through piece by piece. The entrance doorway would then be reconstructed after the funeral in stone and plaster. The passageway, later filled with rubble, stretched about nine yards long and two yards wide. It led down to four chambers: an antechamber and, across that to the left, an annexe cut off by a sealed doorway and, immediately to the right of the antechamber, the burial room with 'magic' bricks in the walls, then, to the far right of the burial chamber with no blockading wall or door, the treasury. Only in the burial chamber were the walls plastered and painted and this was apparently done in great haste by the workmen.

The chambers are all relatively small and prepared clumsily. Carter declares how:

in the annexe the masons' guide and measuring marks in red are still visible upon the unfinished surfaces of the walls and, like elsewhere in the tomb, flakes of limestone scatter the floor. The masons apparently not even having time to clean them up. Even the walls of the burial chamber were prepared in haste. The plaster was not dry when the tomb was sealed whilst parts of the wall are smoke-stained from the oil lamps or torches of the artists.

Reeves believes the tomb was clearly non-royal, a private sepulchre probably meant for Ay when he saw himself ending his days only as Egypt's first minister and nothing else. The person responsible for the actual construction must have been Maya, Overseer of the King's Works. Tutankhamun's last resting place certainly bears no resemblance to many of the tombs of other Pharaohs with their stairways, corridors and pillared halls. Some attempt has been made to pass it off as a royal tomb with glory holes like the annexe and treasury. I doubt if KV62 was meant to be a tomb for anyone, least of all Tutankhamun. KV62, KV55 and what is now known as KV54, the pit, were really storerooms dug in the valley, on the orders of Ay and Maya, to receive the goods and funeral equipment of those royal sarcophagi from El-Amarna.

Carter himself, at the very beginning, when he was clearing the passageway, was puzzled by the scraps and fragments he found bearing the name of Akhenaten, Tuthmosis III and Amenhotep III.

Why this mixture of names? The balance of evidence so far would seem to indicate a cache rather than a tomb and, at this stage in the proceedings, we are inclined more and more to the opinion that we are about to find a miscellaneous collection of objects of the Eighteenth Dynasty Kings, brought from El Amarna by Tutankhamun and deposited here for safety.

In a sense Carter's first reaction is correct. He had found a cache, a storeroom, one of at least of three which, by force of circumstances, was re-used as an imperial tomb. Even when he had realized what he had truly found and examined the contents of the tomb, Carter declared, 'The objects which belong to his [Tutankhamun's] life are the exception.' Carter was fully convinced that KV62 was a poor tomb for a Pharaoh. He writes:

In the place of an elaborate series of corridors, sunken staircases, protective wall and vestibule, further descending passages, antechamber, sepulchral hall, crypt and a series of four storerooms, of the orthodox Theban plan, Tutankhamun's tomb merely comprises a sunken entrance-staircase, a descending passage, an antechamber with annexe, a burial chamber and one storeroom, all small and of the simplest kind. In fact, it only conforms with the Theban pattern of the New Empire royal tomb in orientation, by having its burial chamber alone painted of a golden hue corresponding with 'The Golden Hall', and

[158]

by having, in its walls, niches for the magical figures of the four cardinal points.

When he came to catalogue the contents Carter was also struck by the obvious haste of the craftsmen:

The funerary statues, statuettes, coffins and masks, show a certain hurried workmanship . . . At the risk of being tedious I repeat that, apart from the exploits of the robbers, clearly there was a suggestion, one would even say demonstration, of confusion, or a want of proper system where the objects were originally deposited . . . The tomb itself is not orthodox planned and is much contracted.

Chests and boxes belonged to other reigns. A whipstock bears the name Tuthmosis. The couches were wrongly assembled with inaccurate inscriptions. Fats and unguent jars had been re-used. A number of items belonged to the mysterious Semenkhkare, though that name is never used, but Anekhkheperure, one of his coronation titles. The clappers used by musicians belonged to Queens Tiye and Meritaten. Stone jars date from Tuthmosis III's reign: wine jars, some of them undoubtedly empty when placed there, bore dockets indicating how their contents were some thirty years old. An ivory palette, which belonged to Meritaten, Akhenaten's daughter, was included amongst the grave goods. Many of the statues bear no physical resemblance to Tutankhamun and the shawls which cover them, as well as the black-painted Anubis dog which guarded the entrance to the treasury, were decorated with hieroglyphic script from Akhenaten's reign. A sceptre still displays the symbol of the Aten: two statues of the King depict him on the back of a panther or leopard. One may be Tutankhamun but the other is that of a woman garbed in the regalia of a Pharaoh, possibly a carving of Nefertiti or Meritaten. Bracelets found belonged to Akhenaten and his mysterious co-regent.

This confusion and chaos also extends to more important objects. The very famous throne of state, with its emblem of the rays of the Aten beaming down on Pharaoh and his wife, has been remodelled and fresh inscriptions carved on its surface. One wonders if the figure of the Pharaoh and Queen depicted on the throne, pictures of which are often associated with Tutankhamun's tomb, are indeed this Pharaoh or one of his predecessors. In the small coffinettes Tutankhamun's cartouche covers that of Ankhkheperure. Indeed, the balance of current scholarly thinking is that the coffinettes, the stoppers to the canopic jars (wrongly assembled), the throne of state and, indeed, the shrine around the sarcophagus, the lid of the sarcophagus, as well as the sarcophagus itself, were all borrowed from someone else.

A further example are the two guardian statues: they are similar but not identical. The triangular kilts which adorn them bear Tutankhamun's names and titles but did they orig-inally belong to him? The kilts each had a hollowed recess beneath, to the depth of eight inches, to receive religious texts. However, the hollows are empty, they have been plastered and gilded over. I suspect the statues belonged to someone else. They were inscribed with Tutankhamun's name but the texts referring to their original owner had been removed. The guardian statues were the first things Carter saw when he shone his torch through the antechamber, therefore they must have been the last items seen by the burial party. In their haste, Ay's party simply removed the original texts, their brief for 'guarding' someone else over; then filled in the hollows and inscribed Tutankhamun's name on the kilts to regulate matters.

Tutankhamun's mummy, with its famous face mask, was buried in three coffins and placed in the sarcophagus. This in turn was contained in four shrines of striking beauty, the first being protected by a clumsily built wooden pall frame. Striking differences exist between the funeral mask and the faces of the coffins, particularly the third coffin where the face does not display the serene countenance of Tutankhamun but a harsher, fuller face. Even when Carter examined the mummy itself, he found gold strips around it which must have been used in a previous burial, that of Ankhkheperure, whilst Tutankhamun's skull cap, tied closely round the shaven head, bore references to the Aten. Nothing demonstrates better the incredible haste of Tutankhamun's funeral process than Carter's description of the lid which covered the sarcophagus, as well as the four gilded shrines which protected it.

The lid, made of rose granite, tinted to match the quartzite sarcophagus, was cracked in the middle and firmly embedded in the rebated top edges. The cracks had been carefully cemented and painted over to match the rest, in such a way as to leave no doubt that it had not been tampered with. Undoubtedly the original intention must have been to provide a quartzite lid in keeping with the sarcophagus itself: it would therefore appear that some accident had occurred. It may be that the intended

[161]

lid was not ready in time for the burial of the King, and that this crudely made granite slab was substituted in its place.

Of the shrine itself, Carter writes:

During the process of our work it became clear that the Ancient Egyptian staff of undertakers must have had extreme difficulty in erecting the shrines within that limited space. Their task, however, was perhaps easier than ours, as in their case, the wood was new and pliable, the gold ornamentation firm and strong. In that narrow area it must have been necessary for them to have placed the parts of the four shrines in correct order around the four walls of the chamber: the various parts and panels of the outermost shrine being introduced first, and those of the innermost shrine last. The next logical step in that operation must have been first to erect the innermost shrine and lastly the outermost. And that was what apparently occurred. The carpentry and joinery of those constructions exhibited great skill, and each section was carefully numbered and orientated to show not only how they fitted, but also their correct orientation. Hence the constructors of those shrines were manifestly past-masters in their work, but on the other hand there was evidence that the obsequies had been hurriedly performed, and that the workmen in charge of those last rites were anything but careful men. They had, with little doubt placed those parts around the sarcophagus, but in their carelessness had reversed the order in regard to the four cardinal points. They had leant them against the four walls around the sarcophagus they were to shield, contrary to the instructions written upon the different parts, with a result that, when they were erected, the doors of the shrines faced east instead of west, the foot ends west instead of east, and the side panels were likewise transposed. This may have been a pardonable fault, the chamber being too small for correct orientation, although there were other signs of slovenliness. Sections had obviously been banged together, regardless of the risk of damage to their gilt ornamentation. Deep dents from blows from a heavy hammer-like implement are visible to the present day on the gold-work, parts of the surfaces in some cases had been actually knocked off, and the workmen's refuse, such as chips of wood, had never been cleared away.

Accordingly, Tutankhamun's burial chamber was a small, dingy tomb, poorly decorated with items from other reigns scattered about higgledy-piggledy, even the axles of the chariots had been sawn in two to get them into the tomb. The paintings on the wall are hastily done and show little of the usual boasting of a Pharaoh who had reigned for almost ten years. Couches and beds had been wrongly assembled, wine jars were empty and items had been hastily taken from somewhere else. Even the most sacred canopic jars, which bore the entrails of the dead Pharaoh, appear to be borrowed, as was the sarcophagus, whilst the gold shrine which surrounded it was hastily banged into place. Some of the representations of Tutankhamun, advertised as such in brochures or books, are now being closely questioned. Some are obviously not images of the dead Pharaoh. There is a lack of order, of accuracy, even the food parcels bore the wrong dockets. On the one hand Tutankhamun was sent into eternity with a hoard of treasure which any Pharaoh would have envied but the tomb itself and the way it was prepared would have been the despair of any right-thinking Overseer of the Houses of Eternity.

Not even the coffins escaped. Carter comments:

Lying on the bottom of the sarcophagus beneath this bier were a number of wooden chips bearing traces of gesso-gilt ornamentation. These were at first puzzling, but their presence was accounted for upon further examination. The design on the gesso-gilt surface was identical with that on the edge of the first (outermost) coffin, from which pieces had been crudely hacked away by some sharp instrument like a carpenter's adze. The obvious explanation is that the foot-end of the coffin, as it rested on the bier, was too high to allow the lid of the sarcophagus to be lowered in place, and it was therefore cut down by those whose duty it was to close the sarcophagus. This is evidence of want of forethought on the part of the workmen. This mutilation of the coffin had not been noticed before, owing to its having been hidden by the anointing unguents, the presence of which, in this case only on the feet, might have been an endeavour to cover the disfiguring scar, and thus may not be of religious significance.

Carter's observations on Tutankhamun's tomb, its contents and the mummification process are crucial. Later in his account Carter even begins to question the entire ritual which should

[164]

have surrounded Tutankhamun's burial. If the gold bands which were wrapped round Tutankhamun's corpse belonged to Semenkhkare, then why can't the same be said for the face mask or coffins? This may well explain their different images. If other graves were plundered and this is a certainty rather than a probability, then there may have been a wide range of masks and coffins to choose from, not only Semenkhkare's but that of Akhenaten's elder brother Crown Prince Tuthmosis, as well as any other individuals of the Tuthmosid clan. Moreover, the autopsies of Derry and Harrison confirmed a remarkable similarity in age and appearance between the remains of Semenkhkare and Tutankhamun. If haste was the order of the day, in the gathering of funeral goods etc., such a similarity would have been a boon to Ay's servants.

The ritual of Egyptian mummification has already been described and is now very well known, being analysed and studied in a wide range of publications. All of these quote the two great sources for the process, namely, the Greek historians Herodotus and Diodorus. Every attempt may have been made to pay honour to this ritual in the mummification of Tutankhamun's corpse, bound by hundreds of yards of costly linen, with over a hundred sacred amulets pushed between the folds. The face mask was a work of art, the last coffin was fashioned out of solid gold, so heavy it would take eight strong men to carry it. The toes and fingers of the dead Pharaoh were capped in gold but a close examination of the reports of Derry and Harrison show that Tutankhamun's mummification was as hasty as his burial.

Tutankhamun's corpse would have undergone the same process as other royal cadavers: the withdrawal of the brain, the slit down the sides and the removal of the viscera, all in preparation for the application of natron to dry the body out. Debate rages over how this natron bath was applied. Was it a solution? Or was it powder? Great emphasis is also laid on the seventy-day period of mourning during which the preparation, mummification and burial must take place. However, Ay and his colleagues obviously worked in great haste in burying Tutankhamun and, if they were prepared to borrow the funeral goods of other princes, then why should they observe the seventy-day period? In fact, it was the mummification process which dominated this seventy-day period, so every attempt must have been made to hasten the procedure. One way of doing this was to increase the strength of the natron used. The Egyptologist El-Mahdy has pointed out how a liquid natron brine was much stronger than the powder. I believe this was the case in the mummification of Tutankhamun's corpse, the cadaver became desiccated, dried out, much more so than was intended.

Derry writes: 'The cracked and brittle state of the skin of the head and face . . . was even more marked in the body and limbs.' Harrison observed 'that the sternum and anterior aspect of the ribs had been removed.' The only reason this could have happened is because the breast bone and part of the ribs (already prominent and vulnerable, as shall be discussed later, because of Tutankhamun's medical condition) became so dry they cracked and were pulled away by the embalmers, who then tried to hide their clumsiness by pouring in more than a generous supply of the resin-based unguents. Some Egyptologists have been eager to seize on the absence of the sternum and ribs. They talk of foul play, or a possible accident such as a fall from a fast-moving chariot. However, a fall from a chariot, especially a fast-moving one where the driver usually had the reins either wrapped round his wrists or waist, would have caused multiple injuries and major traumas, not just to the sternum and ribs but everywhere. The body would have been dragged, possibly hundreds of yards, at a very high speed over rocky ground and this would have been obvious to either Derry or Harrison. More importantly, Harrison also discovered that when he examined the remains of Semenkhkare, his sternum and ribs had also been removed. Two Pharaohs falling from their chariots receiving identical injuries in the chest and ribs but nowhere else is very difficult to accept. The obvious answer is that they both shared the same physical condition, 'pectus carinatum', that they were 'pigeon-chested'.

Egyptologists were also excited by Harrison's X-ray of Tutankhamun's skull. It revealed the above-mentioned piece of loose bone but also something else, quite unusual. Sweet-smelling resins had been heated and melted and poured over Tutankhamun's desiccated body, some was also poured into the skull through the nose. The purpose of this was to strengthen the skull by forming some sort of substance within it to lessen any danger of cracking or crumbling. If the King's corpse was lying on a slab, the resin, following the laws of gravity, should settle at the back of the skull: this is the case regarding Tutankhamun's. However, a second layer, at right angles to the first layer of resin, was found inside the top of Tutankhamun's skull. This can only mean that the royal corpse, at some point, was suspended by its feet long enough for a second lot of resin to settle at the top of the skull. Another explanation is that Tutankhamun's body, during this hasty process, was laid out on a fairly small table or slab. At one point its feet would be hanging over the end but, as the embalmers moved to treat the lower part of the corpse, it was pushed up with the neck and head hanging over the table, its features pointed to the ceiling.

However, Harrison also showed that when he carried out his examination he was studying a collection of limbs rather than a complete skeleton. He writes:

When the bandages wrapped around the remains were removed, it was immediately obvious that the mummy is not in one piece. The head and neck were separated from the remainder of the body, and the limbs had been detached from the torso. The remains were still mummified, however, although very markedly carbonized, and in many places black resin still adhered to the rock-hard black tissues. The resin exuded a sweet smell which soon pervaded all through the tomb and became a notable feature of the remainder of the examination. Further investigation showed that the limbs were broken in many places, as well as being detached from the body. The right arm had been broken at the elbow, the upper arm being separated from the forearm and hand, which lay across the torso so that the hand lay on the lower left part of the abdomen. The left arm was also broken at the elbow, and in addition at the wrist, the lower ends of the radius and ulna being broken off. The thumb was missing from the right hand: this and the left hand were later found lying under the body in the sand of the tray, whilst the left forearm itself was found in cotton wool on which the sand tray had lain in the base of the coffin. The left leg was broken at the knee. The right leg was intact, but some indication of the fragility of the remains became apparent when, with the slightest movement, this leg also dislocated at the knee joint. The heads of the right humerus and both femurs had been broken off.

Tutankhamun's mummy was in a fairly parlous condition. Carter and Derry do not dwell as long as Harrison does on the desiccation of the corpse. However, Carter talks, (and Harrison makes reference to this in the section quoted above), 'of the vast amounts of resin-based unguents which were poured over the corpse and into the coffins'. Of course, we must also remember that these unguents, once the sarcophagus was sealed, underwent a chemical change and possibly caused the spontaneous combustion which Carter describes as 'carbonization and decay'. Carter bemoans how, 'The use of the liquids', i.e. the unguents, 'within the wood and metal coffins was the main cause of the extremely bad condition of their contents.' He adds that if it were not for these anointing oils, 'I believe that the wrappings, and all accessories of Tutankhamun's mummy in the solid gold coffin, would have been found practically as perfect as when first placed in the coffin.'

There is no doubt that the amount of unguents used in Tutankhamun's burial procedure are excessive, but why? Again, because of the haste. The embalmers apparently moved quickly, the opening in the left side was 'of a ragged appearance' and is situated somewhat differently from that described by Professor Elliot Smith in the royal mummies he examined: 'In these it was usually placed more vertically and in the left flank extending from near the lower ribs to the anterior superior iliac spine.' In other words the opening cut of eighty-six millimetres was longer, not very cleanly done, and followed the line across the left side rather than the vertical cut down towards the hip. Once the body had been cleaned, it was over-dried, the natron solution being far stronger than it should have been. Consequently, when the embalmers returned to their task, the protuberant sternum and rib cage broke loose and Pharaoh's skull became detached. Harrison does talk of, 'Some repairs to the head were visible in the form of wax between the atlas and the formenum magnum at the base of the skull.'

Tutankhamun's body was not only hastily prepared by the embalmers but, from Carter's own admission, because of the hard resinous material, roughly handled by his own investigation team. Harrison's report, it must be remembered, was written describing the mummy as Carter and Derry had left it. One of the great variables is that we are not too sure how much injury Carter himself inflicted on Tutankhamun's remains. However, Carter and his team only worsened the damage done by the embalmers who'd over-dried the Pharaoh's corpse so that the rib cage and sternum snapped, as did the head from the top of the spine. They would have handled this as if it was a cup, turning it upside down and adding more resin to the top of the skull to strengthen it before uniting it with the rest of Pharaoh's remains.

After this the embalmers continued in haste. The corpse was not fully cleaned of the natron, traces of which were found at the top of the back. The body was packed rather clumsily with the precious ointments which were pushed in so, 'The abdominal wall exhibited a marked bulging on the right side. This was found to be due to the forcing of the packing material across the abdominal cavity to the left side where the embalming incision is situated.' The embalmers

[170]

knew that they had been over-hasty and tried to remedy the situation by pouring in gallons of the hot melting resin-based unguents in the hope that this would glue and keep the corpse together. Carter points out how the embalmers also used unguents to conceal the damage done to the final coffin. In actual fact, these unguents were over-used to cover all the mistakes of this hasty mummification.

To conclude, a close study of Tutankhamun's grave, the goods it contains and the mummy itself provokes questions. Were the rites religiously followed, the liturgy observed in both substance and letter? Carter himself doubts this. He doesn't develop his theory but he certainly raised the possibility that something was very wrong. He writes:

It is manifest, after the actual burial ceremonies, that the tomb must have remained open and have been in the hands of workmen for a long time, for it is obvious that the nest of shrines, covering the sarcophagus, could only have been erected after the great coffins were placed in position, and the sarcophagus closed. In the same way the partition wall, dividing the Antechamber from the Burial Chamber, must have been built after the erection of the shrines, and the furniture filling both chambers subsequently introduced. These last facts open up an interesting question: where were all the valuable and delicate objects that eventually filled those rooms, while these lengthy operations – the erection of the shrines and the building of the partition wall – were being carried out? As we have no evidence that any storeroom existed in the Valley, although there might have been temporary constructions serving for that purpose, does it mean that

[171]

the funerary furniture was brought from the royal work-shop only when their place was ready? If these objects were not brought to the tomb simultaneously, the obsequies would be of a different character from that generally supposed. It has been usually imagined that all of the furniture was carried behind the coffin in the funeral procession, thus forming a gorgeous pageant. But, as we have just seen, it would appear that many of the funerary objects must have been transported to the tomb after the actual burial of the king, when the chambers were ready to receive them.

And again:

Our knowledge gathered from other sources for the period of mummification, shows that it was at least seventy days, or possibly more, but whether the period of mourning was contemporaneous with it is still uncertain, though it seems clear that the funeral took place immediately after the completion of mummification. However this may be, it is now evident that, between a royal burial and the closing of the tomb, some time must have elapsed for the various intricate preparations before the chambers were ready to receive their full equipment, and that consequently it does not seem probable that the whole of the funerary furniture could have been carried in the procession of the mummy. It is difficult to conceive that the great quantity of delicate and extremely valuable articles, not to mention boxes of jewellery and gold vessels, etc., such as filled the Burial Chamber and its adjacent rooms, could have been stacked there, while the

[172]

workmen and tackle necessary for closing the sarcophagus, erecting the shrines and building the thick
masonry partition wall, were present. Further, it would
have been well nigh impossible for the workmen to have
carried out their task, had those chambers been encum-
bered with furniture as we found them. I might here note
that upon the outermost shrine there were distinct
splashes of plaster, whereas the funerary furniture bore
no such evidence.

Carter is not being definitive but this most skilful of the
Egyptologists' suspicions have been aroused. He certainly
believes that the body was buried first and then the goods
placed in the tomb, even that the painting and decoration of
the burial chamber took place after the interment and not
before. Carter must be praised for what can only be determined as a brilliant deduction.

The stumbling point for him is that he finds it hard to
imagine some sort of store in the Valley of Kings. Actually,
there is more to it than that; as shall be shown later, the Valley
of the Kings was the place where Tutankhamun could have
died as well as being prepared for his final journey to the Far
Horizon. If a funeral procession did take place then, again, the
tomb doesn't lie. Depicted on the east wall of Tutankhamun's
tomb is Pharaoh's mummy on a sledge pulled by twelve
courtiers. An inscription above this painting claims: 'The
courtiers of the royal household going in procession with the
Osiris, King Tutankhamun, to the west. They voice: "Oh King
come in peace, Oh God Protector of the Land."'

Commentators call this a unique painting, for the funeral
sledge was usually drawn by oxen who would later be

slaughtered as part of the ritual. I cannot imagine twelve courtiers pulling such a sledge through the Valley of the Kings towards Tutankhamun's tomb. We know a procession took place, not only because of the paintings but because of gold rings found in the tomb, intended 'for the funeral procession'. In fact, the route of this procession was probably not very long. It either originated from Ay's temporary headquarters set up in the Valley of the Kings around KV54, discovered by Davies 'A little distance from the King's tomb where large pottery jars were discovered: their contents proved to be accessories used during the funerary ceremonies of the young King and afterwards gathered together and packed away within jars.' Or the procession started from the great El-Amarna storeroom,' KV55.

Tutankhamun's death and burial were deliberately shrouded in secrecy. To discover the reason, the probable cause of death, as far as reasonably possible, must be established.

5

The End of a Dynasty

The dread of me is in the twilight.

Spell 124: *The Book of the Dead*

Come, so that we may expel and grip hold of your falsehood.
So that the dread of you may be on earth.

Spell 126: *The Book of the Dead*

THERE IS NO DOUBT THAT TUTANKHAMUN WAS A TUTHMOSID PRINCE, whilst all the evidence indicates that his father was Akhenaten. The rather bizarre paintings of Akhenaten have prompted many Egyptologists to discuss whether he had some form of genetic disorder. According to the artists of Amarna, Akhenaten is always presented in what can only be termed a most singular way. The major abnormalities in the heretic Pharaoh's appearance can be listed as: elongated head, slanting eyes, prognathism (protruding chin), long thin neck, long thin arms, spidery fingers (arachnodactyly), breasts or pigeon chest ('pectus carinatum'), protruding belly or possible spinal curvature mimicking it, and finally wide pelvic girdle.

Dr Paul Siggins, MB, BS, an East London general practitioner, deeply interested in famous murders, has studied the medical evidence available on Akhenaten and Tutankhamun. I have discussed with him the possibility that Tutankhamun inherited all or some of his father's abnormal characteristics. Of course there are no paintings of Tutankhamun which depict him in the same style as his father but there again the return from the City of the Aten not only meant the religion of Akhenaten being forsaken but his entire culture, including

[177]

artistic schools of thought. Indeed, it could be argued that any pictorial depiction of Tutankhamun would go to the other extreme and signify a major return to the main stream of Egyptian artistic thought.

Tutankhamun's skeleton indicates he may have inherited his father's genetic disorder which most Egyptologists now agree was Marfan's syndrome, named after the Parisian paediatrician who first described it in 1896. According to Dr Siggins, at least fifteen per cent of Marfan cases arise as a sporadic mutation, the other eighty-five per cent are inherited. However, Dr Siggins warns, the degree to which each individual family member is affected varies greatly. Some will look relatively normal, others will be very tall and display a range of the characteristics described above. However, it is not just the physical appearance of Marfan sufferers which is affected. According to Dr Siggins, seventy per cent of all sufferers will dislocate one or other lens in the eye: the poorly constituted elastic body tissue (another effect of Marfan's) will cause such dislocation. Vision is affected and it can result in blindness or highly impaired eyesight. The same elastic degeneration can also be detected in the major arteries where tissue deteriorates rapidly. Aneurysms (i.e. ballooning) in the biggest artery of the body, the aorta, which feeds the heart, is also quite common. So if that artery or, indeed, any other, ruptures, death follows swiftly. Degeneration of the aorta in Marfan sufferers can appear in many forms as early as two years old and as late as sixty.

Tutankhamun inherited some Marfan characteristics. Derry and Harrison's autopsies show he had the elongated head, whilst the absence of the sternum and part of the rib cage could reflect a pigeon chest which was snapped off, either deliberately or accidentally during the embalming process. It could also explain the presence of so many walking sticks in the tomb, along with over 400 shabtis. Tutankhamun may have been physically weak, experienced poor vision and been mentally impaired, which is reflected in the passive posture of this Pharaoh in so many paintings of him; this may have been a degenerative process which accelerated, according to the medical evidence, as Tutankhamun reached his middle teens.

Dr Siggins has also examined the evidence from Harrison's X-rays, as well as the re-examination of the plate of this film by Dr Gerald Irwin, consultant radiologist at Long Island University, whose advice is quoted by Professor Bob Briers in his work *The Murder of Tutankhamun*. Dr Siggins agrees that the x-ray does show a thinning of the bone at the base of the skull behind the left ear. Nevertheless, he points out that it is the inner skull which is thinning, not the outer, though the latter is, according to the autopsies, slightly protuberant. Dr Siggins agrees that the inner surface of the skull is a little denser than might be expected and agrees with Irwin's description of an area of increased density within the skull which looks like a fluffy cloud and has been identified as possible calcification.

Both Dr Siggins and I, however, disagree that such a trauma was the result of a blow. Dr Siggins declares: 'It is a very funny place to be hit on the head. Indeed, for an accidental blow it is . . . I can't imagine any way that the injury could be sustained there, without the most unlikely contortions.' Dr Siggins and I agree that an assailant usually rains blows down on his victim's head and that a fatal head injury, which is the result of such an attack, usually indicates multiple blows and consequent fractures of the skull. This is not true in

[179]

Tutankhamun's case. Dr Siggins also points out, and I agree, that the Harrison X-ray demonstrates bone thinning and calcification. However, it takes weeks, even months, for calcification to form around a blood clot, whilst the body takes months, if not years, to re-model bone. Accordingly, Dr Siggins points out: 'If Tutankhamun was hit on the head anywhere, suffering a haemorrhage inside the skull but no skull fracture, there would be quite simply no X-ray evidence for all of this if he died within a few weeks of his injury.' In other words, Bob Brier's rather dramatic description of an assassin creeping into the royal bed chamber and striking Pharaoh on the back of the head is highly suspect.

On the one hand the assassin must have been very skilful to evade all the court flunkeys, as well as Pharaoh's personal bodyguard, yet very clumsy in carrying out his dastardly act. Such a blow could only have been delivered by someone very close to the Pharaoh, so why didn't he or she finish the job? Why weren't they more skilful and use some of the potent poisons available? Why a blow there? A dagger thrust to the throat or heart would have been more effective.

The rushed nature of Tutankhamun's mummification and burial indicate that Tutankhamun's death came as a shock to his entourage. It caught Ay and his circle unawares which would not have been the case if Pharaoh had been in a coma for months. Indeed, the latter would have been impossible. Ancient Egyptian doctors simply lacked the technical and medical knowledge to keep a coma patient alive. Starvation, infection and/or dehydration would ensure death followed fairly swiftly. The same can be said of any other theories, such as an accidental blow with a throwing-stick or any other object: thinning of the skull and consequent calcification

Tutankhamun – the remains of a colossus, removed from
Tutankhamun's mortuary temple by Ay for his own use

A hunting scene – Tutankhamun sitting, hunts with the help of his
wife-queen – from a chest found in his tomb

A scene on a casket from Tutankhamun's tomb
showing hordes of Nubians being routed in battle

A relief showing a Nubian slave or prisoner

The place where Howard Carter found Tutankhamun's tomb in the Valley of the Kings

Left: Women mourners

Middle left: From Horemheb's tomb – the sun god makes his nightly journey through the underworld

Below: A scene from Vizier Ramose's tomb depicting a funeral procession

Tutankhamun in his tomb casket, note the wall paintings

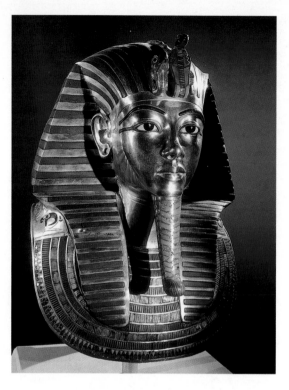

The famous death mask
placed over Tutankhamun

Goddess Nepthys guards
the shrine of Tutankhamun

From the chariot of Tutankhamun –
the Horus Falcon bearing a sun disc

The famous wall painting from Tutankhamun's tomb showing Ay, as Pharaoh, performing the ceremony of the 'opening of the mouth'

From Horemheb's tomb – a painting showing a meeting between Hathor and Pharaoh

Horemheb and his patron god, Horus

Treasurer Maya wearing the gold
collars of Pharaoh's favour

round the clot entails a process of months whilst, if Pharaoh lapsed into a coma, death would have followed swiftly.

Dr Paul Siggins and I have assessed all the possible medical evidence and reached the following conclusions.

- The evidence indicates that Tutankhamun may have been a Marfan sufferer (elongated head, protuberant chest, etc., though not to the same degree as his father Akhenaten).
- Such a condition may have affected his eyesight (a seventy per cent chance) and posed more serious internal weaknesses in the possible thinning and splitting of major arteries and veins.
- The X-rays indicate that, at the back of Tutankhamun's skull, behind his left ear, there was thinning of the inner skull and calcification.
- Both thinning of the skull and calcification are processes which can take months if not years.
- There is very little evidence to indicate that this thinning and calcification was the result of either a deliberate or accidental blow. If Tutankhamun fell into a coma, ancient Egyptian medicine did not have the technological skill or ability to keep a patient alive for long: the victim would have succumbed quickly due to malnutrition, dehydration and infection.
- The cloudy or fluffy area picked up by Dr Irwin could be nothing more than a piece of brain tissue cooked by the hot resins poured into Tutankhamun's skull.
- Tutankhamun certainly suffered some form of serious trauma affecting his head. This is obvious in the way his skull was shaved shortly before death, as well as

[181]

the elaborate rituals implemented to shroud that skull during the embalming process. The shaving of the head indicates continued and hasty exploration by Tutankhamun's physicians searching for the cause of their Master's illness. Such shaving, or re-shaving, must have occurred just before death. The rounded depression on the left cheek just in front of the lobe of the ear . . . 'resembling a scab', noted by Derry, could well be the legacy of Tutankhamun's doctors; 'a possible pressure sore' as Dr Siggins describes it, caused by the physicians in their hasty attempts to diagnose what illness was affecting the back of Pharaoh's skull, just behind his left ear. However, in the last resort, the only firm medical evidence we possess is the thinning of Tutankhamun's skull and Dr Siggins has based his conclusion on this.

He reports:

There is a scenario which can account for Tutankhamun's early demise, the shaving of his head, bone thinning and intracerebral calcification without any contradictions. Every doctor sees patients with persistent headaches; many of them are worried that they have a brain tumour. It is a fact that not every patient with a brain tumour presents head pains as a first symptom. It is as likely that they will suffer a convulsion as a result of brain irritation or bleeding into the tumour, or have a stroke due to bleeding or pressure of the tumour on important brain structures. In any case the headaches of brain tumours are usually a very bad prognostic sign. Pressure within

[182]

the skull, sufficient to produce headaches, means enough pressure to force the brain down through the foramen magnum (literally the 'big hole', where the neck joins onto the skull). In this case the brain is squeezed through this opening like toothpaste from a tube. Pressure on the brain stem quickly affects those parts which control consciousness level, respiration and heart rate. Death, without treatment, is rapid and, without measures to support nutrition, hydration and breathing, even more so . . .

Tumours can be divided into two types, benign and malignant. Benign tumours are those that do not penetrate into the neighbouring tissues, they are usually slow growing and the body often forms a capsule around them. Malignant tumours penetrate the tissues, cells break off them and spread through the body along the lymph channels and veins so that they may appear at points distant from the original or primary tumour. This process is called metastasis, the distant metastases are secondary tumours.

In other words malignant tumours can be primary or secondary. So we now have three possible types of brain tumour:

- Primary malignant
- Secondary malignant
- Primary benign

Many people assume that the commonest type would be primary but, in fact, secondary tumours are more likely, usually from cancer of the lung, kidney or breast. Because metastasizing cancers are more likely in older people, and because primary brain tumours actually occur slightly more commonly in younger people, then, if Tutankhamun had a malignant brain tumour it would be more likely to be primary rather than secondary, given his age. Now these are all pathological definitions. Sadly, benign tumours in the brain, although pathologically benign, are not clinically benign. The confusion arises because benign tumours in the brain are stuck inside a rigid box, the skull. So, no matter how slowly they grow, they will eventually cause pressure in the skull and then symptoms, depending on their position: by and large, this will be a slow process since they grow more slowly. What's more, calcification in these benign growths is common, mostly because there is plenty of time for the process to occur.

One of the commonest types of benign brain tumours is the meningioma. This grows from the outside covering of the brain and very slowly exerts pressure on the brain within it and the skull bone outside it. They commonly produce no symptoms at all for years and the initial symptoms are usually vague, like memory loss and personality change. It is the meninges (the membrane around the brain) and the arteries and veins of the brain which hold the majority of the pain receptors inside the skull so headaches are common as the tumour grows. Tumours inside the brain tissue don't hurt in the early stages because the brain tissue itself has no pain receptors. Tumours are not the only things that cause expanding lesions in and around the brain. Blood vessels have walls that are elastic. If the elastic slowly gives way, the blood vessel swells. This swelling is called an aneurysm. The majority of the brain's blood vessels are found in and around the meninges. If the blood vessel is a major artery then the usual consequence is a sudden dramatic bleed causing a quick death. In other cases, however, the growth is slowly progressive and causes pressure effects rather than a haemorrhage.

I need to introduce you to one more possible cause of a slowly expanding lesion around the brain. This is the arteriovenous malformation. In this case there is an abnormal connection between an artery and a vein. These may only be tiny arteries and veins. The connection between the two raises the pressure in the veins to the pressure of the artery. Consequently the veins begin to slowly stretch and over years a network of expanded blood vessels forms. Tiny clots are common within this system and calcification results. After a long period of slow growth, one of the vessels bursts and a bleed ensues. If this bleed is within the skull death will occur. Both arteriovenous malformations and aneurysms are more common in patients with disorders of connective tissue such as Marfan's syndrome. So, perhaps, it happened like this.

Tutankhamun was born affected by an inherited disease which caused him to have an elongated head and pigeon-like chest. More seriously, tucked away behind his left ear, was a brain lesion he was either born with or which started in his early teens. This slowly grew, pressing on the overlying bone and causing increased density of the inner surface and gradually thinning of the bone. As the lesion grew Tutankhamun began to get headaches as the meninges stretched, he may have begun to act oddly, had temper tantrums or memory lapses. The

[185]

end could have come in two ways: he might have had increasing headaches, lapsed into a coma and died or a blood vessel inside the lesion leaked, causing rising intracranial pressure for seconds, minutes or hours. In either case his physicians shaved his head to see if they could find the disease, but the cause was lost and the most famous Pharaoh of all time was dead.

I agree with Dr Siggins's conclusion. Tutankhamun therefore comes across as a Pharaoh who, as he grew older, weakened both physically and mentally, a token ruler used by Ay and others as the official stamp for their authority. The possible personality changes are fascinating: temper tantrums, memory lapses and behaviour changes would have been noticeable.

Accordingly, Pharaoh Tutankhamun was never healthy but plagued by illness and of simple mind. Nevertheless, he was the last Tuthmosid prince. Ay did not wish him to die, far from it. Tutankhamun was the source of his power and Ay exercised that power very effectively, even over Pharaoh himself. Nevertheless, a constant source of concern must have been Pharaoh's health. The Tuthmosid dynasty was not noted for its longevity, nor were their progeny famous for their robustness. Akhenaten was the only one of Amenhotep's children who survived into adulthood, whilst neither Semenkhkare nor Tutankhamun produced a living heir. So, what would happen if Tutankhamun died? Ay's fear must have been shared by Ankhesenamun.

There was one further worry. Horemheb had emerged as a strong man of Egypt, a commoner from the north who had risen through the ranks by sheer merit and hard work. It is difficult to determine on Horemheb's exact titles and powers during

Tutankhamun's reign but, if the evidence of his tomb at Sakkara is correct, Horemheb was the commander-in-chief who had personally won the allegiance of Egypt's standing army. He had also married into the royal family; for his wife Mutnejdmet he was also preparing a place in his Memphis Necropolis.

Ay must have considered Horemheb a threat, a real rival. If Tutankhamun died, Horemheb would not be the first, and certainly not the last, successful general to seize power. There was tension between the two. Horemheb was certainly excluded from, or not given the proper credit for, Huy's expedition into Nubia. Indeed, once he did seize the throne, Horemheb's personal spite against Ay spilled over. Ay's tomb was desecrated and the dead Pharaoh became a victim of the policy of *Damnatio memoriae*. Horemheb also had little love for Huy, Tutankhamun's Viceroy in Nubia, or for Ankhesenamun, Tutankhamun's widow. Their memory, too, would also suffer.

Very late in the winter of 1324 BC, Ay's nightmare became a reality. Tutankhamun fell ill, most probably of a brain tumour and other complications. Ay, Ankhesenamun and the others moved quickly to exclude Horemheb from any active role in the succession. Horemheb later designated himself as 'Pharaoh's heir' yet no real evidence exists to prove that this title from his inscriptions was legitimate or just the product of his own fertile imagination. However, dynasties came and went and, thanks to Akhenaten, the Tuthmosid, in the minds of many power-brokers, had outstayed its welcome. Tutankhamun had no heir, neither designated nor obvious. Apart from Ankhesenamun, no one of the blood-royal was alive after Tutankhamun's death. Alexander the Great, when asked to whom he left his empire, allegedly replied, 'To the strongest.'

[187]

This was the situation in Egypt when Tutankhamun died: Ay controlled Thebes, the Karnak complex and those troops under Nakhtmin and Mahu. Ay also had one descendant of Amenhotep III, with whom he shared the honour and glory of being grandfather, namely Ankhesenamun. She, too, was a member of the Akhmim clan. However, Horemheb controlled the greater part of Egypt's fighting force and he could always add Ankhesenamun to his list of wives.

From dried flowers found in his tomb, Tutankhamun must have been buried between February and March 1323 BC. Horemheb was probably in the Delta co-ordinating the campaign with his allies against the Hittites some 600 miles away. This provided Ay and his administrators with a window of opportunity. The physicians, led by Pentju, Ay's old friend and colleague from El-Amarna, would be summoned. They would try their best to heal Pharaoh but the medical treatises such as Ebers Papyrus, referred to by Elliot Smith makes it very clear that serious medical conditions like Tutankhamun's were beyond their skill, expertise and knowledge.

Ay kept these proceedings secret. It would not be difficult. During his life Tutankhamun had lived like a recluse, Ay being his ears, eyes and mouth. Ay had kept the boy Tutankhamun at El-Amarna for the first two years of his reign. Most of the images we have of this Pharaoh is one of being confined to royal palaces, hunting and fishing on, or beside, the artificial lakes. Of course, news can leak out. Horemheb must have had his spies in Thebes; nevertheless distance, as well as other factors, were on Ay's side.

In the last stages of his illness, taking the point made by Carter, Tutankhamun was hurriedly moved into the Valley of the Kings, an easy area to control. The entrance to the Valley would be sealed and the pathways into the smaller valleys within it guarded by hand-picked troops and police under General Nakhtmin and Police Chief Mahu. Certain funerary goods were ordered, craftsmen hired but, in the main, the Valley of the Kings contained everything Ay needed. Caverns such as KV55 and KV62 held a treasure hoard of coffins and sarcophagi from El-Amarna. These were opened and preparations begun. Tutankhamun eventually died of his illness. If his corpse wasn't already in the Valley of the Kings, then it was carried there quickly, the entrance sealed and guarded.

If foul play did ensue, then, perhaps, it was in the latter stages of Tutankhamun's illness. Did Ay, fearful of the consequences of the news of Pharaoh's mortal illness, order a mercy killing to alleviate Pharaoh's pain as well as to defend his own political interests? Opiates were known to the likes of physician Pentju, Ay's crony from the Amarna days. It would be so easy to administer an overdose. The evidence for this is scant, except it would fit in with Ay's ruthlessness, his panic as well as his detestation of Horemheb.

More importantly, Egyptologists have not commented on the apparent absence of Tutankhamun's heart from his mummified remains. The ancient Egyptians regarded the heart as the seat of all emotions: it had to be left in the corpse for its Ka to be activated. In many mummies, the heart has simply decayed or disappeared, especially in those roughly handled by robbers or ill-advised trophy-hunters. However, Ramesses II's was found, albeit in the wrong position, but there's no evidence for Tutankhamun's heart. This may be the result of the clumsy embalmers, although that would have been a very serious, blasphemous act of omission.

The other possible source for the heart's absence could be

the result of Carter's and Derry's examination of Tutankhamun's remains, though it is strange neither mention it. One other more macabre explanation is that it was removed by someone who did not wish Pharaoh Tutankhamun to move on, to travel into the Eternal West – or even, eventually, to meet him there. Consequently the case for deliberate murder is extremely weak but, given Ay's unholy haste, did a mercy-killing take place, a hastening on of a painful process? Was the heart secretly removed to prevent any haunting by the victim of the perpetrator?

I have searched for any mention of Tutankhamun's heart but can find no substantial reference either to it or to the powerful heart scarab which was traditionally placed over it. True, the heart and its scarab may still be there, caught up in the mummified rags or covered by that ever-pervasive black resin. This absence may be due to an accident during the burial process or the great discovery some 3,000 years later. Whatever happened, there seems to have been, at the very least, a lack of care over something so vital by those power-brokers so keen to manage everything in Egypt during that fateful spring of 1323 BC.

Ay and Nakhtmin certainly had the power to control travellers along the Nile and those roads to the north. Searches would be made, people who could not be trusted either held or turned back. Meanwhile, in the valley, preparations continued apace. The sarcophagus which would house Tutankhamun's coffin, was placed in what we now know to be Tutankhamun's tomb, KV62; it may have even been there in the first place, as KV62 might also have been one of those storerooms used by Ay to hide what had been taken from the Necropolis at El-Amarna.

The most important part of the process, however, was the mummification. This may have been done in the tomb itself, even in the area which now houses KV54 where linen bundles of natron, used in mummification, were found in 1907. Carter asked what buildings stood in the Valley of the Kings. We have no knowledge of any but it is quite possible that there was some sort of building near KV62. If there wasn't, the tomb itself could have been used. However, Tutankhamun's body was certainly not handed over to the official embalmers in the Houses of Life in Thebes. There would be no Wabet, no Place of Purity or House of Beautification. Instead, the mummification was done hastily under Ay's supervision in the valley itself. The brain was drained, the torso cleared, but they were in such a hurry, the embalmers' cut on the left side was ragged, too long and in the wrong place.

Meanwhile canopic jars and other funerary equipment were brought from other storerooms. Once Tutankhamun's corpse was ready, it was placed in its natron bath. I doubt very much if Ay observed the seventy-day period. The embalmers had been instructed to act reverentially, to treat their Pharaoh's corpse as if it was sacred, but haste was the order of the day. In the embalming process it is essential for the corpse to be fully dried. The embalmers, clumsily, probably working in a poor light, followed these orders to the letter. There was only one way of hastening the drying process and that was to increase the strength of the natron solution, applied not in powder form but as a bath of brine. When the corpse was removed, the embalmers found to their horror that it was fully dried out to the point of desiccation. Because of Tutankhamun's medical condition, which led to a prominent pigeon-like chest, the sternum and ribs jutting out so

[191]

markedly were reduced to nothing more than brittle sticks. Either deliberately or by accident, as in the case of his kinsman Semenkhkare, these were snapped off.

The embalmers, working day and night in poor light, then carried out the task which should have been done in the House of Purification: the embalming of the dried corpse with oils, unguents and perfumes. Under the watchful eye of Ay's hand-picked priests, who would recite texts from the *Book of the Dead* and the other parts of this important liturgy, the corpse was packed with its unguents and perfumed resin. The damage inflicted must have been obvious. The head broke loose, which explains the two levels of resin inside, one at the back to strengthen the skull and one in the top to protect that line of bone. The bandaging followed, the lector priests gabbling their texts, the embalmers working hurriedly amidst clouds of incense and the cloying smells of the melted unguents. They knew a mistake had been made but they tried to rectify it, pouring in the hot resin which would later coagulate and harden, durable as rock.

Ay was not being blasphemous or sacrilegious, nor were the priests under his orders. They were simply in a hurry. The equivalent of a modern news blackout was in operation, Tutankhamun had to be buried before Horemheb found out and took effective action.

Tutankhamun's corpse was wrapped in costly linen: the priests, conscious of their duties and Ay, not wishing to give offence to the dead Pharaoh or to his widow Ankhesenamun, tried desperately to cover that unholy haste with all the aura of public sanctity. Coffin texts, amulets, scarabs, were included in the folds of the linen wrappings. One important item was missing. Many funeral goods were ready-made;

[192]

shabtis, for example, could be taken from another tomb or bought en masse from some supplier and the dead person's name, or the donor, quickly inscribed. Important Egyptians, however, had their personal copy of the *Book of the Dead* buried with them. Tutankhamun did not; it would take too much time and might alert suspicion. Ay tried to compensate by literally smothering Tutankhamun's mummy in amulets and his burial chamber with appropriate coffin texts.

Particular attention was paid to the head, the source of Tutankhamun's illness. This was protected, in the first instance, by a costly linen skull cap inscribed with references to the Aten, the god held responsible for the health of the head. It included appropriate texts from the *Book of the Dead* which harked back to Tutankhamun's illness, especially the phrase: 'Rise up from non-existence, oh Prostrate One, overthrow thine enemies, triumph over what they do against thee.' Carter suggests that the use of the extensive bandaging round the head was also to act as some sort of cushioning effect to protect the skull. The embalmers would certainly be aware of the fragile nature of the skull following their over-exposure of it in the drying process.

Eventually the mummification ceremonies were completed and the corpse was ready for its coffin. The origin of the gorgeous face mask is debatable: the prognosis of Pentju and the other doctors that Tutankhamun's illness was terminal, might have persuaded Ay to have that mask especially made. However, if the gold bands which circled the torso of Tutankhamun's mummy had been looted from Ankhkheperure's coffin then, why not the mask itself, together with the three anthropoid coffins?

At some point everything must have been ready; the tomb,

now known as Tutankhamun's or KV62, with its beautiful quartzite sarcophagus, awaited the royal corpse. However, shortly before the coffin was placed in the sarcophagus, its original lid was either broken or rendered useless and another one was fashioned and hastily painted. This second lid was also cracked but the fissure was covered up. Ay and his colleagues then carried out the ritual funeral procession, as depicted on the east wall of Tutankhamun's burial chamber. Carter describes this painting accurately:

> Wherein the deceased Tutankhamun upon a sledge is being drawn by courtiers to the tomb. The mummy is shown supported upon a lion-shaped bier, within a shrine on a boat, which rests upon the sledge. The bier painted here resembles that actually found in the sarcophagus under the coffins, whilst the shrine is of similar design to that which encloses the canopic chest and jars in the storeroom of this tomb. Over the dead king are festoons of garlands: on the boat in front of the shrine is a sphinx rampant: before and behind the shrine are the mourning goddesses, Nepthys and Isis respectively: and attached to the prow and stern of the boat, as well as on both sides of the shrine, are red and white pennants. The courtiers and high officials forming the cortege are divided up in the following order: a group of five nobles, then two groups of two nobles each, two officials wearing garments such as distinguish the viziers, and lastly a courtier. Each personage wears upon his wig or bare shaven head, as the case may be, a white linen fillet such as is usually found in funeral processions illustrated in private tomb chapels, and like those still used by the

[194]

modern Egyptian on such occasions to distinguish relatives and retainers of the deceased's household. A legend above this procession tells us: 'The Courtiers of the Royal Household going in procession with the Osiris King Tutankhamun to the West. They voice: O King! Come in peace! O God! Protector of the Land!'

Naturally, this procession would not have been a large one. It was not moving from the Malkata palace but from a place in the Valley of the Kings. This is why KV62 had been chosen and hurriedly prepared: it was not a fitting royal mausoleum but, in the circumstances, would have to pass as one. The walls would have been roughly prepared, the doorways and entrances altered, but even here haste was the order of the day. We can imagine these courtiers pulling the sledge that very short distance: the chattering priests, the gusts of incense, the ceremony of the Opening of the Mouth, and then the body being taken down into the burial chamber to be coffined and later placed in the sarcophagus. This was then sealed with a makeshift lid, cracked across the middle, and manhandled clumsily in such an enclosed space by the workmen. Only then did Ay believe he had fulfilled his responsibilities, whilst more pressing matters awaited. I strongly suspect it was just before or after the burial that Ay had himself crowned, perhaps on the same day.

A possible time-line for the events surrounding Tutankhamun's death would be:

- Winter 1324/1323 BC. Tutankhamun falls ill; he is secretly moved into the Valley of the Kings. Ankhesenamun remains in the Malkata palace to sustain the pretence that all was well.

- Early spring–February/March 1323 BC. Tutankhamun dies; a news blackout is imposed. Certain items are ordered but the secret storerooms of Amarna in the Valley of the Kings are opened whilst Tutankhamun's body is embalmed there.
- March 1323 BC. The sarcophagus, coffins and canopic jars are ready; the tomb is inspected by Ankhesenamun. Tutankhamun is buried. Coterminous with this, Ay is crowned.
- April 1323 BC (at the latest): the tomb is painted, its contents moved in and the tomb is sealed. Ay's coup is proclaimed throughout Egypt.

The burial chamber was certainly left unfinished after the burial. Carter comments how 'the ceiling was left plain in its rough and unfinished state.' The workmen moved fast. Beneath the coffin, at the bottom of the sarcophagus, were found the remains of a pole and a greasy rag as well as the shards from the foot of the other outer coffin which had been roughly shaved and cut away so the lid would be secure. The gold-plated shrine which covered the sarcophagus was quickly and roughly assembled. Some of the plates were in the wrong position and roughly hammered together, but the workmen didn't care, the important task had been done. Ay would also have ordered certain paintings. There was very little to celebrate from Tutankhamun's life but the conventions were followed: Tutankhamun's body being brought to the tomb, Tutankhamun's soul being accepted into the Fields of the Blessed and, more importantly, Ay's proclamation that Tutankhamun was dead, that he had performed the funeral rites and, with the support of Ankhesenamun and other powerful courtiers, was to be Pharaoh.

Only then was the news proclaimed throughout Egypt whilst, in the Valley of the Kings, the pathetic finishing touches to the hasty royal burial were carried through. Carter himself points out how the plastering and decoration of the chamber itself must have taken place some time after the burial of the King, the closing of the sarcophagus and the erection of the fourth shrine. Carter explains:

This is proved by the following facts: the introduction of the sarcophagus, the burial, and the placing of the shrines, could not have been effected after the partition wall had been built, the doorway through it being insufficiently large. Again, the plastering and painting that covered the inner face of the partition wall was uniform with the rest of the decoration of the chamber. Thus the plastering and painting of the chamber must necessarily have been done after the erection of the shrines, under exceptionally difficult conditions and in a very confined space, which may account for the crudeness of the workmanship. The surfaces of the walls are covered with small brown fungus growths, the original germs of which were possibly introduced either with the plaster or the sizing of the paint, and were nourished by the enclosed humidity that exuded from the plaster after the chamber had been sealed up.

The different chambers were filled, some of the smaller goods had been brought from the palace but others came from KV55 and other storerooms. Ay must have been pleased.

Tutankhamun was buried, hastily and secretively whilst, at the same time, part of an outstanding problem was solved, namely the distribution of some of the treasure from El-Amarna, including items such as the redundant throne of state displaying the Aten, as well as the canopic jars and other items.

Were those two small coffins which contained the remains of two foetuses truly Tutankhamun's children, or the offspring of some other member of his family? Ay could now resolve that problem, the coffins being placed in Tutankhamun's tomb for decent burial. The younger one had a face mask but the other didn't, though a redundant child's death mask was found amongst the debris of KV54. Ay tried his best but haste took precedence over ritual and the two child corpses were thrust into the dead Pharaoh's tomb.

They and Tutankhamun's burial goods were not just included to give a sense of majesty, a feeling that Pharaoh had been buried with a hoard of goods for the after life. His tomb was also used as a final depository for some of the costly treasures taken from Akhenaten's doomed city. Chamber after chamber was filled with goods garnered from KV55 and other store places. They were brought into the tomb in a hasty, clumsy way, chariots sawn up, clothing wrapped in bundles. Even the food intended for the dead Pharaoh's use was roughly pushed into parcels and inaccurately labelled.

One theme is constant in Carter's report on the clearing of the chambers and the opening of the tomb: how each chamber had to be carefully cleared simply to give his archaeological team the room to manoeuvre. One can imagine servants and officials hurrying down with their goods, putting them in inappropriate places, not caring whether wine jars were empty or linen shawls, such as that which covered the black Anubis-like dog, were relics of Akhenaten's reign. Some attempt was made to change the ownership of certain items but this was often clumsy and, sometimes, even ignored.

The conclusion is inevitable, that Ay ordered as much material as possible be brought into Tutankhamun's tomb; whether it was appropriate or not (for example the wine jars) was irrelevant. Whether it was dropped or broken was also ignored. Ay was paying lip service to the important ritual of royal mummification and burial. Tutankhamun had been buried in accordance with the set rules of the liturgy, his Ka should be safe on its journey into the West.

Eventually the process must have been completed. Ay and his officials hurried back into the Valley of the Kings, the tomb doors were sealed. Ay was in such haste he hadn't his own seals ready, so the dead Pharaoh's were used on the doors to his sepulchre, as well as those of KV55. The funeral meal was hastily eaten, though there again, evidence exists that Ay waited until everything had been brought in and the door sealed before that meal took place, shared with seven others. I suspect these were: Ankhesenamun, Maya, Huy, Nakhtmin, Usermont (the vizier), Pentju and, perhaps, Mahu. Ay didn't even have the patience to remove the remains of this meal, together with other items used in the mummification and burial, to KV54. These were brought out after Maya later resealed the tomb during the turbulence following Ay's death.

Nevertheless, Ay's plot of spring 1323 BC was successful: Tutankhamun was buried, whilst Ay was proclaimed and crowned as Pharaoh. Horemheb could seethe but do little. Ay had the support of others who figure in the funerary arrangements for Tutankhamun's corpse. Nakhtmin and the praetorian guard were loyal, as were Huy and Maya. Ay, both before Tutankhamun's death and certainly afterwards as Pharaoh, could command the allegiance not only of the troops but also of the powerful priests of Thebes and the leading nobles. Ay would be seen as a safe pair of hands. He had put an end to the El-Amarna nonsense, brought Pharaoh back to his proper capital and temples, restored those temples, as well as the wealth and opulence of their priesthood. More importantly, Ay must have had the full and total support of Ankhesenamun. She was a princess, a member of the blood royal, as well as of the Akhenaten and Akhmim clan.

Reeves argues that Ankhesenamun was 'inconsequential'. I disagree. A great deal of evidence regarding Ankhesenamun was swept away by Horemheb and his successors. Indeed, the status of Ankhesenamun raises the question of Ay's audience or, what I call the cracked lid syndrome. There is no doubt Tutankhamun was buried hastily. Yet, every effort was made to make it appear his passing into the West was gloriously triumphant, in strict accord with the Osirian ritual, but for whose benefit was this?

The people of Thebes? Yet they must have been, in the main, totally ignored by Ay's policy of secrecy. The upper strata of Theban society, the nobles, officials and priests, were excluded. Only eight people attended the funeral meal, Ay and his inner circle.

The gods? Ay was propitiating divine favour. However, Ay's theology was, like the Vicar of Bray's allegiances, a matter of seasonal adjustment. He could be the most fervent Atenist but also act as the defender of Amun, and the same could be said for members of his inner circle. Ay had few scruples when it came to hurrying the Osirian ritual along, or getting himself crowned. He had no scruples whatsoever in plundering the dead from El-Amarna, and this includes the gold coffin bands of Ankhkheperure, to bury Tutankhamun as quickly as possible.

Tutankhamun himself? True, Ay may have felt great affection for this Pharaoh, who had been so pliable, so easy to manage. However, Ay still rushed the ritual and, as Pharaoh, he was quite prepared to take Tutankhamun's public monuments as his own.

Post eventum? Horemheb and others might have asked if Tutankhamun was given honourable burial. However, by then, Tutankhamun was gone, buried in his deep cavern. Royal mausoleums were not tourist attractions to be opened to the public or anyone else who might like to wander round. Moreover, there was no mortuary temple for Tutankhamun, no soaring public monument to mark his last resting place. This begs the important question, why did Ay go to such trouble in the burial of Tutankhamun. Why not hurry him to the grave and have done with it?

The cracked sarcophagus lid provides an answer. Tutankhamun's sarcophagus was of golden-yellow quarzite: the original lid was not used, so a red quarzite was employed but painted to match the rest of the sarcophagus. Even so, in their haste, the workers cracked this lid: the crack was then filled with gypsum and painted over, a golden-yellow, to cover up the mistake. Now why should Ay and his party go to such lengths. Who really cared? Who was going to find out? After all the sarcophagus and its cracked lid were soon to be hidden, concealed by four shrines for all eternity.

The answer is obvious: the sarcophagus was to be seen by someone close to Tutankhamun who would demand the best

[201]

for the dead Pharaoh. It would not be seen in the light of day but in the glow of lamps and torches and had to pass inspection. The same applies to many other items in the tomb – only now, with our modern technology, is the true ownership of many of the items being established.

I suggest Ay and his group were addressing one audience, Ankhesenamun. She did support Ay, she must have stayed in the Malkata palace to sustain the illusion that all was well, but she must have been present at the final interment. Whatever happened afterwards in the world of realpolitik, Ankhesenamun must have demanded that her husband be given honourable burial. We can imagine Ankhesenamun coming to the tomb: she sees the hoard of treasure waiting to be moved in, the chests, caskets, boxes and jars. She sees the gold sheets of the shrine leaning in the corridor, she enters the burial chamber with its waiting coffins of gorgeous, precious metal. In the poor light the golden-yellow quarzite sarcophagus glows like an ingot of gold, its lid leaning against the wall. In the end Ankhesenamun saw what she was supposed to see, a gorgeous sarcophagus for her husband, the last Tuthmosid prince. The cracked, hastily painted lid would not be too closely inspected and the same would apply to other items, the guardian statues, the bow, the coffinettes. Ankhesenamun's reaction would be that of Carter's some 3,000 years later, one of delight at such awesome treasure. Eighty years after Carter, we are still trying to decide the true source of many of the items found in Tutankhamun's tomb.

Ankhesenamun would also be satisfied that she was well represented in the tomb on many objects, whilst the rather original paintings of Isis and Hathor on the walls of Tutankhamun's tomb bear an uncanny resemblance to an

Amarnan princess! On the strip of gold depicting Tutankhamun 'smiting' an enemy, Ay takes the place of the God but, if a comparison is made with Tuthmosis IV, Ankhesenamun takes the place of Wadjet the Cobra, Nekhbet's sister Goddess. Indeed, the depiction from the tomb shows Ankhesenamun assuming priestly roles, very similar to those Nefertiti performed for Akhenaten: pouring liquid into ceremonial goblets or anointing her husband. More formal scenes in the shrine depict Ankhesenamun as the goddess Weret Hikau, Mistress of the Palace. Ankhesenamun was not inconsequential but, along with grandfather Ay, a real power behind the throne.

Ankhesenamun would be pleased with what she saw in the tomb: honour was satisfied, Ay had her approbation and why not? She was the last of the Tuthmosid line, daughter of Akhenaten, grand-daughter of Amenhotep the Glorious, widow of Tutankhamun, the restorer of the gods, grand-daughter of the powerful Tiye, daughter of the resolute Nefertiti, the child nursed in the theocratic notions of the City of the Sun Disc. Ankhesenamun was a power in the land, a force to be reckoned with. Ankhesenamun would leave the tomb and the workmen, having hastily assembled the shrine, would seal in their master for the next 3,000 years.

Ankhesenamun must have supported Ay. More importantly, she was a snob, with little love for the commoner Horemheb, the soldier who had risen through the ranks. It was best for the moment if she was seen to support Ay for, at the time, what other choice did she have? Others argue differently and this is where the story takes a dramatic twist.

The source of this dramatic turn of events lies not in the Egyptian archives but with the Hittites whose records office was excavated in its ancient capital at Bogazkale in central Anatolia, now Turkey. There are four sources: the first is from the Deeds of Suppiluliumas written by his son Mursil II and describes a surprising twist in Egyptian-Hittite relationships. The other sources are what are called the First and Second Plague Prayers of Mursil II, as well as a fragment of a Hittite king's letter.

According to the Deeds:

While my father was in the country of Carcemish, he sent Lupakkish and Teshubi . . . to the country of Amki [in the region of Antioch]. They left: they ravaged the country of Amki and brought back to my father prisoners and cattle . . . When the people of Egypt learned of the destruction of Amki they were afraid, for to make matters worse their master, Niphururiya [Nebkheperure, i.e. Tutankhamun] had just died and Dahamunzu the Queen of Egypt sent an ambassador to my father and wrote to him in these terms: 'My husband is dead and I have no son. People say that you have many sons . . . If you send me one of your sons he will become my husband for it is repugnant to me to take one of my subjects to be husband.' When my father learned of this he called together the Council of the Great [and said to them]: 'Since the most ancient times such a thing has never happened before.' He decided to send Hattu-Zittish, his chamberlain, saying: 'Go, bring me information worthy of belief; they may be trying to deceive me; the possibility that they may have a prince, bring me back information worthy of belief.'

While Hattu-Zittish was absent on the soil of Egypt, my father vanquished the city of Carchemish . . . The ambassador of Egypt, my Lord Hani, came to him. Because my father had instructed Hattu-Zittish when he went to the country of Egypt as follows: 'Perhaps they have a prince, they may be trying to deceive me and do not really want one of my sons to reign over them.' The Egyptian Queen answered my father in a letter in these words: 'Why do you say, "They are trying to deceive me?" If I had a son, should I write to a foreign country in a manner humiliating to me and to my country? You do not believe me and you even say so! He who was my husband is dead and I have no son. Should I then perhaps take one of my servants and make of him my husband? I have written to no other country. I have written [only] to you. They say that you have many sons. Give me one of your sons and he will be my husband and lord of the land of Egypt.' My father was generous, he granted the lady's request and decided to send his son.

The second source, the Plague Prayers of Mursil II, continues the story.

Now my father sent men and horses, and they attacked the borderland of Egypt, namely Amki, and then he sent more: and they attacked again. Thereupon the Egyptians were terrified; they came and asked my father to send his son as their king. Accordingly, thereupon my father gave them his son, Zanaanza; thereupon they conducted him to Egypt. Then they murdered him and he was buried there. My father marched into Egypt. The land of Egypt he smote and the men and horses of Egypt they destroyed ... He captured them and brought them back to the land

[205]

of the Hittites. Among the captives the death penalty was adjudged. They were condemned to death. Afterwards the capturers carried them to the land of the Hittites . . . Then in the land of the Hittites, on the same day they were put to death.

A further source is the fragmentary remains of a letter by a Hittite king to a Pharaoh of Egypt on the subject of the death of his son: there can be no doubt that the Hittite king is Suppiluliumas and that accusation and counter-accusation were passed to and fro.

The Hittite texts have been closely analysed by Federn, Sayce, Bryce, Shulman, Reeves, Redford and other Egyptologists. Reeves claims that the Queen of Egypt who asked for Hittite help was Nefertiti. The scenario is developed that, after Akhenaten's death (c.1334 BC), Nefertiti tried to bring a Hittite prince into Egypt only to be frustrated. I have great difficulty with the theories that Nefertiti disappeared from Akhenaten's court and then returned in the guise of the mysterious Semenkhkare. Such a theory is based on a similarity between Semenkhkare's throne names and the titles Akhenaten gave Nefertiti.

Nefertiti disappeared, probably by the fourteenth year of Akhenaten's seventeen-year reign. She had passed her prime and may have fallen from favour. Semenkhkare is not Akhenaten's queen but possibly Akhenaten's half-brother or even his son. The use of a title, even the most formal version, is like the Roman term Augustus or Augusta. It can be applied to different genders. Moreover, the Nefertiti/Semenkhkare theory totally ignores a considerable body of evidence, including the fact that Semenkhkare was married to

Nefertiti's own daughter Meritaten and may have even begotten a child by her. It also ignores the evidence about a male prince of the Tuthmosid line, with a very close physical kinship to Tutankhamun, whose remains were found in KV55 and are too young to be those of Akhenaten. I believe that Semenkhkare was a young male of the Tuthmosid line who became Akhenaten's co-regent and may have survived the heretic Pharaoh by some months.

The Hittites' sources do not actually mention Tutankhamun or that Ankhesenamun was the Queen in question. However, both Niphururiya and Dahamunzu are the transliterations of Egyptian titles into the Hittite language. Most Egyptologists agree that Niphururiya is a Hittite transliteration of Nebkheperure, one of Tutankhamun's throne names, whilst Dahamunzu is not a reference to a personal name but the Hittite translation of the Egyptian phrase for 'the King's wife' or, indeed, 'the King's great wife'. Amki is a reference to the fertile plains around Antioch which formed the border of Egypt's northern territories with the Hittites. The reference to the Hittites 'crossing' into the land of Egypt and harassing the Egyptians does not mean a Hittite army swept through southern Canaan, across Sinai and into the Egyptian Delta, only that they crossed the border into Amki. The Hittites invaded Egypt's client kingdom to the south which they harassed, burnt, plundered and took certain captives back.

The events described in the Hittite records certainly accord with what we know to be Egyptian foreign policy towards the end of Tutankhamun's reign. The Restoration Stela clearly states the Egyptian army was not happy with Akhenaten's inaction as regards their sphere of influence across Sinai. Horemheb's tomb at Sakkara shows western Asiatic prisoners, including Hittites, being captured whilst, as has been mentioned above, evidence suggests that shortly before Tutankhamun's death a border war broke out in the region of the Amki. Most of the fighting was done by Egypt's vassals, stiffened by detachments of Egyptian troops, archers, infantry and chariots, with help from Assyria. The war did not go as well as Egypt would have hoped. The Hittite records talk of at least two attacks on the Amki, the first before the news of Tutankhamun's death reached them and, secondly, after the murder of the Hittite prince.

Some historians, such as Brier, whilst eschewing the Nefertiti theory, have painted the following picture: that Tutankhamun died and that his wife Ankhesenamun used the seventy-day mourning period to despatch a hasty messenger to the Hittite King asking for his son in marriage. Suppiluliumas considered the offer and sent a messenger into Egypt who returned with a high-ranking Egyptian official. Suppiluliumas agreed to the marriage but, when he sent his son Zannanza, the latter was brutally murdered, probably in the Amki region at the behest of Egypt. Suppiluliumas held Egypt responsible. He invaded the Amki, captured those responsible for the death of his son and brought them back into Hittite lands for summary trial and execution. Meanwhile, in Egypt, Ankhesenamun's treachery had been discovered and she paid the penalty, whatever that was. It's an interesting theory and heightens the impression of foul deeds being done, of serious divisions at the Theban court. But both Reeves' and Briers' analyses ignore the basic logistics involved. According to the Hittite records, the sequence of events was as follows:

- News of Tutankhamun's death reaches the Amki

region. Looking at a modern map, the land route from Luxor to Port Said is 600 miles and, from there to Tripoli, in Lebanon 400 miles, following the Palestinian coast northwards; a distance of 1,000 miles across fairly tough terrain. The distance by sea from Port Said to the same port in Lebanon is also about 400 miles.

- Dahamunzu then writes to Suppiluliumas; her messenger has to travel at least 1,000 miles to the area around Carchemish, across inhospitable terrain during a time of war and civil unrest.

- Suppiluliumas then deliberates. He may have even taken the Egyptian envoy back to the Hittite capital – near Bogazkale, involving a further 600-mile journey over the mountains and through the river valleys of Anatolia. We do not know how long these deliberations lasted but, doubtless, they took time.

- Suppiluliumas sends his envoy into Egypt: if the envoy came from the Hittite capital, it is a journey of about 1,600 miles to the palace complexes of Thebes. If the Hittite envoy travelled from the Amki region, it's about 1,000 miles.

- The Hittite envoy would then demand validation and guarantees, his life would depend on this; consequently it would not be a flying visit. He treats, he negotiates then travels 1,000 or 1,600 miles back to Suppiluliumas.

- The Hittites discuss Dahamunzu's second letter, agreement is reached which would have involved another round journey of at least 2,000 miles.

- Prince Zannanza prepares to enter Egypt; this would involve gifts, retinues, etc. He probably left the Hittite capital Bogazkale and made the journey of at least 600 miles into the Amki region. He is ambushed, killed 'and buried there'; so the attack was secret.

- There would be a further time lapse before the Hittites found out what had really happened and openly remonstrated.

Simple calculations of the distances involved in these negotiations, over hostile terrain, during a period of war, of envoys, with escorts, travelling through the heat of the desert, facing the vagaries of the weather on both land and sea, are cause for reflection. Moreover, Suppiluliumas, the destroyer of the Mitanni empire, the war-king who united the Hittites, would not be rushed or fooled. Nor can such negotiations have been secret, Suppiluliumas would never have accepted that. The negotiations must have been supported by the government in Thebes. The Egyptian army could march fifteen to twenty miles a day. Even if the envoys went on horseback (a relative rarity at the time), by chariot or, where possible, by river and sea, the most they could reasonably cover in one day would be twenty-five to thirty miles without mishap. This calculation does not include the time spent at the respective courts or Prince Zannanza preparing to leave on his ill-fated journey. I calculate the entire Dahamunzu incident must have taken at least eighteen months from start to finish. The hypothesis that it all happened during the seventy-day mourning period for Tutankhamun does not bear scrutiny, especially when the evidence indicates that Ay did not even observe the official ten weeks of mourning.

Reeves' argument that Dahamunzu was Nefertiti entails the following:

- Nefertiti, although disappearing around Year 14 of her husband's reign, re-emerged to dominate Egyptian foreign policy for the rest of the reign as Semenkhkare. Considerable evidence indicates, however, that Semenkhkare was a male of the Tuthmosid line who reigned in his own right.

- Reeves argues that Nefertiti's conduct of the Hittite negotiations took some considerable time but is rather vague about the details, although he concedes the process lasted sixteen months. Consequently, if Ankhesenamun was the Queen involved, she must have been conducting these talks secretly during the period Ay was Pharaoh. Reeves finds this 'beyond belief'. I disagree, for I believe Ay supported these negotiations.

- Reeves dismisses Ankhesenamun as 'inconsequential': she was not; she was Ay's co-regent, his grand-daughter and the last surviving member of the Tuthmosid line. True, evidence is scarce about her but Horemheb regarded her and Ay as his enemies; both were included in the *damnatio memoriae* process.

- Reeves argues that the Amki incident is mentioned in the Amarna Letters; these were from archives abandoned at Akhetaten by the end of Tutankhamun's reign. In other words, by the time Ankhesenamun was widowed, the Amarna archives were closed so she cannot be 'Dahamunzu'. In actual fact, the Amarna archives were closed and forgotten by the second year of Tutankhamun's reign, perhaps even earlier, as the beginning of Tutankhamun's reign , coincided with the move back to the old administrative centres. Indeed, Reeves' argument can be turned on its head; if the

[211]

Amki/Hittite episode belonged to the Amarna period, when Nefertiti/Semenkhkare was allegedly in power, why isn't it mentioned, even referred to, in those records?

- Reeves fails to address the question of Hittite validation. Suppiluliumas was apparently suspicious. He sent a high-ranking envoy to check the important fact, that there was no Tuthmosid heir. However, at the end of Akhenaten's reign there was at least one – Tutankhamun. How did Nefertiti explain him away? Suppiuliumas must have been convinced to send his own son. It might be argued that Nefertiti exercised supreme power but the Hittite envoy would have carried out his own research and demanded guarantees. The contradictions persist. Reeves argues that, because of the Hittite affair, Nefertiti was overthrown, her death was one 'in which natural causes played a little part'. Nevertheless, her burial was 'an impressive one'. This is rather bewildering. Nefertiti successfully concluded what Reeves views as a treasonable alliance. She convinces the Hittites whilst successfully hiding the existence of Tutankhamun. However, she is later overthrown, killed for her treason but is still given a state funeral by those responsible for her downfall.

I believe the Hittite incident entailed the following:

- A time when there was no surviving male of the Tuthmosid line.
- A time when there was no clear successor to the imperial throne of Egypt.

[212]

- A period of time when the power-brokers in Egypt, or one party of them, could give strong guarantees that a Hittite prince could enter Egypt and be married to an Egyptian Queen without rivalry from a legitimate heir.
- A period of time when ambassadors from both countries could travel the vast distances back and forth across hostile terrain, stay at each other's courts and conduct open, not secret, negotiations. Suppiluliumas was no fool, if he suspected something was wrong, he would have broken off negotiations: he would certainly not have sent his son, escorted by a bridal party, into Egypt.
- A period of time when, despite the murder of the Hittite prince, Suppiluliumas could still remonstrate with a Pharaoh of Egypt.
- A period of time when, despite the assurances of the power-brokers in Thebes, there was one wild card, someone who had the power to arrange Zannanza's murder.
- A period of time when there was an Egyptian queen capable of bearing a child: the correspondence refers to that. The oft-repeated phrase 'I have no son' indicates that the writer hopes that the Hittite marriage would provide one, an heir for Egypt. Nefertiti's biographer, Joyce Tyledesley, has pointed out that an unfinished limestone statue of Nefertiti in Berlin indicates an ageing woman, well past the age of child-bearing. Tyledesley argues that by Year 12 of Akhenaten's reign, Nefertiti had lost her chance to produce an heir. Reeves, in fact, agrees with this: 'After Year 10, Nefertiti's child-bearing days seem to have drawn to a

close.' However, the writer of the letter to Suppiluliumas must have been capable of bearing a child, and Suppiluliumas would demand validation of this. If Nefertiti was past such a feat by Year 10 of her husband's reign, she certainly wouldn't be a viable candidate some eight to ten years later. Ankhesen-amun, however, at the time in question, would be twenty-one to twenty-two years of age.

Accordingly, the only occasion when all these 'appropriate times' converge was not after Akhenaten's death, or even Tutankhamun's, but during the reign of Ay. Indeed, the theory of Ankhesenamun acting in such a short period of time (or, indeed, a 'resurrected' Nefertiti) seems to totally ignore what we know of ancient Middle East diplomacy and foreign policy. Envoys were special people. They carried tablets of baked clay which served as their warrants. They had to negotiate difficult journeys and, when they arrived at the court to which they had been sent, their difficulties were only beginning.

For example, when the future Ramesses II opened negotiations to sign a lasting peace with the Hittites, the negotiations began in the twenty-first year of his reign, 1259 BC. It was a splendid diplomatic event:

Year 21, First month of Winter, Day 21, under the Majesty of . . . Ramesses II. This day, behold, His Majesty was at the City of Pi-Ramesses, doing the pleasure of the Gods . . . There came the three Royal Envoys of Egypt . . . together with the First and Second Royal Envoys of Hatti, Tili-Teshub and Ramose, and the Envoy of Carchemish,

Yapusili, bearing the silver tablet which the Great Ruler of Hatti, Hattusil III sent to Pharaoh, to request peace frolm the Majesty of Ramesses II.

When the same Pharaoh agreed to the marriage between himself and a Hittite princess, it took at least a year for the negotiations to reach fruition, and this was at a time when Egyptian-Hittite relations were peaceful. At the time of the Amki incident the entire northern territories were in turmoil. Messengers would have to be very careful and be properly accredited so as to gain safe passage. The opening Amarna Letters are full of the chatter surrounding diplomatic activity. In the first one, Amenhotep III complains that the Babylonian king had sent envoys who were nobodies, who seemed unable to tell the truth. In another letter, a ruler complains about how envoys were detained for at least six years, about the inferior quality of the gifts he'd received from Egypt and the lack of invitations to a royal festival at Thebes.

There were real difficulties over the terrain when Ramesses married his Hittite princess. One of Pharaoh's great concerns was the lengthy and arduous journey his bride would have to make and what arrangements he would have to implement to ensure safe passage as well as a comfortable arrival. If we apply all this to the plea by Ankhesenamun the same holds true. Suppiluliumas was one of the great Hittite kings. He had united his own country, destroyed the Mitanni Empire and posed a direct threat to Egyptian imperialism in the Middle East. He would certainly take his time in responding to any marriage overture and the texts prove this. Suppiluliumas was astonished. He sent his own envoy to demand verification and a high-ranking Egyptian lord had to escort that envoy back. I doubt if Suppiluliumas would have been convinced by a simple plea from an Egyptian widow-queen.

The difficulties arise because the impression given by the Hittite sources is telescopic, events have been concertinaed together. However, if the sources are analysed, a different solution emerges, following the death of Tutankhamun. Once that Pharaoh was buried, Ay, supported by Nakhtmin's troops and the priesthood of Amun, had himself proclaimed as Pharaoh. He seized the opportunity, and exploited Horemheb's absence in the north to carry his palace revolution through. Horemheb must have been furious. He was both a soldier and a politician and a very shrewd one to boot. He was a commoner, he had risen from the ranks during the reign of Akhenaten and used Tutankhamun's reign to advance his own political and military career. He was in charge of the army at Memphis and must have played a direct part in the Amki campaign. His absence in the north must have been a boon to Ay who, supported by the different factions in Thebes, assumed the crown.

In this Ay must have won the support of Ankhesenamun. She was Pharaoh's widow, of the blood imperial, and would help to legitimize his claim. She had also been raised in the exclusive tradition of El-Amarna where Pharaoh was regarded as a god incarnate, where Akhenaten's family were seen as distinct, in every way, from everyone else. She also followed in the tradition of powerful Tuthmosid princesses, be they the great Queen Tiye or Nefertiti. Now Ankhesenamun's turn had come. She would need Ay and Ay would need her to face the common enemy, the plebian Horemheb, who had the political and military resources to seize Pharaoh's crown for himself.

Horemheb would have no choice but to accept the status quo. To object or campaign against it would have led to civil war. However, time was on Horemheb's side. Ay was an old man. He had no designated heir, whilst Horemheb would never let another opportunity slip. Horemheb's titles during the reign of Tutankhamun cannot be safely described. We have the evidence of his tomb, as well as the inscription on the back of Horemheb's statue in the Turin Museum. This inscription, published by Gardiner, not only describes Horemheb's coronation but his status beforehand, as the legitimate successor to Pharaoh's throne, though we are not sure who gave him those titles:

He [i.e. Horemheb's predecessor] set him to be supreme chief of the land in order to steer the lords of the Two Regions as hereditary princes of this entire land. He was unique without a second.

He acted as Vice-Regent of the Two Lands over a period of many years.

The eldest son of Horus, being supreme chief and hereditary Prince of this entire land.

The impression given by these inscriptions is that Horemheb not only became Pharaoh but that he was his predecessor's legitimate heir. If that was the case, it was a concession Horemheb wrung from Ay in return for the support of the latter's usurpation of the crown. Nevertheless, there is every possibility that this was all a fiction, part of Horemheb's regularization of his accession. He never actually names his predecessor whilst, later in the reign, he attacked all three predecessors, Akhenaten, Tutankhamun and Ay, and dated his reign from Amenhotep III's. Horemheb had no love for the Akhmim clan. Ay, Ankhesenamun and Nakhtmin were all included in a programme of *damnatio memoriae*.

Ay certainly had to legitimize his own succession. He did not marry Ankhesenamun but there is no doubt that he formed a political alliance with her. In 1932 the Egyptologist Newberry had sight of a small faience ring in the collection of a Cairo dealer named Blanchard. This ring bore the cartouches of Ankhesenamun and the throne name of Ay. At first Egyptologists dismissed this as a fake but, in the 1970s, a museum in Berlin purchased a ring very similar to that described by Newberry. It, too, carried the cartouches of Ay and Ankhesenamun. This ring was scientifically tested and declared genuine. Ankhesenamun and Ay formed a political alliance for two reasons: to give Ay's seizure of Pharaoh's crown a certain legitimacy as well as an alliance against the commoner, Horemheb. However, Ay was a very old man by Egyptian standards, possibly in his early sixties when he succeeded to the throne. Ankhesenamun was in her early twenties. They must have both been pleased at how they had out-manoeuvred Horemheb. The great general could do little except demand assurances about his own future.

However, there is often a slip between cup and lip. Ankhesenamun and Ay had governed Tutankhamun during his life and tended him during his last months. They had him hidden away in the palace and, either shortly before or after his death, had Pharaoh's body taken to a secret place in the Valley of the Kings. Haste was the order of the day. Tutankhamun may have lingered and, if he was murdered, it would be then, given an opiate stronger than was needed and so removed from the political scene. The tomb Tutankhamun had chosen for himself was not ready but Ay, Ankhesenamun and the party of courtiers supporting him, had everything ready as the Valley of the Kings contained storerooms used to hoard other mummies, coffins and funerary objects brought from El-Amarna. The King's corpse was rapidly mummified, other tomb goods plundered and he was buried with unholy haste. Ay and Ankhesenamun used his tomb, filling it with childhood objects from the palace or goods from El-Amarna. Once the body was placed in its sarcophagus, Ay issued the formal proclamation regarding Tutankhamun's death and, supported by Ankhesenamun, had himself shown to both court and priesthood and crowned.

Naturally, they would have to face the day of reckoning. Horemheb would have been furious and put forward his terms. Ay and Ankhesenamun would consider these but, of course, they had planned differently. They were of Akhmim. Ankhesenamun was the daughter of a Pharaoh and a widow to another. Ay was brother to one queen, father of another and grandfather to Meritaten and Ankhesenamun. They may have listened to Horemheb's complaints but would plot a different course of action.

Ankhesenamun and Ay's quandary was Ay's age. He would have been at least sixty and preparing for his own journey to the West. There is no evidence that he had any children and, once he was dead, Horemheb might come into his own. He would demand the crown and Ankhesenamun's hand in marriage. The Akhmims were desperate. Amenhotep III had assured the Babylonian king: 'from time immemorial' no daughter of a Pharaoh was given to any foreign prince. Ankhesenamun was about to break that rule. Supported by the failing Ay, she looked around for an eligible husband, someone with the military force to counter that of Horemheb, and what better prospect than the rising power of the Hittites? Ankhesenamun and Ay would have also recalled how, until the reign of Tutankhamun, relations between Egypt and the Hittites had been cordial. Reeves has pointed out that there was a peace treaty between Akhenaten and Suppiluliumas. Indeed, the Hittite sources quoted above do, in places, refer to a peace treaty which Suppiluliumas mentions. Ankhesenamun and Ay could blame any friction between Egypt and the Hittites in the Amki region on its squabbling princes whilst Egyptian aggression in that region was the policy of Horemheb not the Theban court.

The letter Ankhesenamun sent to Suppiluliumas must have been validated by official seals, as well as by the messengers who carried it. The Hittite king must have been given assurances that this letter reflected the official policy of the Egyptian court. Nevertheless, he was suspicious. He would be astute enough to discern that Ay was a caretaker Pharaoh. What he wanted was verification and validation of Ankhesenamun's claims that there was no other Tuthmosid prince, no legitimate heir in hiding. This also provides an insight into Tutankhamun's reign: the hidden king who sheltered in the shadows of the palace was not well known to this great emerging power across the Sinai. Naturally Suppiluliumas wanted a full inspection and so he sends his own envoy into Egypt.

The Hittite messenger was a chamberlain, a high-ranking official. He must have visited Ankhesenamun and the Theban court and received unreserved guarantees, backed by his own observations, that there was no other legitimate claimant to the throne. What he would see was an ageing, childless Ay and a young widow Queen still capable of bearing sons. He would also require validation from other leading officials that Ankhesenamun's letter reflected the true situation. He then returned with fresh pleas from the Queen and assurances from Ay that all was well.

These were brought by a high-ranking Egyptian official, Lord Hani. Suppululiumas, the cunning Hittite war leader and king, must have been convinced, which means that Ankhesenamun's letters and pleas were backed by the Egyptian court and administration. Horemheb would be simply dismissed as a jumped-up general harbouring pretensions which could be ignored. A careful scrutiny of Ankhesenamun's letter would seem to verify this view. At no time did it say that Egypt did not have a Pharaoh but only, 'My husband is dead and I have no son.' The Hittites would understand this. In their rise to power Suppululiumas had dealt with the Tuthmosid line. Ay may well have been regarded as simply an interlude. Secondly, the Queen is offering the Hittite prince the same legitimacy to rule as she had given to Ay: 'He will become my husband.' Ankhesenamun also insists that the lack of any heir or possible heir has led her to violate Amenhotep III's famous doctrine, 'From time immemorial no Egyptian princess has been married to a foreign ruler.' Again the Queen does not say Egypt doesn't have a Pharaoh. She gives the impression of looking to the future, the legitimate Pharaoh is dead so her new husband, the Hittite prince, will become her husband and lord of the land of Egypt. In other words, Ankhesenamun is saying: 'I have given what is in my power and my gift to decide who will be my next husband and who will be Pharaoh.'

Ankhesenamun comes across as very imperious: she gave Ay legitimacy, she will do so to the Hittite prince. She has

[221]

chosen only him, no other; a Hittite prince is presented as the natural choice. Ankhesenamun also reiterates a very important point, one which Suppiluliumas regarded as vital, there was no eligible heir-apparent in Egypt, no male of the Tuthmosid line (which was the situation following Tutankhamun's death). Ankhesenamun could marry some other foreign prince, which she will not, or a commoner in Egypt, a veiled allusion to the likes of Horemheb, a prospect she regards as repugnant. Suppiluliumas, ostensibly hostile and deeply suspicious, is finally convinced.

The Hittite interlude can only have taken place during Ay's reign and lasted for a period of at least eighteen months. However, Ay was failing. There must have been many in Thebes who fiercely resented the Hittite alliance. Men such as Maya, who would later hold high office under Horemheb, rebelled against it. Horemheb was notified and given the full details of the scheme. A Hittite prince would be brought into Egypt, married to Ankhesenamun and, of course, troops would later follow.

Horemheb did the only thing possible. He stirred up Egyptian allies in the Amki area, reinforced by threats, bribery and cajolery, not to mention Egyptian troops. The Hittite prince crossed the border where he was ambushed and murdered. He had been given assurances by the Egyptian court. He would be armed with letters guaranteeing safe passage and even accompanied by Egyptian nobles, the same process employed years later when the Hittite princess left her kingdom to marry Ramesses II. Ostensibly the Hittites had nothing to fear. They intended to travel safely through Canaan down to Sinai, where another Egyptian escort would be waiting for them but one that never arrived.

The evidence suggests a secret attack when the Hittite party rested at some lonely oasis. One can imagine the war chariots swooping in, reinforced by bowmen and foot soldiers. The Hittite party was massacred and the bodies quietly buried; the Hittite records refer to this. All signs of that massacre were quietly hidden. It would take time for the news of this disaster to seep through both to Thebes and to King Suppiluliumas. The latter does not go to war immediately, he is confused. According to a fragmentary letter, he demanded clarification from Egypt's Pharaoh and concluded that the murder was carried out by men of the Amki region. Ankhesenamun and Ay, horrified at what had happened, their whole scheme brought to nothing, would plead they were innocent of the massacre. Suppiluliumas did not declare outright war. It would take time to establish the truth. Once he had done this he sent soldiers into the Amki region to punish and devastate. The Hittites possessed information on the real perpetrators behind the attack: these were captured and taken back into Hittite territory for summary trial and execution.

Horemheb, of course, could wash his hands, hide his smile of satisfaction and claim it had nothing to do with him. In Horemheb's coronation proclamation, there is a reference to Horemheb being involved in a very serious crisis at Pharaoh's court. The text in question reads: 'He [Horemheb] being summoned before the sovereign when it, the palace, fell into a rage and opened his mouth and answered the King and appeased him with the utterance of his mouth.' This must have been a most serious incident for Horemheb to mention it in his short account of his rise to be Pharaoh. It was also an incident he was very proud of. It cannot have just been a difference in policy. The inscription alludes to something

[223]

Horemheb did which threw the palace into a terrible rage so much so that he was summoned into Pharaoh's presence. The quotation makes a significant three-fold division: Horemheb, the palace, Pharaoh. Horemheb's response is significant. Apparently Horemheb appeased Pharaoh 'with the utterance of his mouth'. He had been accused by the palace of doing great wrong. Backed by his officers, and exercising considerable military influence, Horemheb gave a reply which the Pharaoh and his court had no choice but to accept.

I believe the word 'palace' is a euphemism for Ankhesenamun, the aggressive widow Queen who had no love for the commoner, Horemheb. She had allied herself to the ageing Ay but could now see this old Pharaoh falling into dotage. She had master-minded the Hittite project and Horemheb had brought it to nothing. Ankhesenamun might lay charges against him but Horemheb would point out that he was Ay's commander-in-chief. If something had happened to a Hittite prince, travelling to Egypt to take over that which he should not, then why should Pharaoh be bothered and why should Horemheb be concerned? In a word, the inscription refers to the death of the Hittite. Whatever Horemheb's real involvement in the incident, he emerged unscathed and Ankhesenamun had no choice but to accept this.

This oblique reference to the Hittite prince in Horemheb's coronation proclamation is not an actual confession but it does reveal something of which Horemheb was inordinately proud: a confrontation with the palace over a very serious matter. Horemheb could not boast of it openly, the Hittites would hold him responsible but those in the know, especially his staff officers, his colonels, one of whom Horemheb later named as his successor, would relish the grim joke. They

[224]

would see Horemheb as their deliverer, not only from an unpopular dynasty, but the rule of a foreign prince. Horemheb's Memphis tomb might also bear a reference to this when Horemheb boasts of being 'on the battlefield on *this* day of Slaughtering Asiatics'. This might be an allusion to the Amki campaign. However, the emphasis on '*this* day', alludes to some great occasion in Horemheb's military career and, where better, than when Hittite hopes of usurping the throne of Egypt were dashed?

After a reign of four years Ay died and was hastily buried in the tomb he had chosen in the Valley of the Kings. Some evidence exists that Ay tried once more to circumvent Horemheb's claims by appointing General Nakhtmin as his successor. Nakhtmin's true identity and career have suffered from a lack of evidence. This is due as much as to the process of *damnatio memoriae* as the passage of time. He was, as his name suggests, of the Akhmim clan, possibly Ay's brother or brother-in-law. A bust of Nakhtmin still survives with the title of 'King's Son'. Nakhtmin may have made his bid for power after Ay's death, a period of confusion when those who had worked on Tutankhamun's tomb exploited the time of troubles (as grave-robbers did in ancient Egypt) to return to the hidden sepulchre to plunder it. Nakhtmin was not successful: he was either arrested or killed. Horemheb would be backed by a powerful cohort at the Theban court, led by Maya. Horemheb had served Tutankhamun faithfully. He had supported Ay's investiture as Pharaoh. True, there had been the Hittite incident, as well as the anger and hatred of Ankhesenamun, but now Horemheb came into his own.

The coronation proclamation describing his succession depicts Horemheb as the legitimate heir of his predecessor, who is left vague, whilst great emphasis is placed on how the gods, particularly Amun, Ptah of Memphis and Horus, had always chosen Horemheb for the crown of Pharaoh. There is very little reference to any predecessor. Horemheb openly boasts that he is Pharaoh by divine choice: Amun, king of the Gods had 'nursed him'. Horus had been his guardian: 'The form of a God was his aspect.' In other words, Horemheb proclaimed, as many a military usurper had, and would do so again, he was ruler by the power of his own arm, the force of his personality, as well as that most unanswerable of arguments, ruler by divine choice, grace and favour. Horemheb was also the nation's choice. A powerful general, a defender of Egypt's interests both at home and abroad: the guardian of the established priesthood and temple worship, the darling of his troops and a man who'd bought or cajoled the powerful of Thebes to accept him.

The coronation proclamation depicts Horemheb sweeping into Thebes to a rapturous reception. The Tuthmosid line was dead and gone, no other rival could challenge him. Horemheb would usurp the temples, statues and inscriptions of his three predecessors. He would proclaim himself to be the legitimate successor of Amenhotep III: Akhenaten, Semenkhkare, Tutankhamun, Ay, Nakhtmin and Ankhesenamun would suffer the fate of *damnatio memoriae*, their names and titles would be expunged, their tombs, with the exception of Tutankhamun's, violated. It would be a slow process but one which Horemheb's successors would follow. There would be no more theological nonsense, no more new cities and a rival temple worship dedicated to one god. Egypt would flourish. Horemheb was Pharaoh by divine choice and force of arms, married to the sister of a former queen.

One small problem remained, the fate of Ankhesenamun. In

the Museum of Damascus there is a fragment of a marriage vase found at Ugarit, an ancient city in northern Syria. It shows an Amarnan princess paying homage to her husband Niqmat, King of Ugarit. I can find no trace of an Amarnan princess being married to one of Egypt's allies in north Syria. It is remarkable, especially in view of Amenhotep III's 'from time immemorial' policy on Egyptian princesses marrying foreign rulers. Could this Amarna princess be the widowed Ankhesenamun? Did Horemheb not wish to have the blood of a former queen on his hands, the widow of his previous master Tutankhamun? Did Horemheb see some humour in the policy that, if Ankhesenamun wanted to marry a foreign prince then Horemheb would be only to willing to arrange it? This scant evidence is supplemented by another source.

Relations between Niqmat II of Ugarit and Egypt seemed to have flourished until Year 12 of Akhenaten's reign. Excavations at the royal palace of Ugarit have yielded alabaster vessels from Egypt, indicating close links. There is then a gap in such vessels (presents delivered during diplomatic exchanges) until Horemheb's reign when a more pro-Egyptian ruler succeeded to the Ugarit throne. Was Ankhesenamun part of this Ugarit-Egyptian peace process? Was she packed off to a foreign court where she could spend her time thinking of the hurly-burly following her husband's death? Did she see it as just punishment for the mystery of her husband's lonely tomb in the Valley of the Kings? Tutankhamun may not have been murdered, with malice aforethought, but he died and was buried as if he had been.

[227]

Conclusion

Horemheb, Mighty Bull

I am the lord of the flame who lives on truth, lord of eternity, maker of joy . . . I am he who is in his shrine, master of action who destroys the storm . . . Lord of the winds who announces the north wind . . . Lord of light, maker of light, who lights the sky with his beauty. I am he in his name!

(Ancient Egyptian Coffin Text)

It would have happened like this:

You shine forth beautifully
Oh Amun-Re, in your barge of glory.
All the people give you praise.
The whole land is in jubilee.
Your elder son and heir sails to Luxor.
May you grant him eternity as King of the Two Lands
Everlasting in peaceful years!
Protect him with life, stability and dominion!
Let him appear in glory as a joyful ruler.

The paean of praise rang up to the clear blue skies. The popular hymn, led by the choirs of Karnak and Luxor, wafted across the green glinting water of the Nile. All eyes fastened on the beautiful barge with its fifty oars, its bright red, yellow and blue colours catching the sunlight. Its gilded stern in the form of a ram's head was garlanded with flowers, its jutting prow, the snarling head of Sekhmet. The great rose-tinted sail billowed softly, sending out its own shade for those clustered on board. The silver-tinted beak of the imperial barge,

[231]

the *Effulgence of Amun*, cut through the water, its silver masts creaking in the steady afternoon breeze. On a platform in the stern, Djoserkheperure-Setepenre Horemheb-Merianen, the 'Glory of Horus', 'Mighty Bull', sat slouched on the lion-footed throne, his jewelled fingers resting on striking cobras of silver with green agate eyes which decorated the armrests. Horemheb's square, lined face had a sheen of sweat, his deep-set eyes narrowed against the sunlight. The white padded kilt with the robes of linen over his shoulders were damp with the heat. He wore little ornamentation except a simple gold necklace with a pendant showing Nekhbet the Vulture Goddess; bangles of faience jangled on his wrists. On his shaven head a blue and white nemes fell down to the nape of his neck, silver ear-studs glinted in each lobe. Horemheb felt excited yet hid this well. The beat of his heart, the slight pitch of his stomach must be ignored for this was his day of glory. He, the Son of Horus, was coming into Thebes to be crowned at Karnak. Only the black kohl-ringed eyes betrayed Horemheb's intense pleasure. Already he could smell the different odours of the city, soon it would be in his sight. The barge had left the fields of maize, gold-glinted rye and ripening wheat. The black lands were giving way to the city and the rowers, resting on their oars, now sang in jubilation. They were Horemheb's own men, members of his personal bodyguard, foot soldiers and marines who had followed their master in his rise to power.

'A peaceful landing at Thebes!' one of his standard-bearers intoned and the rest of the crew took up the refrain.

> A peaceful landing at Thebes
> For Heaven's Chosen One!

The sky celebrates.
The earth rejoices.
Our hearts skip with joy!

Horemheb allowed himself a smile and raised his fingers slightly. The manservants at either side of the throne, holding the great flabellum, the pink-tinted ostrich plumes drenched in perfume, moved to allow the breeze to bend these fragrant-smelling fans over this, Egypt's new Pharaoh. An officer, catching his master's eye, snapped his fingers, a Nubian ran up holding a gazelle skin of water. The officer took this and the gold cup the boy carried. He filled it to the brim, tasted it, wetted his lips and passed the cup to Horemheb. Pharaoh drank greedily before handing it to his wife Mutnejdmet who sat at his feet on a gold-fringed cushion.

Mutnejdmet's plump, ripe body was shrouded in a goffered linen robe, a beautiful necklace of cornelian decorated her throat, rings and bangles of silver and gold on her fingers and wrists. On her head a perfume-drenched wig, kept secure by a filletof gold, was spangled with stars of rubies and amethysts. Mutnejdmet took the cup without glancing up. She wanted to savour the water but, most of all, she wanted to relish this moment of glory. Now she would become Pharaoh's Queen. Mutnejdmet's large, dark eyes sparkled with glee. She would sit on the throne, she who had been ignored and ridiculed, packed off from the City of the Aten, despised and ignored as the wife of a commoner. Mutnejdmet had only eyes for the shore, for a glimpse of the crowds lining the banks leading to Thebes. Only that demanded her attention. She wanted to savour that moment. She was almost unaware of her surroundings: the slaves and servants, the

[233]

staff officers from her husband's crack regiments, the court officials, the smell of sweat mixing with the sweetness from the baskets of hyacinths and lotuses, the sweet smelling dates, figs and lemons arranged about the deck. She wanted to see those great ones of Thebes nose the earth. She wanted to see them go down in the dust.

Mutnejdmet shifted slightly and gently caressed her husband's foot in its gold embossed sandal. Horemheb moved his foot in reply then looked to his left and right at the accompanying war barges: this was the power of Egypt, his power! Each was filled with his men, packed with his veterans. They'd accompany him into Thebes and enforce his power. These were not soft-skinned palace guards but dark-skinned from bloody forays across Sinai. They were armed to the teeth with shields, spear, dagger and the curved sword. They were officered by standard-bearers, each of whom had won the golden fly of bravery for killing an enemy in hand-to-hand combat and bringing his head back from the battlefield. They were men of Egypt, sprinkled with mercenaries who fought for gold and silver as well as their personal oath of loyalty to this, Egypt's new Pharaoh; the Shardanna, with their strange curved helmets and guttural tongues, muscular Nubians, in their war kilts of leopard and panther skins, coloured ostrich plumes in their head-bands, quivers of arrows slung across their backs and, in their hands, powerful bows which could bring down a charging lion; Libyans with their clicking tongues; dark-faced desert-wanderers and sand-dwellers.

Horemheb smiled. Oh yes, these would bring peace to Thebes and defend his throne. They would patrol the marble corridors of his palaces and the tree-lined paths of his gardens. Now their task was to clear the river, to keep back all the darting craft which could scuttle across its surface like water beetles. A line of barges stood not far off the bank. The sharp-eyed scouts on board studied the papyrus thickets, the cluster of vegetation which sprouted up so fresh and thick after the great inundation of the Nile. A marvellous place for some hidden assassin to lurk, some fanatic, some priest who still believed in the Aten cult. On the banks, where Horemheb could espy gaps in the crowd, there were further soldiers: phalanx after phalanx of heavily armed infantry and squadrons of slow moving war chariots, their casings of blue-gold electrum dazzling in the sun, the standards of their regiments up against the sky. Ah yes, Horemheb thought, this was the power of Egypt! His lovely boys, his crack troops in all their regiments: the Might of Amun, the Glory of Isis, the Splendour of Seth. Behind him a voice whispered.

'Look, Horemheb and rejoice for they see you as the Panther raging in the south. These are your servants, the dirt under your feet, the ground on which you tread, the seat of your chair, your footstool and the hooves of your horse. They roll on their bellies and backs in the dirt seven times seven.'

Horemheb turned slightly, his gaze held that of his favourite, Colonel Ramesses. His face which always reminded Horemheb of a cobra, narrow and lean, glinting eyes on either side of a great hooked nose, a sneering mouth, a slight man but wiry, a tough fighter. Here was a man who'd protected Horemheb in the heat of battle, commander of the crack regiment, the Glory of Ptah, Horemheb's eyes and ears.

'You are talking of Thebes,' Horemheb whispered.

Ramesses nodded slightly, standing as he always did, one hand on the edge of the throne, shoulder slightly hunched, dark bright eyes unblinking. Horemheb repressed a shiver.

[235]

Ramesses was his man in peace and war but even Horemheb was frightened of him. It was Ramesses who'd brought Thebes into submission after Nakhtmin's futile attempt to seize the throne. Ramesses had sent messages, stark and simple, to the great lords and priests of Thebes: 'If you wish to act rebelliously, you shall die and so shall all your kin. Submit and you might live.' Such a message had wrought its effect. It had been helped by the gold and silver dispensed by Maya, Overseer of the House of Gold, who now stood just behind Ramesses. A plump, merry-looking man, Maya's shrewd eyes were screwed up against the sun, his fat cheeks drenched in oil. Horemheb blinked and turned away. Oh yes, he owed a great deal to these two. He heard the captain of his barge shout orders, the great sail was lowered in a clatter of cordage. More orders rang out, the rowers grasped their oars. The barge was about to make its turn round the final bend which led down to the Great Mooring Place on the Nile. Horemheb eased himself up and licked his lips. A page boy trotted up offering a silver platter full of grapes, iced water melon, sliced pomegranate. Horemheb shook his head, the boy scuttled away. Fresh orders were issued. The oarsmen took up the paean of praise led by their officers:

> Horemheb!
> He of the divine face,
> Exalted of the earth,
> The one who becomes,
> The one who is becoming.
> King of Upper and Lower Egypt.
> Lord of the Two Lands.
> The very image of Re.

[236]

Son of the sun.

Lord of Diadems.

Wearer of the White Crown,

Thou shalt be King of Eternity!

Protector of thy Father.

Heir of Horus, King of the Horizon!

Lion from the abyss.

Panther of the South.

Lover of Horus,

Beloved of Osiris.

The barge turned. Horemheb glimpsed a cluster of trees: palms, sycamores, dates and fig and, above them, the glint of gold-topped obelisks and the carved cornices of the temples and palaces of Thebes. Horemheb leaned slightly forward. He ignored the crowds and stared towards the quayside where the shaven-headed priests were gathered in white gusts of incense and the clash of cymbals and tambourines. Temple girls (or hesets), decked in wreaths of flowers, shook their sistra, the sound of their singing and musical accompaniment, drifting across the water. Danga dwarfs in gaudy rags somersaulted and entertained the crowds held back by the city police. The smell of frankincense, aromatic bark, cassia and incense mingled with the musty smell from the stables and the rather fetid smells from the giraffe and monkey pens. Horemheb glimpsed the milk-white cattle wreathed in garlands who would later be sacrificed. He smiled with pleasure. Soon he would be there. He would walk through the white columns and be solemnly processed through the glowing mass of the temple of Amun. He would be saluted by the palace guard, his every step

[237]

blessed with incense. On the breeze he heard the shrill bray of trumpets. At last he was coming home. The rowers now rested on their oars as the pilot and the captain stood on the prow getting ready to move the barge into its mooring place. Horemheb closed his eyes. He was going back in time, recalling the advice of his mother.

'Do not be a metal-worker cooking at the mouth of his furnace, or a mason without clothing exposed to every wind, wearing out his arms. The weaver squats on his knees, the bleacher on the quay is soaked, the dyer stinks like fish. Become a soldier. Seek the glory.'

Horemheb had. He had dedicated his life to Horus and he had risen fast. He had fought in the dust of the Red Lands, the marshy Black Lands and the craggy windswept valleys of Sinai and the treacherous valleys of Canaan. He had heard the thunder of war chariots, the whirl of sand as the desert-dwellers closed in with sharp-edged sword or axe; battles at night, eyes glinting in the darkness, cruel fingers seeking his throat, running, breathless fights under the burning sun, in desert dunes where the sands drifted up to his knees, or the treacherous swamps of the Delta, battles on the river, hideous fights at sea. He had known the terror of imminent death and he could never forget the cloying tang of blood. He had seen battlefields where the vultures, simply by spreading their wings, could touch each other as they feasted on mounds of corpses, bellies ripe, splitting and spluttering, stinking under the sun. He had been brought to his knees and fought for his life, shield up, sword out. Horemheb had known hunger, thirst, the icy coldness of the desert nights and the dry heat which almost drove him mad. Yet Horus had been with him. He had survived. A standard-bearer here, a standard-bearer

[238]

there, captain of the army, captain and colonel, brigade commander, scribe.

Horemheb opened his eyes. He had to touch himself to make sure he wasn't dreaming. He had become captain of the palace guard under Akhenaten, the mad one, with his long face and strange different coloured eyes glowing with a fervour which turned to insanity. Horemheb had gone into the city of the Sun Disc. He had worshipped whatever god Pharaoh wished but never gave up on Horus who had blessed him since birth. Slowly but surely Horemheb had advanced, been rewarded with Pharaoh's smile, entrusted with this task and that. Horemheb had been as cunning as a mongoose. Any fool could see that Akhenaten could never survive and his dreams would turn to dust. The old viper Ay had patronized him. He'd been given the hand of the Queen's sister in marriage and the post of Scribe of the Army at Memphis. Horemheb had only been too glad to escape there. He had found the garrison slack and lazy, the men not drilled, the war chariots rusting, the horses too plump. Horemheb had imposed order, taking the men out, listening to the reports coming in as Egypt's rule faltered and weakened. He had sent letters to Akhenaten, followed by visits, begging him to send squadrons along the Horus Road into Canaan. Akhenaten, however, had been lost in his god, his mind wine-drenched, his speech slurred. At last Akhenaten had gone into the West.

And Ramesses had appeared, a comrade from earlier days, Ramesses, who had taken him out in his chariot, deep into the Red Lands to a lonely oasis with a gazelle skin full of wine and a basket of dried meats and bread. In the shade of a desiccated palm with only the desert demons to listen, Ramesses had begun to talk and Horemheb had listened to the glories of

[239]

Egypt's past, the great victories of Ahmose and Tuthmosis III. But now Egypt needed a change, a new Pharaoh.

'But Akhenaten had a son,' Horemheb replied. 'Tutankhamun, Princess Kiya's boy.'

'Have you met the boy?' Ramesses replied.

Horemheb had only glimpsed him once.

'Visit him,' Ramesses urged. 'Then we shall come back here and talk again.'

Of course Horemheb had. How could he forget that young boy with his strange statue-like face, elongated head and eerie sloe-shaped eyes? A boy who smiled, who played with his throwing-stick and attempted a game of senet. Horemheb had watched him closely. Sometimes the boy found it difficult to move but it wasn't his body, more his mind, as if he was elsewhere, concentrating on something else, drifting in a dream. A pleasant, harmless lad, Horemheb had felt sorry for him. Horemheb had returned from the City of the Sun Disc back to the barracks of Memphis. He continued to build his tomb and listen to the rumours coming out of the city of the Sun Disc, how a new Pharaoh, Semenkhkare, had been proclaimed. Once again Ramesses had taken him out to that oasis and laid before him the grievances of Egypt. Horemheb recognized Ramesses' words. He had heard similar mutterings in the barracks and at parties thrown for his officers, mutterings about heresy, about the great gods of Egypt being forsaken, their allies across Sinai forgotten.

'One day soon,' Ramesses had whispered, 'the door will open for a truly strong man to go in and seize that which the gods have prepared for him.' Horemheb had agreed, the die was cast. Semenkhkare had followed Akhenaten into the West. Only children remained: eight-year-old Tutankhamun and his half-sister Ankhesenamun.

Horemheb broke from his reverie. The barge was beginning to move, very slowly. It would take some time before
it was moored. Horemheb's mind drifted again as he smelt
a wisp of perfume from a nearby alabaster jar: it reminded
him of Ankhesenaten who had changed her name to
Ankhesenamun! A true, royal bitch! She and her grandfather
Ay, two cheeks of the same arse! Horemheb could still feel
the rage teeming within him. He had overlooked her, under-
estimated Ankhesenamun. Young girls become women and
she was Nefertiti's daughter, born to treachery as a viper is
to striking. He and his officers, Ramesses included, had been
invited to a banquet at the city of the Sun Disc. Ay was there,
cunning as a monkey, sly-eyed, with his dry mouth which
he was for ever licking. Horemheb would always remember
that meeting. Ay could act so many parts. They had sat and
discussed what was to be done next. How Egypt had suffered
because of the Aten cult and Akhenaten's madness.
Horemheb had spoken for the army, Ay had listened and
nodded sagely. He had surprised them all. Old Ay the chariot
general had fooled them. He had agreed to all their demands
and, in doing so, won not only the support of nobles like
Huy and Maya, but even many of his own officers. Of course,
General Nakhtmin and others of the Akhmim gang had been
there: Nakhtmin still controlled the best regiments of Egypt.
Ay had been truly brilliant, he had outflanked them all. Even
Ramesses had been surprised.

The Aten cult would be forgotten, allowed to wither like a
leaf on the branch. The young Tutankhamun would be
removed back to Thebes. He would be crowned there. The
temples would be restored, the army would be refurbished.

[241]

The gods of Egypt would come into their own and mete out justice to their enemies. Horemheb and Ramesses had been surprised. Ay and the entire Akhmim gang were deserting the Aten with as much skill and ease as a whore would roll off a couch. In fact, they'd revealed how they'd already persuaded the former Pharaoh to put out peace-feelers to the nobles of Thebes and the priesthood of Amun. They'd already won over men like Maya and Huy, whilst the entire Aten gang would be faced with a choice, return to Amun or stay in the City of the Sun Disc and wither with it. Horemheb had asked about the Necropolis at Akhenaten's city, Ay had waved his stubby jewelled fingers and whispered it was nothing to worry about, he'd take care of it.

Horemheb and Ramesses had struck back with demands of their own. They wanted the changes to be published on stelae up and down the Kingdom of the Two Lands, from the Third Cataract to the Delta. Ay had clapped his perfumed hands and nodded, his clever eyes never leaving Horemheb's. Oh, Ay had cooed and whispered, taken their demands as if they were his own. Horemheb remembered how heated he had become whilst Ay had remained calm. Ramesses had demanded that the Restoration Stela be carved at Memphis. Ay had agreed. Horemheb had stipulated that the Opet Festival must be restored. Ay had agreed. Ramesses had insisted that military help be sent to their allies across Sinai. Ay had agreed to something being done, 'when all the circumstances were right'. Nubia, the vile Kushites, had to be taught a lesson, Ay had agreed, all the time that enigmatic smile.

Horemheb closed his eyes and ground his teeth. Ramesses was correct. The entire Akhmim clan were a nest of vipers. They had agreed to everything and acted as if they were the authors of the return to Egypt's grandeur and the restoration of the old gods. Ay had been so cunning. Hadn't he danced and pranced before Akhenaten? Hadn't he been the most zealous of the Aten cult, nosing the ground before Nefertiti, grovelling in the dust before Akhenaten's throne? Ay had taken the young Tutankhaten and had him crowned, changed his name to Tutankhamun. He married him to his grand-daughter Ankhesenamun and then they had all come back to Thebes to play happy families. Horemheb had been given titles: master of this and master of that. He had been sent into Kush but Huy had taken the glory, whilst Ay had been cautious about what should happen about the growing power of the Hittites. He'd shook his head and said Egypt wasn't ready, that peace treaties between the Hittites and Pharaohs should be respected. Horemheb had watched. He remembered Ramesses whispering and, whenever he was at court, studied the young Pharaoh's face.

Sometimes the boy was active yet, as he grew older, he'd been withdrawn more and more into the pleasure rooms of the palace. Horemheb had heard the rumours. How young Pharaoh seemed distracted, very frail and weak. There were rumours of Ankhesenamun being pregnant but this was only Ay's hoped for longings. Horemheb had tensed himself like a falcon. If Tutankhamun died then who would become Pharaoh? Ay had bought the priests and the nobles of Thebes body and soul. Horemheb had the support of some of the army. But, then it happened: quite abruptly, Ay gave permission for troops and military assistance to be given to their allies in Canaan.

Horemheb and his officers moved to Avaris in the Delta. They became busy sending troops and liaising with those of

Assyria. The campaign had not gone well. Suppiluliumas drove back the Assyrians and crossed the border into Amki with fire and sword, quickly dispersing the Egyptian-controlled levies.

Horemheb had been distracted when the news came, like one of those sudden sand storms which could sweep in, black and lowering, along the coasts of the Great Green, blocking out sky and sea. Tutankhamun was dead! Pharaoh had gone to the Far Horizon. Ay was Pharaoh, supported by the priests, the garrison of Thebes and, of course, Ankhesenamun. Horemheb was completely taken by surprise. He had his own spies in Thebes, and so did Ramesses, yet Ay had struck fast and furious. Tutankhamun's body had been transported into the Valley of the Kings and secretly embalmed for burial. Ay had opened the store-houses full of the bric-a-brac he had brought from the City of the Sun Disc. It had all been over in a matter of days. No one had known, not until Ay and Ankhesenamun had appeared at the Window of Appearances.

Horemheb gnawed his lip. He would investigate that. Just how cleverly they had done it. And what could he have done but accept the will of Amun-Re? He had tried to force Ay to nominate him as his heir but Ay grew frail and Ankhesenamun had contacted the Hittites. Oh, he had known all about it, who wouldn't, with envoys going backwards and forwards like vultures in the sky? He could do little at first but watch. Horemheb played with the bracelets round his wrist, the Hittite plot had proven too much for men like Maya. They'd had enough. Horemheb smiled in satisfaction. Ramesses had organized an end to all that. Letters and gold were despatched along the Horus Road and the Hittite prince died in some lonely oasis. Horemheb didn't even want to know the details. Let Ay explain, make excuses. What did Horemheb care? Ay was now dead. Horemheb would seal him in his tomb and quietly pay some priest to curse his name for all eternity.

The rest of the Akhmim gang had been killed or fled after Nakhtmin's stupid plot to seize the throne. As for Ankhesenamun? The barge was now moving. Horemheb watched the young priestesses on the quayside, their sinuous perfume-drenched bodies moving to the music. Horemheb wetted his lips. Ankhesenamun was under house arrest and Horemheb had plans for her, not the slaughter yard but a marriage somewhere far away where everyone could forget her! Horemheb watched the oars come up. He'd also take care of the rest: Nakhtmin was dead. The palace guard would be purged, as would the temple priesthood, the court officials and the army. He'd wait then take revenge against Ay and all the Akhmim gang. He'd shake Egypt like a wet rag and squeeze out all the dirt, take the kingdom back to the glory days of Amenhotep III and forget all the rest. The City of the Sun Disc could rot, he'd plunder it, leave not one stone upon the other! Ay and the other heretics would not be allowed to rest in peace. Horemheb recalled the gentle eyes of Tutankhamun, the hapless man child. Horemheb relaxed, he'd allow that one to pass. He would impale those who had plundered Pharaoh's tomb, tell Maya to re-seal it, leave it to be forgotten for all Eternity.

Glorious are you.
Beloved of Horus.
He who holds the sweet breath of Amun!

[245]

The barge was nosing fast towards the quayside. Ramesses was beside him, ready to steady him. Horemheb got to his feet. Ramesses clutched his wrist. For a brief second Horemheb remembered. Hadn't he done the same for Tutankhamun? Even to Ay? He glanced quickly at Ramesses. The colonel stared blankly back.

'You've come home!' Ramesses whispered. 'You have come into your own!'

Annotated Bibliography

Prologue

I have deliberately kept the number of authorities cited to those having a direct bearing on the circumstances surrounding the mysterious death of Tutankhamun. A few general books, however, are worth a close study.

Eugen Struhal, *Life of the Ancient Egyptians*, Liverpool University Press, 1996

Alberto Siliotti, *A Guide to the Valley of the Kings*, Weidenfeld and Nicolson, 1993

R. O. Faulkner, *The Ancient Egyptian Book of the Dead*, British Museum Publications, 1977

Bill Manley, *The Penguin Historical Atlas of Ancient Egypt*, Penguin, 1990

Joseph Nunn, *Ancient Egyptian Medicine*, British Museum Press, 1996

Christine El Mahdy, *Mummies, Myths and Magic*, Thames and Hudson, 1989

Howard Carter's *The Tomb of Tutankhamun*, BCA Publications, 1972, should be read in its entirety. Carter very skilfully allows his doubts to surface regarding the accepted story. Carter's fascinating account is most thought provoking. Carter's real intention is to describe Tutankhamun's tomb and its contents: his disquiet about the accepted story surfaces in the occasional paragraph or sentence.

The British Museum publication *The Treasures of Tutankhamun* gives a thorough listing of the tomb treasures. This is only equalled by Nicholas Reeves' splendid book *The Complete Tutankhamun*, Thames and Hudson, 1990. For example, see this book for an explanation of self bows (p. 174).

Chapters 1 and 2

A number of fascinating books are published on Amenhotep III and the last rulers of the Tuthmosid dynasty.

Christine El Mahdy, *Tutankhamun, the Life and Death of a Boy King*, Headline, 1999

Christian Desroches-Noblecourt, *Life and Death of a Pharaoh Tutankhamun*, Michael Joseph, 1969

Barbara Watterson, *Amarna: Ancient Egypt's Age of Revolution*, Tempest Books, 1999

Nicholas Reeves, *Egypt's False Prophet Akhenaten*, Thames and Hudson, 2001

The most readable and enjoyable work, however, is:

Joanne Fletcher, *Egypt's Sun King, Amenhotep III: an Intimate Chronicle of Ancient Egypt's Most Glorious Pharaoh*, Duncan Baird Press, 2000

The following books provide a fascinating insight:

Donald B. Redford, *Akhenaten, the Heretic King*, Princeton University Press, 1984

Joyce Tyledesley, *Nefertiti, Egypt's Sun Queen*, Viking, 1998

On the general life of the Egyptians I would recommend:

Hilary Wilson, *People of the Pharaohs, Brockhampton Press*, 1996

Another most readable account is Time-Life's publication:

What Life Was Like on the Banks of the Nile, 1999

On the Gods and temples of Ancient Egypt, I would recommend:

Barbara Watterson, *The Gods of Ancient Egypt*, Sutton Publications, 1996

Richard H. Wilkinson, *The Complete Temples of Ancient Egypt*, Thames & Hudson, 2000

All these publications give an insight into the life of priests, scribes and soldiers.

I would also recommend :

Ronald Partridge, *Transport in Ancient Egypt*, Rubicon Press, 1996

Dilwyn Jones, *Boats*, British Museum Press, 1995

R. O. Falconer, 'Egyptian Military Organisation', *Journal of Egyptian Archaelogy*: Volumes 39–40, 1953–1954, page 32 *et seq.* is still worth a read.

Finally, Bob Briers, *The Murder of Tutankhamun*, Putnam, 1998, very clearly sets the scene, although I totally disagree with his conclusions.

On Sohag, the Akhmim Gang and the rise of Ay, I would recommend:

Joyce Tyledesley, *Nefertiti*

Barbara Watterson, *Amarna*

Joanne Fletcher, *Egypt's Sun King, Amenhotep III*

Christine El Mahdy, *Tutankhamun*

In addition Percy E. Newberry's article, 'King Ay, the Successor of Tutankhamun', *Journal of Egyptian Archaeology*: Volume 18, 1932, pages 50 *et seq.* is still valuable, as is Otto Schaden's 'Clearance of the Tomb of King Ay', *Journal of Egyptian Archaeology*, Volume 21, 1984, pages 39 *et seq.*

On Egyptian foreign policy:

The Amarna Letters, edited by John Moran, Johns Hopkins University Press, 1997

On Akhenaten and the Amarna age:

Nicholas Reeves' most recent publication, *Akhenaten: the Heretic King* provides a graphic description and erudite analysis, though I disagree with his conclusions.

Joyce Tyledesley's *Nefertiti* and Barbara Watterson's *Armana* are also useful.

On Akhenaten's mysterious co-regents:

I would recommend: James P. Allen, 'Akhenaten's Mysterious Co-regent and Successor', *Amarna Letters*, Volume 1: Autumn 1991, pages 74 *et seq.*

On Tomb 55, all the above-mentioned works on Akhenaten and Tutankhamun provide their theories. I would also recommend:

Aidan Dobson, 'Kings Valley Tomb 55 and the Fate of the Amarna Kings' *Amarna Letters*, Volume 3: Winter 1994, page 92 *et seq.*

Also:

George B. Johnson, 'Who Owned What in KV55', *KMT*, Volume 19: Spring 1998, page 57, *et seq.*

On Tutankhamun's parentage:

Bob Briers, *The Murder of Tutankhamun*, pages 80–5.

On the Restoration Stela:

J. Bennet, 'The Restoration Inscription of Tutankhamun', *Journal of Egyptian Archaelogy*, Volume 25, 1939 pages 8–15

On Ancient Thebes:

Nigel & Helen Strudwick: *Thebes in Egypt*, British Museum Press, 1999

On the role of women in ancient Egypt:

Barbara Watterson: *Women in Ancient Egypt*, Sutton Press, 1999

On Horemheb:

The standard works on Akhenaten and Tutankhamun bear a number of references to this ambitious general and his second wife.

[249]

However, my main source has been Sir Alan Gardiner's two articles: 'The Memphite Tomb of the General Haremhab' and 'The Coronation of King Haremhab', *Journal of Egyptian Archaelogy*, Volumes 39–40, 1953–1954, page 3 *et seq.* and page 13 *et seq.*

Denis Forbes' article 'The New Kingdoms In Between Pharaoh', *KMT*, volume 9, No. 1, Spring 1998, pages 31 *et seq.* is also interesting.

The standard histories also makes reference to Nakhtmin but also see:

Aidan Dobson, 'Two Who Might Have Been King', *Amarna Letters*, Volume 1: Autumn 1991, page 26 *et seq.*

Chapter 3

The best summaries of Tutankhamun's reign are given in Reeves' *The Complete Tutankhamun* (pages 16–32) and Desroches-Noblecourt's *Tutankhamun* (pages 173–92).

Tomb 55 is discussed in the above-mentioned authorities.

For Viceroy Huy:

N. de G. Davies and A. H. Gardiner, *The Tomb of Huy, Viceroy of Nubia in the Reign of King Tutankhamun*, Theban Tomb series: Egyptian Exploration Fund, London, 1926.

A good readable account of Egypt's relationship with Nubia can be found in the above cited authorities but I would also recommend John Taylor, *Egypt and Nubia*, British Museum Press, 1991

The theory that other tombs in the Valley of the Kings were used to house the remains from Amarna:

Susan James, Volume 'The Mummy – Elder Lady', *KMT*, Volume 12, No. 2, Summer 2001, page 42 *et seq.*

Egyptian foreign policy across Sinai is covered by the published histories of Tutankhamun. The clearest and most analytical is Redford's *Akhenaten*, chapter 11, page 185 *et seq.* and Chapter 13, page 212 *et seq.* I would also recommend K. A. Kitchen's brilliant study: *Supliluliuma and the Amarna Pharaohs*, Liverpool University Press, 1962. Also John Moran, *The Amarna Letters*, EA9, page 18.

The two definitive books on Tutankhamun's tomb are Howard Carter's *The Tomb of Tutankhamun* and Reeves' extremely detailed study of each chamber and its contents, *The Complete Tutankhamun*. Carter's book also has two appendices of great significance: Appendix 1: 'A Report Upon the Examination of Tutankhamun's Mummy' by Douglas G. Derry (page 224 *et seq.*). The timing of Tutankhamun's burial is dated by the floral wreaths found in the tomb: this forms Appendix 2 of Carter's book: 'A Report on the Floral Wreaths Found in the Coffins of Tutankhamun' by P. E. Newberry (paqe 232 *et seq.*).

On a more recent examination of Tutankhamun's remains: G. Harrison, 'The Remains of Tutankhamun', *Antiquity*, XLVI, 1972 page 8 *et seq.*

Two fascinating supplementary works are G. Elliot Smith's *The Royal Mummies*, Duckworth Press Edition, 2000 and Christine El Mahdy's *Mummies, Myth and Magic*, page 159 *et seq.*

Briers' *The Murder of Tutankhamun*, page 159 et seq. summarizes the medical findings on both Tutankhamun and Semenkhkare.

On the ownership of articles in the tomb:

Reeves': *Complete Tutankhamun* draws attention to the inconsistencies. Certain items are very carefully examined in *After Tutankhamun*, edited by C. M. Reeves, Kegan Paul, 1992, page 73 *et seq.* and page 85 *et seq.*

On the disputed wall painting which, in turn, has been described as being of Akhenaten/Semenkhkare and Tutankhamun:

Reeves, *Akhenaten*, page 158; El Mahdy, *Tutankhamun*, between pages 88–9; and Desroches-Noblecourt, *Tutankhamun*, page 166, plate 98.

On mortality rates in ancient Egypt:

Susan James' above-mentioned article, Rosalind and Jacques Janssen's *Growing Up in Ancient Egypt*, Rubicon Press, 1990; and their *Getting Old in Ancient Egypt*, Rubicon Press, 1996.

For Ramesses II:

K .A. Kitchen's *Pharaoh Triumphant: the Life and Times of Ramesses II*, Aris and Phillips, 1982.

On Egyptian co-regencies:

W. J. Murnane, *Egyptian Co-regencies*, Chicago University Press, 1997

On the strip of gold depicting Tutankhamun 'smiting' before Ay:

Desroches-Noblecourt: *Tutankhamun*, page 202, figure 121. This strip should be compared with the photograph of Tuthmosis IV's arm brace which can be seen in Fletcher's *Amenhotep III*, page 21.

Chapter 5
On Pit 54:

The best summary is given by Reeves in *The Complete Tutankhamun*, pages 34–9 and Carter's book, *The Tomb of Tutankhamun*, page 36.

On the importance of the heart and heart-scarab:

El Mahdy, *Mummies, Myths and Magic*, pages 58, 94, 150 and 153. This should be read in conjunction with Elliot Smith's interesting work, *The Royal Mummies*.

On Ankhesenamun and the Amki affair:

L. Green, 'A Lost Queen of Ancient Egypt . . . Ankhesenamun, *KMT*, Winter 1991, page 23 *et seq*. This article also deals with the famous Newberry ring and refers to the hostility between Horemheb and Ankhesenamun.

Also, Reeves, *Akhenaten*, pages 174–182; A. R. Schulman, 'Ankhesenamun, Nofretity and the Amki Affair', *Journal of the American Research Centre in Egypt*, Volume 15, 1997, page 43 *et seq*.

A.H. Sayce, 'The Hittite Correspondence With Tutankhamun's Widow', *Ancient Egypt*, part 2, 1927, pages 33–5 and 'What Happened After the Death of Tutankhamun', *Journal of Egyptian Archaelogy*, Volume 12, 1926, page 168 *et seq*.

Walter Federn, "Dahumunzu' *Journal of Cuneiform Studies* (Volume 14, 1960), page 33.

Trevor B. Bryce, 'The Death of Niphururiya and Its Aftermath', *Journal of Egyptian Archaelogy*, Volume 76, 1980, page 97 *et seq*.

Redford, *Akhenaten*, pages 217 *et seq*. is also interesting.

On Horemheb:

Gardiner's two articles on Horemheb in the *Journal of Egyptian Archaeology*, Volume 39–40, 1953–1954, pages 3–31.

On distances in Ancient Egypt:

The Penguin Atlas of Ancient Egypt, and K. A. Kitchen, *Pharaoh Triumphant*, page 50 *et seq*. and page 75 *et seq*.

On the 'time immemorial' letter of Amenhotep III:

Moran, *The Amarna Letters*, page 8.

On Horemheb's links with Ugarit:

The fragment of vase with the Amarna princess can be seen in Desroches-Noblecourt, *Tutankhamun*, page 279, figure 181.

Also see Kitchen, *Suppiluliuma and the Amarna Kings*, page 74.

Index